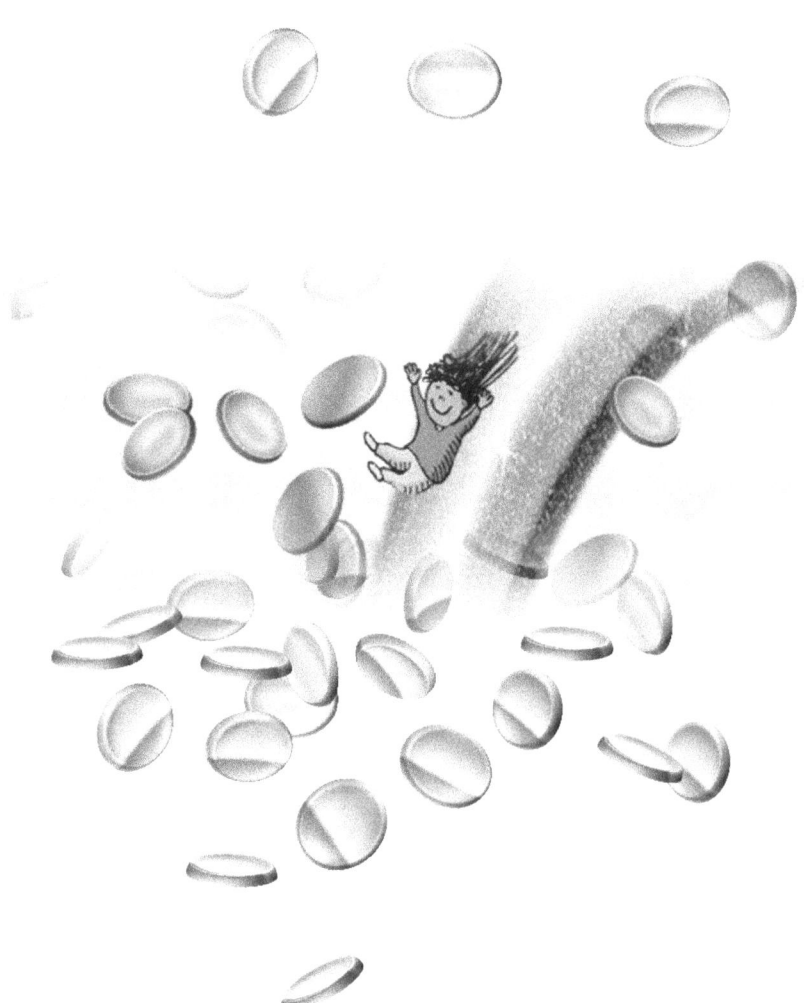

Table of Contents

Introduction - Why Budgeting
FAQ's

Why Budgeting?

As an accounting consultant, the most frequent situation I encounter is people not knowing how to navigate the 21st century.

This is not just a problem of younger people, there are many older people who find themselves struggling to get their finances to balance without the partner who handled everything.

Yes, there are things that are complicated, like figuring out mortgage terms, or capital gains…but that knowledge tends not to be needed frequently and when it is needed there are professionals who will be involved simply to assist you.

But when you have a situation where you know you will need to make a major purchase in the future, or you don't know where your money went -but you have a huge credit card bill, few people can offer advice other than…'oh well create a budget' or – If you PAY to take this class, they will help you.

This budgeting book is simple. It has chapters of different common financial scenarios and how to successfully budget for them. Are you sleeping on a cot in the shelter? There's a budget to help you get your own place.   Are you supporting a stay at home spouse and an elderly parent or a child and you want to move to a house? There is a budget for that also.

From paying off a car loan to paying off a student loan you will find simple budgets you can follow for success and wealth.

Frequently Asked Questions:

Q: Why does it Start on January 4, 2019?
A: It starts on that date because that was the First Friday (traditionally 'pay day) that was on the calendar the year this book was started. The dates are one week apart.

Q: What if my paycheck is higher/lower than the budget that I selected?
A: If your paycheck is higher than either add money to your savings category, your 'gifts and pets' category, or to your emergency savings. If it is lower, subtract money from those categories.

Q: My parents/ friends/ relatives won't accept my rent.
A: Put it in a separate account so you are used to paying it out. You could use it for moving expenses or you could throw a party for your parents/friends when you move out.

Q: What if I don't have a pet?
A: Then spend the money on yourself. What about a movie once a month? Bowling?

Q: I need more than $50 a week to feed myself.
A: No, you do not. Sit down and PLAN your meals. The healthier the meal, the less expense you will have. Here is a link to a $50 grocery list for a week of healthy eating.

Q: What if my car insurance is HIGHER that the figures you have?
A: If your insurance is higher or lower make up the difference in your 'Gifts and pets' Category.

Q: Why can't I buy any clothes or shoes?
A: You can. Use the money from your 'Gifts and Pets' catagory and do not be afraid to ask relatives and friends for clothing or gift cards at birthdays or holidays

Q: What if someone dies and I have to go to a funeral?
A: That is what your emergency fund is for. Do not be afraid to spend it in an emergency.

Q: Can I use my emergency savings if I start a New job and have to purchase my own uniform?
A: Yes. So if you have to spend $50.00 of your 'emergency' cash on uniforms, then contribute an extra $5.00 every week for 10 weeks to make it up.

Q: I have to pay out $100.00 toward the 'bridesmaid fund' for my cousin's wedding. Can I take this from emergency funds?
A: No. That is not an emergency. Instead put in $5 or $10 a week from your 'Gifts and Pets' category until you've given the entire $100.00

Q: How do I make MY OWN spreadsheet - the ones here do not cover everything I need?
A: If you are not familiar with EXCEL SPREADSHEETS You will find a brief guide to setting one up at the end of the book

CHAPTER ZERO

Starting with Nothing

This budget is for a person who has nothing but a backpack full of clothes and a cot to sleep on at night. You just got a full time job @ $8.00 per hour (40 hours per week) your goal is to save a total of $13,000.00 . $5,000.00 to qualify for a place to live and $8,000.00 to get a car for work and transportation.

♦ Rent : You are currently not paying rent. But you will be paying it eventually. So pay yourself 'rent' by putting this amount in a separate bank savings account, and you will be able to use this toward a security deposit when you reach your budget goals.

♦ Misc. Food: You may HAVE to buy prepared food most of the time due to your situation. It is expensive to do this so try to look for places that serve community meals to save some money. You will find a grocery and meal planner at the backof this book.

♦ Cell phone. If you have one, then it is time to start paying back the person who keeps it turned on for you. If you do not have one, you will need a way for people (your boss) to stay in touch with you. Save up for an inexpensive phone and plan. Put this ampount aside to get a cell phone in a couple of months.

♦ Save for a place to live and a Used Car: This exact amount should be put in to a separate bank account every week. At the end of 206 weeks you will be able to qualify for a room or small apartment AND pay cash for your car. If you put it in a savings account that earns .91% or better, you will have slightly more.

♦ Health Insurance: Your employer may withhold this amount from your check in weekly increments.

♦ Transportation: You cannot walk to work every day, and if there is no one to give you a lift...there will be occasional days when you need to take a bus.

♦ Gifts/Fun: Allow yourself a little bit of FUN money so you do not get depressed. So you need to put it in your budget. You do not have to spend that much, but do not spend more.

♦ Emergency Savings: Put this amount aside every week in case of a Real emergency. Medical or a death in the family qualify.

♦ Balance in Bank: That is what you should have in your bank account at the end of all transactions in order to stay on your budget.

♦ Paycheck: This is an average, because tax laws vary from state to state and even from city to city. A $10 a week pay increase is built in to the second year.

♦ Balance forward: This is what is left after you pay your expenses. This money cannot be spent – it is carried forward to the next period. This is the main point of a budget – to not spend every bit of money that comes into your hands.

Chapter Zero	4-Jan-19	11-Jan-19	18-Jan-19	25-Jan-19	1-Feb-19	8-Feb-19	15-Feb-19	22-Feb-19
Rent/Mortgage					-50			
Meals @ $10 per day	-70	-70	-70	-70	-70	-70	-70	-70
Cell	0				-70			
Saving $20K for room + car	0	0	0	0	-50	-50	-50	-50
Health insurance	-40				-40			
Auto/transportation	-40	-40	-40	-40	-40	-40	-40	-40
Gifts/ fun/pets	0	0	0	0	0	0	0	0
Emergency Savings	0	0	0	0	0	0	0	0
Balance in bank	0	84	208	332	456	370	444	518
Paycheck (After approx taxes)	234	234	234	234	234	234	234	234
Balance forward	84	208	332	456	370	444	518	592

Figure One

Notes:

Chapter Zero	1-Mar-19	8-Mar-19	15-Mar-19	22-Mar-19	29-Mar-19	5-Apr-19	12-Apr-19	19-Apr-19
Rent/Mortgage	-50				-50			
Meals @ $10 per day	-70	-70	-70	-70	-70	-70	-70	-70
Cell	-70				-70			
Saving $20K for room + car	-50	-50	-50	-50	-50	-50	-50	-50
Health insurance	-40				-40			
Auto/transportation	-40	-40	-40	-40	-40	-40	-40	-40
Gifts/ fun/pets	0	0	0	0	-5	-5	-5	-5
Emergency Savings	0	0	0	0	-5	-5	-5	-5
Balance in bank	592	506	580	654	728	632	696	760
Paycheck (After approx taxes)	234	234	234	234	234	234	234	234
Balance forward	506	580	654	728	632	696	760	824

Figure Two

Notes:

Chapter Zero	26-Apr-19	3-May-19	10-May-19	17-May-19	24-May-19	31-May-19	7-Jun-19	14-Jun-19
Rent/Mortgage		-50				-50		
Meals @ $10 per day	-70	-70	-70	-70	-70	-70	-70	-70
Cell		-70				-70		
Saving $20K for room + car	-50	-50	-50	-50	-50	-50	-50	-50
Health insurance		-40				-40		
Auto/transportation	-40	-40	-40	-40	-40	-40	-40	-40
Gifts/ fun/pets	-5	-5	-5	-5	-5	-5	-5	-5
Emergency Savings	-5	-5	-5	-5	-5	-5	-5	-5
Balance in bank	824	888	792	856	920	984	888	952
Paycheck (After approx taxes)	234	234	234	234	234	234	234	234
Balance forward	888	792	856	920	984	888	952	1016

Figure Three

Chapter Zero	21-Jun-19	28-Jun-19	5-Jul-19	12-Jul-19	19-Jul-19	26-Jul-19	2-Aug-19	9-Aug-19
Rent/Mortgage		-50					-50	
Meals @ $10 per day	-70	-70	-70	-70	-70	-70	-70	-70
Cell		-70					-70	
Saving $20K for room + car	-50	-60	-60	-60	-60	-60	-60	-60
Health insurance		-40					-40	
Auto/transportation	-40	-40	-40	-40	-40	-40	-40	-40
Gifts/ fun/pets	-5	-5	-5	-5	-5	-5	-5	-5
Emergency Savings	-5	-5	-5	-5	-5	-5	-5	-5
Balance in bank	1016	1080	974	1028	1082	1136	1190	1084
Paycheck (After approx taxes)	234	234	234	234	234	234	234	234
Balance forward	1080	974	1028	1082	1136	1190	1084	1138

Figure Four

Chapter Zero	16-Aug-19	23-Aug-19	30-Aug-19	6-Sep-19	13-Sep-19	20-Sep-19	27-Sep-19	4-Oct-19
Rent/Mortgage			-50					-50
Meals @ $10 per day	-70	-70	-70	-70	-70	-70	-70	-70
Cell			-70					-70
Saving $20K for room + car	-60	-60	-60	-60	-60	-60	-60	-60
Health insurance			-40					-40
Auto/transportation	-40	-40	-40	-40	-40	-40	-40	-40
Gifts/ fun/pets	-5	-5	-5	-5	-5	-5	-5	-5
Emergency Savings	-5	-5	-5	-5	-5	-5	-5	-5
Balance in bank	1138	1192	1246	1140	1194	1248	1302	1356
Paycheck (After approx taxes)	234	234	234	234	234	234	234	234
Balance forward	1192	1246	1140	1194	1248	1302	1356	1250

Figure Five

Chapter Zero	11-Oct-19	18-Oct-19	25-Oct-19	1-Nov-19	8-Nov-19	15-Nov-19	22-Nov-19	29-Nov-19
Rent/Mortgage				-50				-50
Meals @ $10 per day	-70	-70	-70	-70	-70	-70	-70	-70
Cell				-70				-70
Saving $20K for room + car	-60	-60	-60	-60	-60	-60	-60	-60
Health insurance				-40				-40
Auto/transportation	-40	-40	-40	-40	-40	-40	-40	-40
Gifts/ fun/pets	-5	-5	-5	-5	-5	-5	-5	-5
Emergency Savings	-5	-5	-5	-5	-5	-5	-5	-5
Balance in bank	1250	1304	1358	1412	1306	1360	1414	1468
Paycheck (After approx taxes)	234	234	234	234	234	234	234	234
Balance forward	1304	1358	1412	1306	1360	1414	1468	1362

Figure Six

Chapter Zero	6-Dec-19	13-Dec-19	20-Dec-19	27-Dec-19	3-Jan-20	10-Jan-20	17-Jan-20	24-Jan-20
Rent/Mortgage					-50			
Meals @ $10 per day	-70	-70	-70	-70	-70	-70	-70	-70
Cell					-70			
Saving $20K for room + car	-60	-60	-60	-60	-60	-60	-60	-60
Health insurance					-40			
Auto/transportation	-40	-40	-40	-40	-40	-40	-40	-40
Gifts/ fun/pets	-5	-5	-50	-5	-5	-5	-5	-5
Emergency Savings	-5	-5	-5	-5	-5	-5	-5	-5
Balance in bank	1362	1416	1470	1479	1533	1427	1481	1535
Paycheck (After approx taxes)	234	234	234	234	234	234	234	234
Balance forward	1416	1470	1479	1533	1427	1481	1535	1589

Figure Seven

Chapter Zero	31-Jan-20	7-Feb-20	14-Feb-20	21-Feb-20	28-Feb-20	6-Mar-20	13-Mar-20	20-Mar-20
Rent/Mortgage	-50				-50			
Meals @ $10 per day	-70	-70	-70	-70	-70	-70	-70	-70
Cell	-70				-70			
Saving $20K for room + car	-60	-60	-60	-60	-60	-60	-60	-60
Health insurance	-40				-40			
Auto/transportation	-40	-40	-40	-40	-40	-40	-40	-40
Gifts/ fun/pets	-5	-5	-5	-5	-5	-5	-5	-5
Emergency Savings	-5	-5	-5	-5	-5	-5	-5	-5
Balance in bank	1589	1483	1537	1591	1645	1539	1593	1647
Paycheck (After approx taxes)	234	234	234	234	234	234	234	234
Balance forward	1483	1537	1591	1645	1539	1593	1647	1701

Figure Eight

Chapter Zero	27-Mar-20	3-Apr-20	10-Apr-20	17-Apr-20	24-Apr-20	1-May-20	8-May-20	15-May-20
Rent/Mortgage	-50					-50		
Meals @ $10 per day	-70	-70	-70	-70	-70	-70	-70	-70
Cell	-70					-70		
Saving $20K for room + car	-60	-60	-60	-60	-60	-60	-60	-60
Health insurance	-40					-40		
Auto/transportation	-40	-40	-40	-40	-40	-40	-40	-40
Gifts/ fun/pets	-5	-5	-5	-5	-5	-5	-5	-5
Emergency Savings	-5	-5	-5	-5	-5	-5	-5	-5
Balance in bank	1701	1595	1649	1703	1757	1811	1705	1759
Paycheck (After approx taxes)	234	234	234	234	234	234	234	234
Balance forward	1595	1649	1703	1757	1811	1705	1759	1813

Figure Nine

Chapter Zero	22-May-20	29-May-20	5-Jun-20	12-Jun-20	19-Jun-20	26-Jun-20	3-Jul-20	10-Jul-20
Rent/Mortgage		-50					-50	
Meals @ $10 per day	-70	-70	-70	-70	-70	-70	-70	-70
Cell		-70					-70	
Saving $20K for room + car	-60	-60	-60	-60	-60	-60	-60	-60
Health insurance		-40					-40	
Auto/transportation	-40	-40	-40	-40	-40	-40	-40	-40
Gifts/ fun/pets	-5	-5	-5	-5	-5	-5	-5	-5
Emergency Savings	-5	-5	-5	-5	-5	-5	-5	-5
Balance in bank	1813	1867	1761	1815	1869	1923	1977	1871
Paycheck (After approx taxes)	234	234	234	234	234	234	234	234
Balance forward	1867	1761	1815	1869	1923	1977	1871	1925

Figure Ten

Chapter Zero	17-Jul-20	24-Jul-20	31-Jul-20	7-Aug-20	14-Aug-20	21-Aug-20	28-Aug-20	4-Sep-20
Rent/Mortgage			-50					-50
Meals @ $10 per day	-70	-70	-70	-70	-70	-70	-70	-70
Cell			-70					-70
Saving $20K for room + car	-60	-60	-60	-60	-60	-60	-60	-60
Health insurance			-40					-40
Auto/transportation	-40	-40	-40	-40	-40	-40	-40	-40
Gifts/ fun/pets	-5	-5	-5	-5	-5	-5	-5	-5
Emergency Savings	-5	-5	-5	-5	-5	-5	-5	-5
Balance in bank	1925	1979	2033	1927	1981	2035	2089	2143
Paycheck (After approx taxes)	234	234	234	234	234	234	234	234
Balance forward	1979	2033	1927	1981	2035	2089	2143	2037

Figure Eleven

Chapter Zero	11-Sep-20	18-Sep-20	25-Sep-20	2-Oct-20	9-Oct-20	16-Oct-20	23-Oct-20	30-Oct-20
Rent/Mortgage				-50				
Meals @ $10 per day	-70	-70	-70	-70	-70	-70	-70	-70
Cell				-70				
Saving $20K for room + car	-60	-60	-60	-60	-60	-60	-60	-60
Health insurance				-40				
Auto/transportation	-40	-40	-40	-40	-40	-40	-40	-40
Gifts/ fun/pets	-5	-5	-5	-5	-5	-5	-5	-5
Emergency Savings	-5	-5	-5	-5	-5	-5	-5	-5
Balance in bank	2037	2091	2145	2199	2093	2147	2201	2255
Paycheck (After approx taxes)	234	234	234	234	234	234	234	234
Balance forward	2091	2145	2199	2093	2147	2201	2255	2309

Figure Twelve

Chapter Zero	6-Nov-20	13-Nov-20	20-Nov-20	27-Nov-20	4-Dec-20	11-Dec-20	18-Dec-20	25-Dec-20
Rent/Mortgage	-50				-50			
Meals @ $10 per day	-70	-70	-70	-70	-70	-70	-70	-70
Cell	-70				-70			
Saving $20K for room + car	-60	-60	-60	-60	-60	-60	-60	-60
Health insurance	-40				-40			
Auto/transportation	-40	-40	-40	-40	-40	-40	-40	-40
Gifts/ fun/pets	-5	-5	-5	-5	-5	-5	-50	-5
Emergency Savings	-5	-5	-5	-5	-5	-5	-5	-5
Balance in bank	2309	2203	2257	2311	2365	2259	2313	2322
Paycheck (After approx taxes)	234	234	234	234	234	234	234	234
Balance forward	2203	2257	2311	2365	2259	2313	2322	2376

Figure Thirteen

Chapter Zero	1-Jan-21	8-Jan-21	15-Jan-21	22-Jan-21	29-Jan-21	5-Feb-21	12-Feb-21	19-Feb-21
Rent/Mortgage	-50					-50		
Meals @ $10 per day	-70	-70	-70	-70	-70	-70	-70	-70
Cell	-70					-70		
Saving $20K for room + car	-60	-60	-60	-60	-60	-60	-60	-60
Health insurance	-40					-40		
Auto/transportation	-40	-40	-40	-40	-40	-40	-40	-40
Gifts/ fun/pets	-5	-5	-5	-5	-5	-5	-5	-5
Emergency Savings	-5	-5	-5	-5	-5	-5	-5	-5
Balance in bank	2376	2270	2324	2378	2432	2486	2380	2434
Paycheck (After approx taxes)	234	234	234	234	234	234	234	234
Balance forward	2270	2324	2378	2432	2486	2380	2434	2488

Figure Fourteen

Chapter Zero	26-Feb-21	5-Mar-21	12-Mar-21	19-Mar-21	26-Mar-21	2-Apr-21	9-Apr-21	16-Apr-21
Rent/Mortgage		-50				-50		
Meals @ $10 per day	-70	-70	-70	-70	-70	-70	-70	-70
Cell		-70				-70		
Saving $20K for room + car	-60	-60	-60	-60	-60	-60	-60	-60
Health insurance		-40				-40		
Auto/transportation	-40	-40	-40	-40	-40	-40	-40	-40
Gifts/ fun/pets	-5	-5	-5	-5	-5	-5	-5	-5
Emergency Savings	-5	-5	-5	-5	-5	-5	-5	-5
Balance in bank	2488	2542	2436	2490	2544	2598	2492	2546
Paycheck (After approx taxes)	234	234	234	234	234	234	234	234
Balance forward	2542	2436	2490	2544	2598	2492	2546	2600

Figure Fifteen

Chapter Zero	23-Apr-21	30-Apr-21	7-May-21	14-May-21	21-May-21	28-May-21	4-Jun-21	11-Jun-21
Rent/Mortgage			-50				-100	
Meals @ $10 per day	-70	-70	-70	-70	-70	-70	-70	-70
Cell			-70				-70	
Saving $20K for room + car	-60	-60	-60	-60	-60	-60	-60	-60
Health insurance			-40				-40	
Auto/transportation	-40	-40	-40	-40	-40	-40	-40	-40
Gifts/ fun/pets	-5	-5	-5	-5	-5	-5	-5	-5
Emergency Savings	-5	-5	-5	-5	-5	-5	-5	-5
Balance in bank	2600	2654	2708	2602	2656	2710	2764	2608
Paycheck (After approx taxes)	234	234	234	234	234	234	234	234
Balance forward	2654	2708	2602	2656	2710	2764	2608	2662

Figure Sixteen

.

Chapter Zero	18-Jun-21	25-Jun-21	2-Jul-21	9-Jul-21	16-Jul-21	23-Jul-21	30-Jul-21	6-Aug-21
Rent/Mortgage			-100				-100	
Meals @ $10 per day	-70	-70	-70	-70	-70	-70	-70	-70
Cell			-70				-70	
Saving $20K for room + car	-60	-60	-60	-60	-60	-60	-60	-80
Health insurance			-40				-40	
Auto/transportation	-40	-40	-40	-40	-40	-40	-40	-40
Gifts/ fun/pets	-5	-5	-5	-5	-5	-5	-5	-5
Emergency Savings	-5	-5	-5	-5	-5	-5	-5	-5
Balance in bank	2662	2716	2770	2614	2668	2722	2776	2620
Paycheck (After approx taxes)	234	234	234	234	234	234	234	234
Balance forward	2716	2770	2614	2668	2722	2776	2620	2654

Figure Seventeen

Chapter Zero	13-Aug-21	20-Aug-21	27-Aug-21	3-Sep-21	10-Sep-21	17-Sep-21	24-Sep-21	1-Oct-21
Rent/Mortgage				-100				-100
Meals @ $10 per day	-70	-70	-70	-70	-70	-70	-70	-70
Cell				-70				-70
Saving $20K for room + car	-80	-80	-80	-80	-80	-80	-80	-80
Health insurance				-40				-40
Auto/transportation	-40	-40	-40	-40	-40	-40	-40	-40
Gifts/ fun/pets	-5	-5	-5	-5	-5	-5	-5	-5
Emergency Savings	-5	-5	-5	-5	-5	-5	-5	-5
Balance in bank	2654	2688	2722	2756	2580	2614	2648	2682
Paycheck (After approx taxes)	234	234	234	234	234	234	234	234
Balance forward	2688	2722	2756	2580	2614	2648	2682	2506

Figure Eighteen

Chapter Zero	8-Oct-21	15-Oct-21	22-Oct-21	29-Oct-21	5-Nov-21	12-Nov-21	19-Nov-21	26-Nov-21
Rent/Mortgage					-100			
Meals @ $10 per day	-70	-70	-70	-70	-70	-70	-70	-70
Cell					-70			
Saving $20K for room + car	-80	-80	-80	-80	-80	-80	-80	-80
Health insurance					-40			
Auto/transportation	-40	-40	-40	-40	-40	-40	-40	-40
Gifts/ fun/pets	-5	-5	-5	-5	-5	-5	-5	-5
Emergency Savings	-5	-5	-5	-5	-5	-5	-5	-5
Balance in bank	2506	2540	2574	2608	2642	2466	2500	2534
Paycheck (After approx taxes)	234	234	234	234	234	234	234	234
Balance forward	2540	2574	2608	2642	2466	2500	2534	2568

Figure Nineteen

Chapter Zero	3-Dec-21	10-Dec-21	17-Dec-21	24-Dec-21	31-Dec-21	7-Jan-22	14-Jan-22	21-Jan-22
Rent/Mortgage	-100					-100		
Meals @ $10 per day	-70	-70	-70	-70	-70	-70	-70	-70
Cell	-70					-70		
Saving $20K for room + car	-80	-80	-80	-80	-80	-80	-80	-80
Health insurance	-40					-40		
Auto/transportation	-40	-40	-40	-40	-40	-40	-40	-40
Gifts/ fun/pets	-5	-5	-5	-50	-5	-5	-5	-5
Emergency Savings	-5	-5	-5	-5	-5	-5	-5	-5
Balance in bank	2568	2392	2426	2460	2449	2483	2307	2341
Paycheck (After approx taxes)	234	234	234	234	234	234	234	234
Balance forward	2392	2426	2460	2449	2483	2307	2341	2375

Figure Twenty

Chapter Zero	28-Jan-22	4-Feb-22	11-Feb-22	18-Feb-22	25-Feb-22	4-Mar-22	11-Mar-22	18-Mar-22
Rent/Mortgage		-100				-100		
Meals @ $10 per day	-70	-70	-70	-70	-70	-70	-70	-70
Cell		-70				-70		
Saving $20K for room + car	-80	-80	-80	-80	-80	-80	-80	-80
Health insurance		-40				-40		
Auto/transportation	-40	-40	-40	-40	-40	-40	-40	-40
Gifts/ fun/pets	-5	-5	-5	-5	-5	-5	-5	-5
Emergency Savings	-5	-5	-5	-5	-5	-5	-5	-5
Balance in bank	2375	2409	2233	2267	2301	2335	2159	2193
Paycheck (After approx taxes)	234	234	234	234	234	234	234	234
Balance forward	2409	2233	2267	2301	2335	2159	2193	2227

Figure Twenty -One

Chapter Zero	25-Mar-22	1-Apr-22	8-Apr-22	15-Apr-22	22-Apr-22	29-Apr-22	6-May-22	13-May-22
Rent/Mortgage		-100				-100		
Meals @ $10 per day	-70	-70	-70	-70	-70	-70	-70	-70
Cell		-70				-70		
Saving $20K for room + car	-80	-80	-80	-80	-80	-80	-80	-80
Health insurance		-40				-40		
Auto/transportation	-40	-40	-40	-40	-40	-40	-40	-40
Gifts/ fun/pets	-5	-5	-5	-5	-5	-5	-5	-5
Emergency Savings	-5	-5	-5	-5	-5	-5	-5	-5
Balance in bank	2227	2261	2085	2119	2153	2187	2011	2045
Paycheck (After approx taxes)	234	234	234	234	234	234	234	234
Balance forward	2261	2085	2119	2153	2187	2011	2045	2079

Figure Twenty-Two

Chapter Zero	20-May-22	27-May-22	3-Jun-22	10-Jun-22	17-Jun-22	24-Jun-22	1-Jul-22	8-Jul-22
Rent/Mortgage			-100				-100	
Meals @ $10 per day	-70	-70	-70	-70	-70	-70	-70	-70
Cell			-70				-70	
Saving $20K for room + car	-80	-80	-80	-80	-80	-80	-100	-100
Health insurance			-40				-40	
Auto/transportation	-40	-40	-40	-40	-40	-40	-40	-40
Gifts/ fun/pets	-10	-10	-10	-10	-10	-10	-10	-10
Emergency Savings	-10	-10	-10	-10	-10	-10	-10	-10
Balance in bank	2079	2103	2127	1941	1965	1989	2013	1807
Paycheck (After approx taxes)	234	234	234	234	234	234	234	234
Balance forward	2103	2127	1941	1965	1989	2013	1807	1811

Three

Chapter Zero	15-Jul-22	22-Jul-22	29-Jul-22	5-Aug-22	12-Aug-22	19-Aug-22	26-Aug-22	2-Sep-22
Rent/Mortgage				-100				-100
Meals @ $10 per day	-70	-70	-70	-70	-70	-70	-70	-70
Cell				-70				-70
Saving $20K for room + car	-100	-100	-100	-100	-100	-100	-100	-100
Health insurance				-40				-40
Auto/transportation	-40	-40	-40	-40	-40	-40	-40	-40
Gifts/ fun/pets	-10	-10	-10	-10	-10	-10	-10	-10
Emergency Savings	-10	-10	-10	-10	-10	-10	-10	-10
Balance in bank	1811	1815	1819	1823	1617	1621	1625	1629
Paycheck (After approx taxes)	234	234	234	234	234	234	234	234
Balance forward	1815	1819	1823	1617	1621	1625	1629	1423

Figure Twenty - Four

Chapter Zero	9-Sep-22	16-Sep-22	23-Sep-22	30-Sep-22	7-Oct-22	14-Oct-22	21-Oct-22	28-Oct-22
Rent/Mortgage					-100			
Meals @ $10 per day	-70	-70	-70	-70	-70	-70	-70	-70
Cell					-70			
Saving $20K for room + car	-100	-100	-100	-100	-100	-100	-100	-100
Health insurance					-40			
Auto/transportation	-40	-40	-40	-40	-40	-40	-40	-40
Gifts/ fun/pets	-10	-10	-10	-10	-10	-10	-10	-10
Emergency Savings	-10	-10	-10	-10	-10	-10	-10	-10
Balance in bank	1423	1427	1431	1435	1439	1233	1237	1241
Paycheck (After approx taxes)	234	234	234	234	234	234	234	234
Balance forward	1427	1431	1435	1439	1233	1237	1241	1245

Figure Twenty- Five

Chapter Zero	4-Nov-22	11-Nov-22	18-Nov-22	25-Nov-22	2-Dec-22	9-Dec-22		
Rent/Mortgage	-100				-100			
Meals @ $10 per day	-70	-70	-70	-70	-70	-70		
Cell	-70				-70			
Saving $20K for room + car	-100	-100	-100	-100	-100	-100		
Health insurance	-40				-40			
Auto/transportation	-40	-40	-40	-40	-40	-40		
Gifts/ fun/pets	-10	-10	-10	-10	-10	-10		
Emergency Savings	-10	-10	-10	-10	-10	-10		
Balance in bank	1245	1039	1043	1047	1051	845		
Paycheck (After approx taxes)	234	234	234	234	234	234		
Balance forward	1039	1043	1047	1051	845	849		

Figure Twenty - Six

CHAPTER ONE

Living at Home – First Job

This budget is best for a person who still lives at home and has a full time job (40 hours per week) earning no less than $10.00 per hour, and your goal is to save $10,000.00 to buy a car.

- Rent to parents or Guardian: If you have a job, it is time to learn to pay rent. $200.00 a month is reasonable for a 'starter' rent. If they won't 'accept' rent, then either add it to your savings or ask them to put it in a separate account for you.

- Misc. Food: You will probably begin to eat meals away from home, so it is a good idea to budget for it. You can also spend this money on your personal snacks, or add it to savings. You will find a grocery and meal planner at the backof this book.

- Cell: You can either get your own Phone plan or reimburse your parents for using theirs.

- Internet/Entertainment: You may have an on line subscription or something similar, like Hulu or Xbox gold.

- Heat, Water, Electric: You probably won't be paying these if you are at home, but it is a good idea to remember you will have to budget for them in the future.

- Save for Car: This exact amount should be put in to a separate bank account every week. At the end of 108 weeks you will be able to pay cash for your car. If you put it in a savings account that earns .91% or better, you will have slightly more.

- Health Insurance: You may have a personal policy that you pay monthly. Your employer may withhold this amount from your check in weekly increments.

- Transportation: Even if you skateboard to work, there will be occasional days when you need to take a bus, or Uber.

- Gifts/Fun: It is going to happen so you need to put it in your budget. You do not have to spend that much, but do not spend more.

- Emergency Savings: Put this amount aside every week in case of a Real emergency. Medical or a death in the family qualify.

- Balance in Bank: That is what you should have in your bank account at the end of all transactions in order to stay on your budget. At the beginning of this budget you must start with $200.00 in your bank. That is possible if you deposited your first pay check the week before.

- Paycheck: This is an average, because tax laws vary from state to state and even from city to city. A $10 a week pay increase is built in to the second year. You will be shown how to change this number to match your paycheck in the next section

- Balance forward: This is what is left after you pay your expenses. This money cannot be spent – it is carried forward to the next period. This is the main point of a budget – to not spend every bit of money that comes into your hands.

Chapter One	3-Jan-19	10-Jan-19	17-Jan-19	24-Jan-19	31-Jan-19	7-Feb-19	14-Feb-19	21-Feb-19
Rent to parents or guardian	-200				-200			
Misc. Food	-50	-50	-50	-50	-50	-50	-50	-50
Cell	-35				-35			
Internet/ Entertainment	-25				-25			
Heat								
Electric								
Water								
Save for car		-96	-96	-96	-96	-96	-96	-96
Health insurance	-85				-85			
Transportation	-25	-25	-25	-25	-25	-25	-25	-25
Gifts/ fun/pets	-15	-15	-15	-15	-15	-15	-50	-15
Emergency Savings	-25	-25	-25	-25	-25	-25	-25	-25
Balance in bank	200	50	149	248	347	101	200	264
Paycheck (After approx taxes)	310	310	310	310	310	310	310	310
Balance forward	50	149	248	347	101	200	264	363

Figure 1 - The first 8 weeks

Notes:

Chapter One	28-Feb-19	7-Mar-19	14-Mar-19	21-Mar-19	28-Mar-19	4-Apr-19	11-Apr-19	18-Apr-19
Rent to parents or guardian	-200				-200			
Misc. Food	-50	-50	-50	-50	-50	-50	-50	-50
Cell	-35				-35			
Internet/ Entertainment	-25				-25			
Heat								
Electric								
Water								
Save for car	-96	-96	-96	-96	-96	-96	-96	-96
Health insurance	-85				-85			
Transportation	-25	-25	-25	-25	-25	-25	-25	-25
Gifts/ fun/pets	-15	-15	-25	-30	-40	-40	-40	-50
Emergency Savings	-25	-25	-25	-25	-25	-25	-25	-25
Balance in bank	363	117	216	305	389	118	192	266
Paycheck (After approx taxes)	310	310	310	310	310	310	310	310
Balance forward	117	216	305	389	118	192	266	330

Figure 2 - The second 8 weeks

Notes:

Chapter One	25-Apr-19	2-May-19	9-May-19	16-May-19	23-May-19	30-May-19	6-Jun-19	13-Jun-19
Rent to parents or guardian		-200				-200		
Misc. Food	-50	-50	-50	-50	-50	-50	-50	-50
Cell		-35				-35		
Internet/ Entertainment		-25				-25		
Heat								
Electric								
Water								
Save for car	-96	-96	-96	-96	-96	-96	-96	-96
Health insurance		-85				-85		
Transportation	-25	-25	-25	-25	-25	-25	-25	-25
Gifts/ fun/pets	-40	-40	-40	-40	-40	-50	-40	-40
Emergency Savings	-25	-25	-25	-25	-25	-25	-25	-25
Balance in bank	330	404	133	207	281	355	74	148
Paycheck (After approx taxes)	310	310	310	310	310	310	310	310
Balance forward	404	133	207	281	355	74	148	222

Figure 3 - The third 8 weeks

Notes:

Chapter One	20-Jun-19	27-Jun-19	4-Jul-19	11-Jul-19	18-Jul-19	25-Jul-19	1-Aug-19	8-Aug-19
Rent to parents or guardian		-200					-200	
Misc. Food	-50	-50	-50	-50	-50	-50	-50	-50
Cell		-35					-35	
Internet/ Entertainment		-25					-25	
Heat								
Electric								
Water								
Save for car	-96	-96	-96	-96	-96	-96	-96	-96
Health insurance		-85					-85	
Transportation	-25	-25	-25	-25	-25	-25	-25	-25
Gifts/ fun/pets	-40	-40	-50	-30	-25	-25	-25	-25
Emergency Savings	-25	-25	-25	-25	-25	-25	-25	-25
Balance in bank	222	296	25	89	173	262	351	95
Paycheck (After approx taxes)	310	310	310	310	310	310	310	310
Balance forward	296	25	89	173	262	351	95	184

Figure 4 - The fourth 8 weeks

Notes:

Chapter One	15-Aug-19	22-Aug-19	29-Aug-19	5-Sep-19	12-Sep-19	19-Sep-19	26-Sep-19	3-Oct-19
Rent to parents or guardian			-200					-200
Misc. Food	-50	-50	-50	-50	-50	-50	-50	-50
Cell			-35					-35
Internet/ Entertainment			-25					-25
Heat								
Electric								
Water								
Save for car	-96	-96	-96	-96	-96	-96	-96	-96
Health insurance			-85					-85
Transportation	-25	-25	-25	-25	-25	-25	-25	-25
Gifts/ fun/pets	-25	-25	-25	-75	-25	-25	-25	-25
Emergency Savings	-25	-25	-25	-25	-25	-25	-25	-25
Balance in bank	184	273	362	106	145	234	323	412
Paycheck (After approx taxes)	310	310	310	310	310	310	310	310
Balance forward	273	362	106	145	234	323	412	156
	Figure 5 - The Fifth 8 weeks							
	Notes:							

Chapter One	10-Oct-19	17-Oct-19	24-Oct-19	31-Oct-19	7-Nov-19	14-Nov-19	21-Nov-19	28-Nov-19
Rent to parents or guardian				-200				-200
Misc. Food	-50	-50	-50	-50	-50	-50	-50	-50
Cell				-35				-35
Internet/ Entertainment				-25				-25
Heat								
Electric								
Water								
Save for car	-96	-96	-96	-96	-96	-96	-96	-96
Health insurance				-85				-85
Transportation	-25	-25	-25	-25	-25	-25	-25	-25
Gifts/ fun/pets	-25	-25	-25	-50	-25	-25	-40	-25
Emergency Savings	-25	-25	-25	-25	-25	-25	-25	-25
Balance in bank	156	245	334	423	142	231	320	394
Paycheck (After approx taxes)	310	310	310	310	310	310	310	310
Balance forward	245	334	423	142	231	320	394	138
Figure 6 - The Sixth 8 weeks								
Notes:								

Chapter One	5-Dec-19	12-Dec-19	19-Dec-19	26-Dec-19	2-Jan-20	9-Jan-20	16-Jan-20	23-Jan-20
Rent to parents or guardian					-200			
Misc. Food	-50	-50	-50	-50	-50	-50	-50	-50
Cell					-35			
Internet/ Entertainment					-25			
Heat								
Electric								
Water								
Save for car	-96	-96	-96	-96	-96	-96	-96	-96
Health insurance					-85			
Transportation	-25	-25	-25	-25	-25	-25	-25	-25
Gifts/ fun/pets	-25	-150	-50	-25	-25	-25	-25	-25
Emergency Savings	-25	-25	-25	-25	-25	-25	-25	-25
Balance in bank	138	227	191	255	344	88	177	266
Paycheck (After approx taxes)	310	310	310	310	310	310	310	310
Balance forward	227	191	255	344	88	177	266	355

Figure 7 - The Seventh 8 weeks

Notes:

Chapter One	30-Jan-20	6-Feb-20	13-Feb-20	20-Feb-20	27-Feb-20	5-Mar-20	12-Mar-20	19-Mar-20
Rent to parents or guardian	-200				-200			
Misc. Food	-50	-50	-50	-50	-50	-50	-50	-50
Cell	-35				-35			
Internet/ Entertainment	-25				-25			
Heat								
Electric								
Water								
Save for car	-96	-96	-96	-96	-96	-96	-96	-96
Health insurance	-85				-85			
Transportation	-25	-25	-25	-25	-25	-25	-25	-25
Gifts/ fun/pets	-25	-25	-50	-25	-25	-25	-25	-50
Emergency Savings	-25	-25	-25	-25	-25	-25	-25	-25
Balance in bank	355	99	188	252	341	85	174	263
Paycheck (After approx taxes)	310	310	310	310	310	310	310	310
Balance forward	99	188	252	341	85	174	263	327

Figure 8- The eighth 8 weeks

Notes:

Chapter One	26-Mar-20	2-Apr-20	9-Apr-20	16-Apr-20	23-Apr-20	30-Apr-20	7-May-20	14-May-20
Rent to parents or guardian	-200					-200		
Misc. Food	-50	-50	-50	-50	-50	-50	-50	-50
Cell	-35					-35		
Internet/ Entertainment	-25					-25		
Heat								
Electric								
Water								
Save for car	-96	-96	-96	-96	-96	-96	-96	-96
Health insurance	-85					-85		
Transportation	-25	-25	-25	-25	-25	-25	-25	-25
Gifts/ fun/pets	-25	-25	-25	-25	-25	-25	-50	-50
Emergency Savings	-25	-25	-25	-25	-25	-25	-25	-25
Balance in bank	327	71	160	249	338	427	171	235
Paycheck (After approx taxes)	310	310	310	310	310	310	310	310
Balance forward	71	160	249	338	427	171	235	299

Figure 9 - The Ninth 8 weeks

Notes:

Chapter One	21-May-20	28-May-20	4-Jun-20	11-Jun-20	18-Jun-20	25-Jun-20	2-Jul-20	9-Jul-20
Rent to parents or guardian		-200					-200	
Misc. Food	-50	-50	-50	-50	-50	-50	-50	-50
Cell		-35					-35	
Internet/ Entertainment		-25					-25	
Heat								
Electric								
Water								
Save for car	-96	-96	-96	-96	-96	-96	-96	-96
Health insurance		-85					-85	
Transportation	-25	-25	-25	-25	-25	-25	-25	-25
Gifts/ fun/pets	-50	-50	-50	-50	-50	-50	-100	-40
Emergency Savings	-25	-25	-25	-25	-25	-25	-25	-25
Balance in bank	299	373	102	176	250	324	398	77
Paycheck (After approx taxes)	320	320	320	320	320	320	320	320
Balance forward	373	102	176	250	324	398	77	161

Figure 10 - The Tenth 8 weeks — Note the pay increase. This takes into account your hard work.

Notes:

Chapter One	16-Jul-20	23-Jul-20	30-Jul-20	6-Aug-20	13-Aug-20	20-Aug-20	27-Aug-20	3-Sep-20
Rent to parents or guardian			-200					-200
Misc. Food	-50	-50	-50	-50	-50	-50	-50	-50
Cell			-35					-35
Internet/ Entertainment			-25					-25
Heat								
Electric								
Water								
Save for car	-96	-96	-96	-96	-96	-96	-96	-96
Health insurance			-85					-85
Transportation	-25	-25	-25	-25	-25	-25	-25	-25
Gifts/ fun/pets	-40	-40	-35	-40	-40	-40	-100	-40
Savings	-25	-25	-25	-25	-25	-25	-25	-25
Balance in bank	161	245	329	73	157	241	325	349
Paycheck (After approx taxes)	320	320	320	320	320	320	320	320
Balance forward	245	329	73	157	241	325	349	88

Figure 11 - The Eleventh 8 weeks
Notes:

Chapter One	10-Sep-20	17-Sep-20	24-Sep-20	1-Oct-20	8-Oct-20	15-Oct-20	22-Oct-20	29-Oct-20
Rent to parents or guardian			-200					-200
Misc. Food	-50	-50	-50	-50	-50	-50	-50	-50
Cell			-35					-35
Internet/ Entertainment			-25					-25
Heat								
Electric								
Water								
Save for car	-96	-96	-96	-96	-96	-96	-96	-96
Health insurance			-85					-85
Transportation	-20	-20	-25	-25	-25	-25	-25	-25
Gifts/ fun/pets	-40	-40	-35	-30	-35	-35	-35	-35
Savings	-25	-25	-25	-25	-25	-25	-25	-25
Balance in bank	88	177	266	10	104	193	282	371
Paycheck (After approx taxes)	320	320	320	320	320	320	320	320
Balance forward	177	266	10	104	193	282	371	115

Figure 12 -
Notes:

Chapter One	5-Nov-20	12-Nov-20	19-Nov-20	26-Nov-20	3-Dec-20	10-Dec-20	17-Dec-20	24-Dec-20
Rent to parents or guardian				-200				
Misc. Food	-50	-50	-50	-50	-50	-50	-50	-50
Cell				-35				
Internet/ Entertainment				-25				
Heat								
Electric								
Water								
Save for car	-96	-96	-96	-96	-96	-96	-96	-96
Health insurance				-85				
Transportation	-25	-25	-25	-25	-25	-25	-25	-25
Gifts/ fun/pets	-35	-35	-35	-50	-35	-35	-150	-35
Emergency Savings	-25	-25	-25	-25	-25	-25	-25	-25
Balance in bank	115	204	293	382	111	200	289	263
Paycheck (After approx taxes)	320	320	320	320	320	320	320	320
Balance forward	204	293	382	111	200	289	263	352

Figure 13 - Almost Done

Notes:

Chapter One	31-Dec-20	7-Jan-21
Rent to parents or guardian	-200	
Misc. Food	-50	-50
Cell	-35	
Internet/ Entertainment	-25	
Heat		
Electric		
Water		
Save for car	-96	-96
Health insurance	-85	
Transportation	-25	-25
Gifts/ fun/pets	-50	-50
Emergency Savings	-25	-25
Balance in bank	352	81
Paycheck (After approx taxes)	320	320
Balance forward	81	155

Figure 14 - You can buy the car!

Notes:

CHAPTER TWO

Living at Home – Student Debt

This budget is best for a person who has moved back home after completing a minimum of 2-4 years of Trade School or College, has $20,000.00 of student loan debt, and is working at an entry level $10.00 job. Your goal is to pay off the student loans.

♦ Rent to parents or Guardian: If you have a job, it is time to learn to pay rent. $200.00 a month is reasonable for a 'starter' rent.

♦ Misc. Food: You will probably begin to eat meals away from home, so it is a good idea to budget for it. You can also spend this money on your personal snacks. You will find a grocery and meal planner at the backof this book.

♦ Cell: You can either get your own discount phone plan or reimburse your parents for using theirs.

♦ Internet/Entertainment: You may have an on line subscription or something similar, like Hulu or Xbox gold.

♦ Heat, Water, Electric: You probably won't be paying these if you are at home, but it is a good idea to remember you will have to budget for them in the future.

♦ Pay off Student Loan: This exact amount should be paid on your loan every week. Even though they bill you monthly, if you go ahead and pay them weekly, you will pay off the loan faster because you will be reducing the interest faster. If they have an on-line portal, you can pay there. Otherwise get the correct mailing address and a bunch of stamps and envelopes and go to town. Remember: **weekly payments reduce debt faster** by helping to reduce interest payments.

♦ Health Insurance: You may have a personal policy that you pay monthly. Your employer may withhold this amount from your check in weekly increments. If you do not have insurance, save this amount in the bank in case you need to see a doctor in the future.

♦ Transportation: Even if you skateboard to work, there will be occasional days when you need to take a bus, or Uber.

♦ Gifts/Fun: It is going to happen so you need to put it in your budget. You do not have to spend that much, but do not spend more.

♦ Emergency Savings: Put this amount aside every week in case of a Real emergency. Medical or a death in the family qualify.

♦ Balance in Bank: That is what you should have in your bank account at the end of all transactions in order to stay on your budget. At the beginning of this budget you must start with $200.00 in your bank. That is possible if you deposited your first pay check the week before.

♦ Paycheck: This is an average, because tax laws vary from state to state and even from city to city. If you are on salary, your pay will be the same every week. You can copy the exact figure from your pay stub. If you are an hourly worker, your net pay will change from week to week. Some companies give annual or even semi-annual pay increases. When your pay increases you can contribute more to your savings plan!

♦ Balance forward: This is what is left after you pay your expenses. This money cannot be spent – it is carried forward to the next period. This is the main point of a budget – to not spend every bit of money that comes into your hands.

Chapter 2	4-Jan-19	11-Jan-19	18-Jan-19	25-Jan-19	1-Feb-19	8-Feb-19	15-Feb-19	22-Feb-19
Rent to parents or guardian	-200				-200			
Misc. Food	-50	-50	-50	-50	-50	-50	-50	-50
Cell	-35				-35			
Internet/ Entertainment	-25				-25			
Heat								
Electric								
Water								
Pay Off $20k loan*		-121	-121	-121	-121	-121	-121	-121
Health insurance	-85				-85			
transportation	-25	-25	-25	-25	-25	-25	-25	-25
Gifts/ fun/pets	-5	-5	-5	-5	-5	-10	-40	-10
Emergency Savings			-5	-5	-5	-10	-10	-10
Balance in bank	200	85	194	298	402	161	255	319
Paycheck (After approx taxes)	310	310	310	310	310	310	310	310
Balance forward	85	194	298	402	161	255	319	413
	Notes:		Figure One: First Eight week period					

Chapter 2	1-Mar-19	8-Mar-19	15-Mar-19	22-Mar-19	29-Mar-19	5-Apr-19	12-Apr-19	19-Apr-19
Rent to parents or guardian	-200				-200			
Misc. Food	-50	-50	-50	-50	-50	-50	-50	-50
Cell	-35				-35			
Internet /Entertainment	-25				-25			
Heat								
Electric								
Water								
Pay Off $20k loan*	-121	-121	-121	-121	-121	-121	-121	-121
Health insurance	-85				-85			
Transportation	-25	-25	-25	-25	-25	-25	-25	-25
Gifts/ fun/pets	-10	-10	-40	-20	-20	-20	-20	-20
Emergency Savings	-10	-10	-10	-10	-10	-10	-10	-10
Balance in bank	413	162	256	320	404	143	227	311
Paycheck (After approx taxes)	310	310	310	310	310	310	310	310
Balance forward	162	256	320	404	143	227	311	395
		Figure Two: Second Eight week period						

Chapter 2	26-Apr-19	3-May-19	10-May-19	17-May-19	24-May-19	31-May-19	7-Jun-19	14-Jun-19
Rent to parents or guardian		-200				-200		
Misc. Food	-50	-50	-50	-50	-50	-50	-50	-50
Cell		-35				-35		
Internet/ Entertainment		-25				-25		
Heat								
Electric								
Water								
Pay Off $20k loan*	-121	-121	-121	-121	-121	-121	-121	-121
Health insurance		-85				-85		
transportation	-25	-25	-25	-25	-25	-25	-25	-25
Gifts/ fun/pets	-20	-20	-20	-20	-20	-40	-20	-20
Emergency Savings	-10	-10	-10	-10	-10	-10	-10	-10
Balance in bank	395	479	218	302	386	470	189	273
Paycheck (After approx taxes)	310	310	310	310	310	310	310	310
Balance forward	479	218	302	386	470	189	273	357

Figure Three: Third Eight week period

Chapter 2	21-Jun-19	28-Jun-19	5-Jul-19	12-Jul-19	19-Jul-19	26-Jul-19	2-Aug-19	9-Aug-19
Rent to parents or guardian		-200					-200	
Misc. Food	-50	-50	-50	-50	-50	-50	-50	-50
Cell		-35					-35	
Internet/Entertainment		-25					-25	
Heat								
Electric								
Water								
Pay Off $20k loan*	-121	-121	-121	-121	-121	-121	-121	-121
Health insurance		-85					-85	
Transportation	-25	-25	-25	-25	-25	-25	-25	-25
Gifts/ fun/pets	-20	-20	-40	-20	-20	-20	-20	-20
Emergency Savings	-10	-10	-10	-10	-10	-10	-10	-10
Balance in bank	357	441	180	244	328	412	496	235
Paycheck (After approx taxes)	310	310	310	310	310	310	310	310
Balance forward	441	180	244	328	412	496	235	319

Figure Four: Fourth Eight week period

Chapter 2	16-Aug-19	23-Aug-19	30-Aug-19	6-Sep-19	13-Sep-19	20-Sep-19	27-Sep-19	4-Oct-19
Rent to parents or guardian			-200					-200
Misc. Food	-50	-50	-50	-50	-50	-50	-50	-50
Cell			-35					-35
Internet/ Entertainment			-25					-25
Heat								
Electric								
Water								
Pay Off $20k loan*	-121	-121	-121	-121	-121	-121	-121	-121
Health insurance			-85					-85
transportation	-25	-25	-25	-25	-25	-25	-25	-25
Gifts/ fun/pets	-20	-20	-20	-40	-20	-20	-20	-20
Emergency Savings	-10	-10	-10	-10	-10	-10	-10	-10
Balance in bank	319	403	487	226	290	374	458	542
Paycheck (After approx taxes)	310	310	310	310	310	310	310	310
Balance forward	403	487	226	290	374	458	542	281

Figure Five: Fifth Eight week period

Chapter 2	11-Oct-19	18-Oct-19	25-Oct-19	1-Nov-19	8-Nov-19	15-Nov-19	22-Nov-19	29-Nov-19
Rent to parents or guardian				-200				-200
Misc. Food	-50	-50	-50	-50	-50	-50	-50	-50
Cell				-35				-35
Internet/ Entertainment				-25				-25
Heat								
Electric								
Water								
Pay Off $20k loan*	-121	-121	-121	-121	-121	-121	-121	-121
Health insurance				-85				-85
Transportation	-25	-25	-25	-25	-25	-25	-25	-25
Gifts/ fun/pets	-20	-20	-20	-40	-20	-20	-20	-20
Emergency Savings	-10	-10	-10	-10	-10	-10	-10	-10
Balance in bank	281	365	449	533	252	336	420	504
Paycheck (After approx taxes)	310	310	310	310	310	310	310	310
Balance forward	365	449	533	252	336	420	504	243

Figure Six: Sixth Eight week period

Chapter 2	6-Dec-19	13-Dec-19	20-Dec-19	27-Dec-19	3-Jan-20	10-Jan-20	17-Jan-20	24-Jan-20
Rent to parents or guardian					-200			
Misc. Food	-50	-50	-50	-50	-50	-50	-50	-50
Cell					-35			
Internet/ Entertainment					-25			
Heat								
Electric								
Water								
Pay Off $20k loan*	-121	-121	-121	-121	-121	-121	-121	-121
Health insurance					-85			
transportation	-25	-25	-25	-25	-25	-25	-25	-25
Gifts/ fun/pets	-20	-40	-150	-20	-40	-20	-20	-20
Emergency Savings	-10	-10	-10	-10	-10	-10	-10	-10
Balance in bank	243	327	391	345	429	148	232	316
Paycheck (After approx taxes)	310	310	310	310	310	310	310	310
Balance forward	327	391	345	429	148	232	316	400

FigureSeven: Seventh Eight week period

Chapter 2	31-Jan-20	7-Feb-20	14-Feb-20	21-Feb-20	28-Feb-20	6-Mar-20	13-Mar-20	20-Mar-20
Rent to parents or guardian	-200				-200			
Misc. Food	-50	-50	-50	-50	-50	-50	-50	-50
Cell	-35				-35			
Internet/Entertainment	-25				-25			
Heat								
Electric								
Water								
Pay Off $20k loan*	-121	-121	-121	-121	-121	-121	-121	-121
Health insurance	-85				-85			
Transportation	-25	-25	-25	-25	-25	-25	-25	-25
Gifts/ fun/pets	-20	-20	-40	-20	-20	-20	-40	-20
Emergency Savings	-10	-10	-10	-10	-10	-10	-10	-10
Balance in bank	400	139	223	287	371	110	194	258
Paycheck (After approx taxes)	310	310	310	310	310	310	310	310
Balance forward	139	223	287	371	110	194	258	342

Figure Six: Sixth Eight week period

Chapter 2	27-Mar-20	3-Apr-20	10-Apr-20	17-Apr-20	24-Apr-20	1-May-20	8-May-20	15-May-20
Rent to parents or guardian	-200					-200		
Misc. Food	-50	-50	-50	-50	-50	-50	-50	-50
Cell	-35					-35		
Internet/ Entertainment	-25					-25		
Heat								
Electric								
Water								
Pay Off $20k loan*	-121	-121	-121	-121	-121	-121	-121	-121
Health insurance	-85					-85		
transportation	-25	-25	-25	-25	-25	-25	-25	-25
Gifts/ fun/pets	-20	-20	-20	-20	-20	-20	-20	-20
Emergency Savings	-10	-10	-10	-10	-10	-10	-10	-10
Balance in bank	342	81	165	249	333	417	156	240
Paycheck (After approx taxes)	310	310	310	310	310	310	310	310
Balance forward	**81**	**165**	**249**	**333**	**417**	**156**	**240**	**324**

FigureSeven: Seventh Eight week period

Chapter 2	22-May-20	29-May-20	5-Jun-20	12-Jun-20	19-Jun-20	26-Jun-20	3-Jul-20	10-Jul-20
Rent to parents or guardian		-200					-200	
Misc. Food	-50	-50	-50	-50	-50	-50	-50	-50
Cell		-35					-35	
Internet/ Entertainment		-25					-25	
Heat								
Electric								
Water								
Pay Off $20k loan*	-121	-121	-121	-121	-121	-121	-121	-121
Health insurance		-85					-85	
Transportation	-25	-25	-25	-25	-25	-25	-25	-25
Gifts/ fun/pets	-20	-40	-20	-20	-20	-20	-50	-20
Emergency Savings	-10	-10	-10	-10	-10	-10	-10	-10
Balance in bank	324	408	127	221	315	409	503	222
Paycheck (After approx taxes)	310	310	320	320	320	320	320	320
Balance forward	**408**	**127**	**221**	**315**	**409**	**503**	**222**	**316**

Figure Six: Sixth Eight week period

Chapter 2	17-Jul-20	24-Jul-20	31-Jul-20	7-Aug-20	14-Aug-20	21-Aug-20	28-Aug-20	4-Sep-20
Rent to parents or guardian			-200					-200
Misc. Food	-50	-50	-50	-50	-50	-50	-50	-50
Cell			-35					-35
Internet/Entertainment			-25					-25
Heat								
Electric								
Water								
Pay Off $20k loan*	-121	-121	-121	-121	-121	-121	-121	-121
Health insurance			-85					-85
transportation	-25	-25	-25	-25	-25	-25	-25	-25
Gifts/ fun/pets	-20	-20	-20	-20	-20	-20	-20	-40
Emergency Savings	-10	-10	-10	-10	-10	-10	-10	-10
Balance in bank	316	410	504	253	347	441	535	629
Paycheck (After approx taxes)	320	320	320	320	320	320	320	320
Balance forward	410	504	253	347	441	535	629	358

FigureSeven: Seventh Eight week period

Chapter 2	11-Sep-20	18-Sep-20	25-Sep-20	2-Oct-20	9-Oct-20	16-Oct-20	23-Oct-20	30-Oct-20
Rent to parents or guardian			-200					-200
Misc. Food	-50	-50	-50	-50	-50	-50	-50	-50
Cell			-35					-35
Internet/ Entertainment			-25					-25
Heat								
Electric								
Water								
Pay Off $20k loan*	-121	-121	-121	-121	-121	-121	-121	-121
Health insurance			-85					-85
Transportation	-25	-25	-25	-25	-25	-25	-25	-25
Gifts/ fun/pets	-20	-20	-20	-20	-20	-20	-20	-40
Emergency Savings	-10	-10	-10	-10	-10	-10	-10	-10
Balance in bank	358	452	546	295	389	483	577	671
Paycheck (After approx taxes)	320	320	320	320	320	320	320	320
Balance forward	452	546	295	389	483	577	671	400

Figure Six: Sixth Eight week period

Chapter 2	6-Nov-20	13-Nov-20	20-Nov-20	27-Nov-20	4-Dec-20	11-Dec-20	18-Dec-20	25-Dec-20
Rent to parents or guardian				-200				
Misc. Food	-50	-50	-50	-50	-50	-50	-50	-50
Cell				-35				
Internet/Entertainment				-25				
Heat								
Electric								
Water								
Pay Off $20k loan*	-121	-121	-121	-121	-121	-121	-121	-121
Health insurance				-85				
transportation	-25	-25	-25	-25	-25	-25	-25	-25
Gifts/ fun/pets	-20	-20	-30	-20	-20	-40	-150	-20
Emergency Savings	-10	-10	-10	-10	-10	-10	-10	-10
Balance in bank	400	494	588	672	421	515	589	553
Paycheck (After approx taxes)	320	320	320	320	320	320	320	320
Balance forward	494	588	672	421	515	589	553	647

FigureSeven: Seventh Eight week period

Chapter 2	1-Jan-21	8-Jan-21	15-Jan-21
Rent to parents or guardian	-200		
Misc. Food	-50	-50	-50
Cell	-35		
Internet/Entertainment	-25		
Heat			
Electric			
Water			
Pay Off $20k loan*	-121	-121	0
Health insurance	-85		
Transportation	-25	-25	-25
Gifts/ fun/pets	-50	-20	-20
Emergency Savings	-10	-10	-10
Balance in bank	647	366	460
Paycheck (After approx taxes)	320	320	321
Balance forward	366	460	676

Figure Six: Sixth Eight week period

CHAPTER THREE

Living at Home – You want to move

You are at least 18, you live at home, and you own a car. Your goal is to save enough money to move into a small apartment or shared house with rent at $500.00 a month. In order to successfully move, you need to save $6,450.00. You just started working at a full-time $11.00 per hour job.

♦ Rent to parents or Guardian: If you have a job, it is time to learn to pay rent. $200.00 a month is reasonable for a 'starter' rent.

♦ Misc. Food: You will probably begin to eat meals away from home, so it is a good idea to budget for it. You can also spend this money on your personal snacks. You will find a grocery and meal planner at the backof this book.

♦ Cell: You can either get your own Discount plan or reimburse your parents for using theirs.

♦ Internet/Entertainment: You may have an on line subscription or something similar, like Hulu or Xbox gold.

♦ Heat, Water, Electric: You probably won't be paying these if you are at home, but it is a good idea to remember you will have to budget for them in the future.

♦ Save to Move Out: This exact amount should be put in to a separate bank account every week. This must be a savings account that pays interest. The interest is not likely to be a LOT. It will most likely be 1% or less. But as it accumulates in YOUR account it will make certain that you reach your goals faster. In addition to having a security deposit and the first month's rent, you need kitchen stuff, furniture, moving expenses, and at least $4,300.00 in 'fall back' funds in the bank. Follow this carefully and at the end of 108 weeks you will have the funds necessary to move.

♦ Health Insurance: You may have a personal policy that you pay monthly. Your employer may withhold this amount from your check in weekly increments. If you do not have insurance, save this amount in the bank in case you need to see a doctor in the future.

♦ Transportation: Even if you skateboard to work, there will be occasional days when you need to take a bus, or Uber.

♦ Gifts/Fun: It is going to happen so you need to put it in your budget. You do not have to spend that much, but do not spend more.

♦ Emergency Savings: Put this amount aside every week in case of a Real emergency. Medical or a death in the family qualify.

♦ Balance in Bank: That is what you should have in your bank account at the end of all transactions in order to stay on your budget. At the beginning of this budget you must start with $320.00 in your bank. That is possible if you deposited your first pay check the week before.

♦ Paycheck: This is an average, because tax laws vary from state to state and even from city to city. If you are on salary, your pay will be the same every week. You can copy the exact figure from your pay stub. If you are an hourly worker, your net pay will change from week to week. Some companies give annual or even semi-annual pay increases. You will be shown how to change the pay rate figure to match your paycheck in Chapter

♦ Balance forward: This is what is left after you pay your expenses. This money cannot be spent – it is carried forward to the next period. This is the main point of a budget – to not spend every bit of money that comes into your hands.

Chapter 3	4-Jan-19	11-Jan-19	18-Jan-19	25-Jan-19	1-Feb-19	8-Feb-19	15-Feb-19	22-Feb-19
Rent to parents or guardian	-200				-200			
Misc. Food	-50	-50	-50	-50	-50	-50	-50	-50
Cell	-45				-45			
Internet/ Entertainment	-25				-25			
Heat								
Electric								
Water								
Save to MOVE OUT	-95	-95	-95	-95	-95	-95	-95	-95
Health insurance	-85				-85			
Auto/transportation	-35	-35	-35	-35	-35	-35	-35	-35
Gifts/ fun/pets		-30	-30	-30	-30	-30	-30	-30
Emergency Savings			-5	-5	-5	-5	-5	-5
Car Ins. @ $600 per year.	-50				-50			
Balance in bank	320	55	165	270	375	75	180	285
Paycheck (After approx taxes)	320	320	320	320	320	320	320	320
Balance forward	55	165	270	375	75	180	285	390

Figure one - The First 8 Weeks

Notes:

Chapter 3	1-Mar-19	8-Mar-19	15-Mar-19	22-Mar-19	29-Mar-19	5-Apr-19	12-Apr-19	19-Apr-19
Rent to parents or guardian	-200				-200			
Misc. Food	-50	-50	-50	-50	-50	-50	-50	-50
Cell	-45				-45			
Internet/ Entertainment	-25				-25			
Heat								
Electric								
Water								
Save to MOVE OUT	-95	-95	-95	-95	-95	-95	-95	-95
Health insurance	-85				-85			
Auto/transportation	-35	-35	-35	-35	-35	-35	-35	-35
Gifts/ fun/pets	-30	-30	-30	-30	-30	-30	-30	-30
Emergency Savings	-5	-5	-5	-5	-5	-5	-10	-10
Car Ins. @ $600 per year.	-50				-50			
Balance in bank	390	90	195	300	405	105	210	310
Paycheck (After approx taxes)	320	320	320	320	320	320	320	320
Balance forward	90	195	300	405	105	210	310	410

Figure Two - The Second 8 Weeks

Chapter 3	26-Apr-19	3-May-19	10-May-19	17-May-19	24-May-19	31-May-19	7-Jun-19	14-Jun-19
Rent to parents or guardian		-200				-200		
Misc. Food	-50	-50	-50	-50	-50	-50	-50	-50
Cell		-45				-45		
Internet/ Entertainment		-25				-25		
Heat								
Electric								
Water								
Save to MOVE OUT	-95	-95	-95	-95	-95	-95	-95	-95
Health insurance		-85				-85		
Auto/transportation	-35	-35	-35	-35	-35	-35	-35	-35
Gifts/ fun/pets	-30	-30	-30	-30	-30	-30	-30	-30
Emergency Savings	-10	-10	-10	-10	-10	-10	-15	-15
Car Ins. @ $600 per year.		-50				-50		
Balance in bank	410	510	205	305	405	505	200	295
Paycheck (After approx taxes)	320	320	320	320	320	320	320	320
Balance forward	510	205	305	405	505	200	295	390

Figure Three - The Third 8 Weeks

Chapter 3	21-Jun-19	28-Jun-19	5-Jul-19	12-Jul-19	19-Jul-19	26-Jul-19	2-Aug-19	9-Aug-19
Rent to parents or guardian		-200					-200	
Misc. Food	-50	-50	-50	-50	-50	-50	-50	-50
Cell		-45					-45	
Internet/ Entertainment		-25					-25	
Heat								
Electric								
Water								
Save to MOVE OUT	-95	-95	-95	-95	-95	-95	-95	-95
Health insurance		-85					-85	
Auto/transportation	-35	-35	-35	-35	-35	-35	-35	-35
Gifts/ fun/pets	-30	-30	-30	-30	-30	-30	-30	-30
Emergency Savings	-15	-15	-15	-15	-15	-15	-15	-15
Car Ins. @ $600 per year.		-50					-50	
Balance in bank	390	485	175	270	365	460	555	245
Paycheck (After approx taxes)	320	320	320	320	320	320	320	320
Balance forward	485	175	270	365	460	555	245	340

Figure Four - The Fourth 8 Weeks

Chapter 3	16-Aug-19	23-Aug-19	30-Aug-19	6-Sep-19	13-Sep-19	20-Sep-19	27-Sep-19	4-Oct-19
Rent to parents or guardian			-200					-200
Misc. Food	-50	-50	-50	-50	-50	-50	-50	-50
Cell			-45					-45
Internet/ Entertainment			-25					-25
Heat								
Electric								
Water								
Save to MOVE OUT	-95	-95	-95	-95	-95	-95	-95	-95
Health insurance			-85					-85
Auto/transportation	-35	-35	-35	-35	-35	-35	-35	-35
Gifts/ fun/pets	-30	-30	-30	-30	-30	-30	-30	-30
Emergency Savings	-15	-15	-15	-15	-15	-15	-20	-20
Car Ins. @ $600 per year.			-50					-50
Balance in bank	340	435	530	220	315	410	505	595
Paycheck (After approx taxes)	320	320	320	320	320	320	320	320
Balance forward	435	530	220	315	410	505	595	280

Figure Five - The Fifth 8 Weeks

Chapter 3	11-Oct-19	18-Oct-19	25-Oct-19	1-Nov-19	8-Nov-19	15-Nov-19	22-Nov-19	29-Nov-19
Rent to parents or guardian				-200				-200
Misc. Food	-50	-50	-50	-50	-50	-50	-50	-50
Cell				-45				-45
Internet/ Entertainment				-25				-25
Heat								
Electric								
Water								
Save to MOVE OUT	-95	-95	-95	-95	-95	-95	-95	-95
Health insurance				-85				-85
Auto/transportation	-35	-35	-35	-35	-35	-35	-35	-35
Gifts/ fun/pets	-30	-30	-30	-30	-30	-30	-30	-30
Emergency Savings	-20	-20	-20	-20	-20	-20	-20	-20
Car Ins. @ $600 per year.				-50				-50
Balance in bank	280	370	460	550	235	325	415	505
Paycheck (After approx taxes)	320	320	320	320	320	320	320	320
Balance forward	370	460	550	235	325	415	505	190

Figure Six - The Sixth 8 Weeks

Chapter 3	6-Dec-19	13-Dec-19	20-Dec-19	27-Dec-19	3-Jan-20	10-Jan-20	17-Jan-20	24-Jan-20
Rent to parents or guardian					-200			
Misc. Food	-50	-50	-50	-50	-50	-50	-50	-50
Cell					-45			
Internet/ Entertainment					-25			
Heat								
Electric								
Water								
Save to MOVE OUT	-95	-95	-95	-95	-95	-95	-95	-95
Health insurance					-85			
Auto/transportation	-35	-35	-35	-35	-35	-35	-35	-35
Gifts/ fun/pets	-30	-30	-150	-30	-30	-30	-30	-30
Emergency Savings	-20	-20	-20	-20	-20	-20	-20	-20
Car Ins. @ $600 per year.					-50			
Balance in bank	190	280	370	340	430	115	205	295
Paycheck (After approx taxes)	320	320	320	320	320	320	320	320
Balance forward	280	370	340	430	115	205	295	385

Figure Seven - The Seventh 8 Weeks

Chapter 3	31-Jan-20	7-Feb-20	14-Feb-20	21-Feb-20	28-Feb-20	6-Mar-20	13-Mar-20	20-Mar-20
Rent to parents or guardian	-200					-200		
Misc. Food	-50	-50	-50	-50	-50	-50	-50	-50
Cell	-45					-45		
Internet/ Entertainment	-25					-25		
Heat								
Electric								
Water								
Save to MOVE OUT	-95	-95	-95	-95	-95	-95	-95	-95
Health insurance	-85					-85		
Auto/transportation	-35	-35	-35	-35	-35	-35	-35	-35
Gifts/ fun/pets	-30	-30	-30	-30	-30	-30	-30	-30
Emergency Savings	-20	-30	-30	-30	-30	-30	-30	-30
Car Ins. @ $600 per year.	-50					-50		
Balance in bank	385	70	150	230	310	390	65	145
Paycheck (After approx taxes)	320	320	320	320	320	320	320	320
Balance forward	70	150	230	310	390	65	145	225

Figure Eight- The Eighth 8 Weeks

Chapter 3	27-Mar-20	3-Apr-20	10-Apr-20	17-Apr-20				
Rent to parents or guardian		-200						
Misc. Food	-50	-50	-50	-50				
Cell		-45						
Internet/Entertainment		-25						
Heat								
Electric								
Water								
Save to MOVE OUT	-95	-95	-95	-95				
Health insurance		-85						
Auto/transportation	-35	-35	-35	-35				
Gifts/ fun/pets	-30	-30	-30	-30				
Emergency Savings	-30	-30	-30	-30				
Car Ins. @ $600 per year.		-50						
Balance in bank	225	305	-20	60				
Paycheck (After approx taxes)	320	320	320	320				
Balance forward	305	-20	60	140	.	.	.	.

Figure Nine- The Final Month

CHAPTER FOUR

Renting -You want to Buy a house

You've just moved into the rental unit you were saving for in Chapter 3. Now, you are paying rent on a small apartment or a shared house or condo. You decided that you want to OWN a place, not rent. You own a car. Your goal is to save $25,600.00 for moving expenses and down payment on a $200,000.00 home. You just started working at a full-time $11.00 per hour job.

- Rent : Your $500.00 per month rent includes the few utilities you use when at home

- Groceries: This may not look like a lot, but if you create menus, cook at home and plan your food budget properly you can save yourself a lot of heartache and money. Not to mention eating healthier! Suggested menus and grocery lists are included at the end of the book!

- Cell: You can choose from many good phone plans and a lot of them have discounts.

- Internet/Entertainment: You may have an on line subscription or something similar, like Hulu or Amazon Prime

- Heat, Water, Electric: The presumption is that these are included in your rent. It is a good idea to remember you will have to budget for them in the future.

- Save for a Home: This exact amount should be put in to a separate bank account every week. This must be a savings account that pays interest. The interest is not likely to be a LOT. It will most likely be 1% or less. But as it accumulates in YOUR account it will make certain that you reach your goals faster. In addition to your $20,000.00 down payment , you need kitchen stuff, more furniture, moving expenses, and some 'fall back' funds in the bank. So, at the end of only 260 weeks you will have the funds necessary to purchase a home.

- Health Insurance: You may have a personal policy that you pay monthly. Your employer may withhold this amount from your check in weekly increments. If you do not have insurance, save this amount in the bank in case you need to see a doctor in the future.

- Transportation: Even if you skateboard to work, there will be occasional days when you need to get to work some other way.

- Gifts/Fun: It is going to happen so you need to put it in your budget. You do not have to spend that much, but do not spend more.

- Emergency Savings: Put this amount aside every week in case of a Real emergency. Medical or a death in the family qualify.

- Balance in Bank: That is what you should have in your bank account at the end of all transactions in order to stay on your budget. At the beginning of this budget you are starting with the $4,300.00 in your bank acount that you had 'saved' in Chapter 3.

- Paycheck: This is an average, because tax laws vary from state to state and even from city to city. If you are on salary, your pay will be the same every week. You can copy the exact figure from your pay stub. If you are an hourly worker, your net pay will change from week to week. Some companies give annual or even semi-annual pay increases. Most companies give merit pay increases. If you do not get an annual pay review, begin to look for a better paying job.

- Balance forward: This is what is left after you pay your expenses. This money cannot be spent – it is carried forward to the next period. This is the main point of a budget – to not spend every bit of money that comes into your hands.

Chapter 4	4-Jan-19	11-Jan-19	18-Jan-19	25-Jan-19	1-Feb-19	8-Feb-19	15-Feb-19	22-Feb-19
Rent/Mortgage	-500				-500			
Groceries	-71	-71	-71	-71	-71	-71	-71	-71
Cell	-40				-40			
Internet/Entertainment	-25				-25			
Heat								
Electric								
Water								
Save for House	-95	-95	-95	-95	-95	-95	-95	-95
Health insurance	-85				-85			
Auto/transportation	-25	-25	-25	-25	-25	-25	-25	-25
Gifts/ fun/pets	-5	-5	-5	-5	-5	-5	-5	-5
Car Ins. @ $600 per year.	-50				-50			
Balance in bank	4,300	3734	3868	4002	4136	3570	3704	3838
Paycheck (After approx taxes)	330	330	330	330	330	330	330	330
Balance forward	3734	3868	4002	4136	3570	3704	3838	3972

Figure One	Notes:							

Chapter 4	1-Mar-19	8-Mar-19	15-Mar-19	22-Mar-19	29-Mar-19	5-Apr-19	12-Apr-19	19-Apr-19
Rent/Mortgage	-500				-500			
Groceries	-71	-71	-71	-71	-71	-71	-71	-71
Cell	-40				-40			
Internet/Entertainment	-25				-25			
Heat								
Electric								
Water								
Save for House	-95	-95	-95	-95	-95	-95	-95	-95
Health insurance	-85				-85			
Auto/transportation	-25	-25	-25	-25	-25	-25	-25	-25
Gifts/ fun/pets	-5	-5	-5	-5	-5	-5	-5	-5
Car Ins. @ $600 per year.	-50				-50			
Balance in bank	3972	3406	3540	3674	3808	3242	3376	3510
Paycheck (After approx taxes)	330	330	330	330	330	330	330	330
Balance forward	3406	3540	3674	3808	3242	3376	3510	3644

Figure Two	Notes:							

Chapter 4	26-Apr-19	3-May-19	10-May-19	17-May-19	24-May-19	31-May-19	7-Jun-19	14-Jun-19
Rent/Mortgage		-500				-500		
Groceries	-71	-71	-71	-71	-71	-71	-71	-71
Cell		-40				-40		
Internet/Entertainment		-25				-25		
Heat								
Electric								
Water								
Save for House	-95	-100	-100	-100	-100	-100	-100	-100
Health insurance		-85				-85		
Auto/transportation	-25	-25	-25	-25	-25	-25	-25	-25
Gifts/ fun/pets	-5	-5	-5	-5	-5	-5	-5	-5
Car Ins. @ $600 per year.		-50				-50		
Balance in bank	3644	3778	3207	3336	3465	3594	3023	3152
Paycheck (After approx taxes)	330	330	330	330	330	330	330	330
Balance forward	3778	3207	3336	3465	3594	3023	3152	3281
Figure Three	Notes:							

Chapter 4	21-Jun-19	28-Jun-19	5-Jul-19	12-Jul-19	19-Jul-19	26-Jul-19	2-Aug-19	9-Aug-19
Rent/Mortgage		-500					-500	
Groceries	-71	-71	-71	-71	-71	-71	-71	-71
Cell		-40					-40	
Internet/Entertainment		-25					-25	
Heat								
Electric								
Water								
Save for House	-100	-100	-100	-100	-100	-100	-100	-100
Health insurance		-85					-85	
Auto/transportation	-25	-25	-25	-25	-25	-25	-25	-25
Gifts/ fun/pets	-5	-5	-5	-5	-5	-5	-5	-5
Car Ins. @ $600 per year.		-50					-50	
Balance in bank	3281	3410	2839	2968	3097	3226	3355	2784
Paycheck (After approx taxes)	330	330	330	330	330	330	330	330
Balance forward	3410	2839	2968	3097	3226	3355	2784	2913
Figure Four	Notes:							

Chapter 4	16-Aug-19	23-Aug-19	30-Aug-19	6-Sep-19	13-Sep-19	20-Sep-19	27-Sep-19	4-Oct-19
Rent/Mortgage			-500					-500
Groceries	-71	-71	-71	-71	-71	-71	-71	-71
Cell			-40					-40
Internet/Entertainment			-25					-25
Heat								
Electric								
Water								
Save for House	-100	-100	-100	-100	-100	-100	-100	-100
Health insurance			-85					-85
Auto/transportation	-25	-25	-25	-25	-25	-25	-25	-25
Gifts/ fun/pets	-5	-5	-5	-5	-5	-5	-5	-5
Car Ins. @ $600 per year.			-50					-50
Balance in bank	2913	3042	3171	2600	2729	2858	2987	3116
Paycheck (After approx taxes)	330	330	330	330	330	330	330	330
Balance forward	3042	3171	2600	2729	2858	2987	3116	2545

Figure Five	Notes:							

Chapter 4	11-Oct-19	18-Oct-19	25-Oct-19	1-Nov-19	8-Nov-19	15-Nov-19	22-Nov-19	29-Nov-19
Rent/Mortgage				-500				-500
Groceries	-71	-71	-71	-71	-71	-71	-71	-71
Cell				-40				-40
Internet/Entertainment				-25				-25
Heat								
Electric								
Water								
Save for House	-100	-100	-100	-100	-100	-100	-100	-100
Health insurance				-85				-85
Auto/transportation	-25	-25	-25	-25	-25	-25	-25	-25
Gifts/ fun/pets	-5	-5	-5	-5	-5	-5	-5	-5
Car Ins. @ $600 per year.				-50				-50
Balance in bank	2545	2674	2803	2932	2361	2490	2619	2748
Paycheck (After approx taxes)	330	330	330	330	330	330	330	330
Balance forward	2674	2803	2932	2361	2490	2619	2748	2177

Figure Sic	Notes:							

Chapter 4	6-Dec-19	13-Dec-19	20-Dec-19	27-Dec-19	3-Jan-20	10-Jan-20	17-Jan-20	24-Jan-20
Rent/Mortgage					-500			
Groceries	-71	-71	-71	-71	-71	-71	-71	-71
Cell					-40			
Internet/Entertainment					-25			
Heat								
Electric								
Water								
Save for House	-100	-100	-100	-100	-100	-100	-100	-100
Health insurance					-85			
Auto/transportation	-25	-25	-25	-25	-25	-25	-25	-25
Gifts/ fun/pets	-5	-5	-60	-5	-5	-5	-5	-5
Car Ins. @ $600 per year.					-50			
Balance in bank	2177	2306	2435	2509	2638	2067	2196	2325
Paycheck (After approx taxes)	330	330	330	330	330	330	330	330
Balance forward	2306	2435	2509	2638	2067	2196	2325	2454

Figure Seven	Notes:							

Chapter 4	31-Jan-20	7-Feb-20	14-Feb-20	21-Feb-20	28-Feb-20	6-Mar-20	13-Mar-20	20-Mar-20
Rent/Mortgage	-500				-500			
Groceries	-71	-71	-71	-71	-71	-71	-71	-71
Cell	-40				-40			
Internet/Entertainment	-25				-25			
Heat								
Electric								
Water								
Save for House	-100	-100	-100	-100	-100	-100	-100	-100
Health insurance	-85				-85			
Auto/transportation	-25	-25	-25	-25	-25	-25	-25	-25
Gifts/ fun/pets	-5	-5	-5	-5	-5	-5	-5	-5
Car Ins. @ $600 per year.	-50				-50			
Balance in bank	2454	1883	2022	2161	2300	1739	1878	2017
Paycheck (After approx taxes)	330	340	340	340	340	340	340	340
Balance forward	1883	2022	2161	2300	1739	1878	2017	2156

Figure Eight	Notes:	Most Minimum wage jobs will give you a $1.00 raise the first year						

Chapter 4	27-Mar-20	3-Apr-20	10-Apr-20	17-Apr-20	24-Apr-20	1-May-20	8-May-20	15-May-20
Rent/Mortgage	-500					-500		
Groceries	-71	-71	-71	-71	-71	-71	-71	-71
Cell	-40					-40		
Internet/Entertainment	-25					-25		
Heat								
Electric								
Water								
Save for House	-100	-100	-100	-100	-100	-100	-100	-100
Health insurance	-85					-85		
Auto/transportation	-25	-25	-25	-25	-25	-25	-25	-25
Gifts/ fun/pets	-5	-5	-5	-5	-5	-5	-5	-5
Car Ins.@ $600 per year.	-50					-50		
Balance in bank	2156	1595	1734	1873	2012	2151	1590	1729
Paycheck (After approx taxes)	340	340	340	340	340	340	340	340
Balance forward	1595	1734	1873	2012	2151	1590	1729	1868
Figure Nine	Notes:							

Chapter 4	22-May-20	29-May-20	5-Jun-20	12-Jun-20	19-Jun-20	26-Jun-20	3-Jul-20	10-Jul-20
Rent/Mortgage		-500					-500	
Groceries	-71	-71	-71	-71	-71	-71	-71	-71
Cell		-40					-40	
Internet/Entertainment		-25					-25	
Heat								
Electric								
Water								
Save for House	-100	-100	-100	-100	-100	-100	-100	-100
Health insurance		-85					-85	
Auto/transportation	-25	-25	-25	-25	-25	-25	-25	-25
Gifts/ fun/pets	-5	-5	-5	-5	-5	-5	-5	-5
Car Ins. @ $600 per year.		-50					-50	
Balance in bank	1868	2007	1446	1585	1724	1863	2002	1441
Paycheck (After approx taxes)	340	340	340	340	340	340	340	340
Balance forward	2007	1446	1585	1724	1863	2002	1441	1580
Figure Ten	Notes:							

Chapter 4	17-Jul-20	24-Jul-20	31-Jul-20	7-Aug-20	14-Aug-20	21-Aug-20	28-Aug-20	4-Sep-20
Rent/Mortgage			-500					-500
Groceries	-71	-71	-71	-71	-71	-71	-71	-71
Cell			-40					-40
Internet/Entertainment			-25					-25
Heat								
Electric								
Water								
Save for House	-100	-100	-100	-100	-100	-100	-100	-100
Health insurance			-85					-85
Auto/transportation	-25	-25	-25	-25	-25	-25	-25	-25
Gifts/ fun/pets	-5	-5	-5	-5	-5	-5	-5	-5
Car Ins. @ $600 per year.			-50					-50
Balance in bank	1580	1719	1858	1297	1436	1575	1714	1853
Paycheck (After approx taxes)	340	340	340	340	340	340	340	340
Balance forward	1719	1858	1297	1436	1575	1714	1853	1292
Figure Eleven	Notes:							

Chapter 4	11-Sep-20	18-Sep-20	25-Sep-20	2-Oct-20	9-Oct-20	16-Oct-20	23-Oct-20	30-Oct-20
Rent/Mortgage			-500					-500
Groceries	-71	-71	-71	-71	-71	-71	-71	-71
Cell			-40					-40
Internet/Entertainment			-25					-25
Heat								
Electric								
Water								
Save for House	-100	-100	-100	-100	-100	-100	-100	-100
Health insurance			-85					-85
Auto/transportation	-25	-25	-25	-25	-25	-25	-25	-25
Gifts/ fun/pets	-5	-5	-5	-5	-5	-5	-5	-5
Car Ins. @ $600 per year.			-50					-50
Balance in bank	1292	1431	1570	1009	1148	1287	1426	1565
Paycheck (After approx taxes)	340	340	340	340	340	340	340	340
Balance forward	1431	1570	1009	1148	1287	1426	1565	1004
Figure Twelve	Notes:							

Chapter 4	6-Nov-20	13-Nov-20	20-Nov-20	27-Nov-20	4-Dec-20	11-Dec-20	18-Dec-20	25-Dec-20
Rent/Mortgage				-500				
Groceries	-71	-71	-71	-71	-71	-71	-71	-71
Cell				-40				
Internet/Entertainment				-25				
Heat								
Electric								
Water								
Save for House	-100	-100	-100	-100	-100	-100	-100	-100
Health insurance				-85				
Auto/transportation	-25	-25	-25	-25	-25	-25	-25	-25
Gifts/ fun/pets	-5	-5	-5	-5	-5	-5	-50	-5
Car Ins. @ $600 per year.				-50				
Balance in bank	1004	1143	1282	1421	860	999	1138	1232
Paycheck (After approx taxes)	340	340	340	340	340	340	340	340
Balance forward	1143	1282	1421	860	999	1138	1232	1371
Figure Thirteen	Notes:							

Chapter 4	1-Jan-21	8-Jan-21	15-Jan-21	22-Jan-21	29-Jan-21	5-Feb-21	12-Feb-21	19-Feb-21
Rent/Mortgage	-500				-500			
Groceries	-71	-71	-71	-71	-71	-71	-71	-71
Cell	-40				-40			
Internet/Entertainment	-25				-25			
Heat								
Electric								
Water								
Save for House	-100	-100	-100	-100	-100	-100	-100	-100
Health insurance	-85				-85			
Auto/transportation	-25	-25	-25	-25	-25	-25	-25	-25
Gifts/ fun/pets	-5	-5	-5	-5	-5	-5	-5	-5
Car Ins. @ $600 per year.	-50				-50			
Balance in bank	1371	810	949	1088	1227	666	805	944
Paycheck (After approx taxes)	340	340	340	340	340	340	340	340
Balance forward	810	949	1088	1227	666	805	944	1083
Figure Fourteen	Notes:							

Chapter 4	26-Feb-21	5-Mar-21	12-Mar-21	19-Mar-21	26-Mar-21	2-Apr-21	9-Apr-21	16-Apr-21
Rent/Mortgage		-500				-500		
Groceries	-71	-71	-71	-71	-71	-71	-71	-71
Cell		-40				-40		
Internet/Entertainment		-25				-25		
Heat								
Electric								
Water								
Save for House	-100	-100	-100	-100	-100	-100	-100	-100
Health insurance		-85				-85		
Auto/transportation	-25	-25	-25	-25	-25	-25	-25	-25
Gifts/ fun/pets	-5	-5	-5	-5	-5	-5	-5	-5
Car Ins. @ $600 per year.		-50				-50		
Balance in bank	1083	1222	661	800	954	1108	562	716
Paycheck (After approx taxes)	340	340	340	355	355	355	355	355
Balance forward	1222	661	800	954	1108	562	716	870
Figure Fifteen	Notes:							

You should be earning $12.70 per hour for a 40 hour week. If not…look for another job.

Chapter 4	23-Apr-21	30-Apr-21	7-May-21	14-May-21	21-May-21	28-May-21	4-Jun-21	11-Jun-21
Rent/Mortgage			-500				-500	
Groceries	-71	-71	-71	-71	-71	-71	-71	-71
Cell			-40				-40	
Internet/Entertainment			-25				-25	
Heat								
Electric								
Water								
Save for House	-100	-100	-100	-100	-100	-100	-100	-100
Health insurance			-85				-85	
Auto/transportation	-25	-25	-25	-25	-25	-25	-25	-25
Gifts/ fun/pets	-5	-5	-5	-5	-5	-5	-5	-5
Car Ins. @ $600 per year.			-50				-50	
Balance in bank	870	1024	1178	632	786	940	1094	548
Paycheck (After approx taxes)	355	355	355	355	355	355	355	355
Balance forward	1024	1178	632	786	940	1094	548	702
Figure Sixteen	Notes:							

Chapter 4	18-Jun-21	25-Jun-21	2-Jul-21	9-Jul-21	16-Jul-21	23-Jul-21	30-Jul-21	6-Aug-21
Rent/Mortgage			-500				-500	
Groceries	-71	-71	-71	-71	-71	-71	-71	-71
Cell			-40				-40	
Internet/Entertainment			-25				-25	
Heat								
Electric								
Water								
Save for House	-100	-100	-100	-100	-100	-100	-100	-100
Health insurance			-85				-85	
Auto/transportation	-25	-25	-25	-25	-25	-25	-25	-25
Gifts/ fun/pets	-5	-5	-5	-5	-5	-5	-5	-5
Car Ins. @ $600 per year.			-50				-50	
Balance in bank	702	856	1010	464	618	772	926	380
Paycheck (After approx taxes)	355	355	355	355	355	355	355	355
Balance forward	856	1010	464	618	772	926	380	534

Figure Seventeen	Notes:							

Chapter 4	13-Aug-21	20-Aug-21	27-Aug-21	3-Sep-21	10-Sep-21	17-Sep-21	24-Sep-21	1-Oct-21
Rent/Mortgage				-500				-500
Groceries	-71	-71	-71	-71	-71	-71	-71	-71
Cell				-40				-40
Internet/Entertainment				-25				-25
Heat								
Electric								
Water								
Save for House	-100	-100	-100	-100	-100	-100	-100	-100
Health insurance				-85				-85
Auto/transportation	-25	-25	-25	-25	-25	-25	-25	-25
Gifts/ fun/pets	-5	-5	-5	-5	-5	-5	-5	-5
Car Ins. @ $600 per year.				-50				-50
Balance in bank	534	688	842	996	450	604	758	912
Paycheck (After approx taxes)	355	355	355	355	355	355	355	355
Balance forward	688	842	996	450	604	758	912	366

Figure Eighteen	Notes:							

Chapter 4	8-Oct-21	15-Oct-21	22-Oct-21	29-Oct-21	5-Nov-21	12-Nov-21	19-Nov-21	26-Nov-21
Rent/Mortgage				-500				
Groceries	-71	-71	-71	-71	-71	-71	-71	-71
Cell				-40				
Internet/Entertainment				-25				
Heat								
Electric								
Water								
Save for House	-100	-100	-100	-100	-100	-100	-100	-100
Health insurance				-85				
Auto/transportation	-25	-25	-25	-25	-25	-25	-25	-25
Gifts/ fun/pets	-5	-5	-5	-5	-5	-5	-5	-5
Car Ins. @ $600 per year.				-50				
Balance in bank	366	520	674	828	282	436	590	744
Paycheck (After approx taxes)	355	355	355	355	355	355	355	355
Balance forward	520	674	828	282	436	590	744	898
Figure Nineteen	Notes:							

Chapter 4	3-Dec-21	10-Dec-21	17-Dec-21	24-Dec-21	31-Dec-21	7-Jan-22	14-Jan-22	21-Jan-22
Rent/Mortgage	-500					-500		
Groceries	-71	-71	-71	-71	-71	-71	-71	-71
Cell	-40					-40		
Internet/Entertainment	-25					-25		
Heat								
Electric								
Water								
Save for House	-100	-100	-100	-100	-100	-100	-100	-100
Health insurance	-85					-85		
Auto/transportation	-25	-25	-25	-25	-25	-25	-25	-25
Gifts/ fun/pets	-5	-5	-50	-5	-5	-5	-5	-5
Car Ins. @ $600 per year.	-50					-50		
Balance in bank	898	352	506	615	769	873	377	531
Paycheck (After approx taxes)	355	355	355	355	355	355	355	355
Balance forward	352	506	615	769	873	377	531	685
Figure Twenty	Notes:							

Chapter 4	28-Jan-22	4-Feb-22	11-Feb-22	18-Feb-22	25-Feb-22	4-Mar-22	11-Mar-22	18-Mar-22
Rent/Mortgage		-500				-500		
Groceries	-71	-71	-71	-71	-71	-71	-71	-71
Cell		-40				-40		
Internet/Entertainment		-25				-25		
Heat								
Electric								
Water								
Save for House	-100	-100	-100	-100	-100	-100	-95	-95
Health insurance		-85				-85		
Auto/transportation	-25	-25	-25	-25	-25	-25	-25	-25
Gifts/ fun/pets	-5	-5	-5	-5	-5	-5	-5	-5
Car Ins. @ $600 per year.		-50				-50		
Balance in bank	685	839	293	447	601	755	209	368
Paycheck (After approx taxes)	355	355	355	355	355	355	355	355
Balance forward	839	293	447	601	755	209	368	527
Figure Twenty One	Notes:							

Chapter 4	25-Mar-22	1-Apr-22	8-Apr-22	15-Apr-22	22-Apr-22	29-Apr-22	6-May-22	13-May-22
Rent/Mortgage		-500					-500	
Groceries	-71	-71	-71	-71	-71	-71	-71	-71
Cell		-40					-40	
Internet/Entertainment		-25					-25	
Heat								
Electric								
Water								
Save for House	-95	-95	-95	-95	-95	-95	-95	-95
Health insurance		-85					-85	
Auto/transportation	-25	-25	-25	-25	-25	-25	-25	-25
Gifts/ fun/pets	-5	-5	-5	-5	-5	-5	-5	-5
Car Ins. @ $600 per year.		-50					-50	
Balance in bank	527	686	145	304	463	622	781	240
Paycheck (After approx taxes)	355	355	355	355	355	355	355	355
Balance forward	686	145	304	463	622	781	240	399
Figure Twenty Two	Notes:							

Chapter 4	20-May-22	27-May-22	3-Jun-22	10-Jun-22	17-Jun-22	24-Jun-22	1-Jul-22	8-Jul-22
Rent/Mortgage			-500				-500	
Groceries	-71	-71	-71	-71	-71	-71	-71	-71
Cell			-40				-40	
Internet/Entertainment			-25				-25	
Heat								
Electric								
Water								
Save for House	-95	-95	-95	-95	-95	-95	-95	-95
Health insurance			-85				-85	
Auto/transportation	-25	-25	-25	-25	-25	-25	-25	-25
Gifts/ fun/pets	-5	-5	-5	-5	-5	-5	-5	-5
Car Ins. @ $600 per year.			-50				-50	
Balance in bank	399	558	717	176	335	494	653	112
Paycheck (After approx taxes)	355	355	355	355	355	355	355	355
Balance forward	558	717	176	335	494	653	112	271
Figure Twenty Three	Notes:							

Chapter 4	15-Jul-22	22-Jul-22	29-Jul-22	5-Aug-22	12-Aug-22	19-Aug-22	26-Aug-22	2-Sep-22
Rent/Mortgage				-500				-500
Groceries	-71	-71	-71	-71	-71	-71	-71	-71
Cell				-40				-40
Internet/Entertainment				-25				-25
Heat								
Electric								
Water								
Save for House	-95	-95	-95	-95	-95	-95	-95	-95
Health insurance				-85				-85
Auto/transportation	-25	-25	-25	-25	-25	-25	-25	-25
Gifts/ fun/pets	-5	-5	-5	-5	-5	-5	-5	-5
Car Ins. @ $600 per year.				-50				-50
Balance in bank	271	430	589	748	207	366	525	684
Paycheck (After approx taxes)	355	355	355	355	355	355	355	355
Balance forward	430	589	748	207	366	525	684	143
Figure Twenty Four	Notes:							

Chapter 4	9-Sep-22	16-Sep-22	23-Sep-22	30-Sep-22	7-Oct-22	14-Oct-22	21-Oct-22	28-Oct-22
Rent/Mortgage					-500			
Groceries	-71	-71	-71	-71	-71	-71	-71	-71
Cell					-40			
Internet/Entertainment					-25			
Heat								
Electric								
Water								
Save for House	-95	-95	-95	-95	-95	-95	-95	-95
Health insurance					-85			
Auto/transportation	-25	-25	-25	-25	-25	-25	-25	-25
Gifts/ fun/pets	-5	-5	-5	-5	-5	-5	-5	-5
Car Ins. @ $600 per year.					-50			
Balance in bank	143	302	461	620	779	238	397	556
Paycheck (After approx taxes)	355	355	355	355	355	355	355	355
Balance forward	302	461	620	779	238	397	556	715
Figure Twenty Five	Notes:							

Chapter 4	4-Nov-22	11-Nov-22	18-Nov-22	25-Nov-22	2-Dec-22	9-Dec-22	16-Dec-22	23-Dec-22
Rent/Mortgage	-500				-500			
Groceries	-71	-71	-71	-71	-71	-71	-71	-71
Cell	-40				-40			
Internet/Entertainment	-25				-25			
Heat								
Electric								
Water								
Save for House	-95	-95	-95	-95	-95	-95	-95	-95
Health insurance	-85				-85			
Auto/transportation	-25	-25	-25	-25	-25	-25	-25	-25
Gifts/ fun/pets	-5	-5	-5	-5	-5	-5	-5	-5
Car Ins. @ $600 per year.	-50				-50			
Balance in bank	715	174	333	492	651	110	269	428
Paycheck (After approx taxes)	355	355	355	355	355	355	355	355
Balance forward	174	333	492	651	110	269	428	587
Figure Twenty Six	Notes:							

Chapter 4	30-Dec-22	6-Jan-23	13-Jan-23	20-Jan-23	27-Jan-23	3-Feb-23	10-Feb-23	17-Feb-23
Rent/Mortgage		-500				-500		
Groceries	-71	-71	-71	-71	-71	-71	-71	-71
Cell		-40				-40		
Internet/Entertainment		-25				-25		
Heat								
Electric								
Water								
Save for House	-95	-95	-95	-95	-95	-95	-95	-95
Health insurance		-85				-85		
Auto/transportation	-25	-25	-25	-25	-25	-25	-25	-25
Gifts/ fun/pets	-5	-5	-5	-5	-5	-5	-5	-5
Car Ins. @ $600 per year.		-50				-50		
Balance in bank	587	746	205	364	523	682	141	300
Paycheck (After approx taxes)	355	355	355	355	355	355	355	355
Balance forward	746	205	364	523	682	141	300	459
Figure Twenty Seven	Notes:							

Chapter 4	24-Feb-23	3-Mar-23	10-Mar-23	17-Mar-23	24-Mar-23	31-Mar-23	7-Apr-23	14-Apr-23
Rent/Mortgage		-500					-500	
Groceries	-71	-71	-71	-71	-71	-71	-71	-71
Cell		-40					-40	
Internet/Entertainment		-25					-25	
Heat								
Electric								
Water								
Save for House	-95	-95	-95	-95	-95	-95	-95	-95
Health insurance		-85					-85	
Auto/transportation	-25	-25	-25	-25	-25	-25	-25	-25
Gifts/ fun/pets	-5	-5	-5	-5	-5	-5	-5	-5
Car Ins. @ $600 per year.		-50					-50	
Balance in bank	459	618	77	236	395	554	713	172
Paycheck (After approx taxes)	355	355	355	355	355	355	355	355
Balance forward	618	77	236	395	554	713	172	331
Figure Twenty Eight	Notes:							

Chapter 4	21-Apr-23	28-Apr-23	5-May-23	12-May-23	19-May-23	26-May-23	2-Jun-23	9-Jun-23
Rent/Mortgage			-500				-500	
Groceries	-71	-71	-71	-71	-71	-71	-71	-71
Cell			-40				-40	
Internet/Entertainment			-25				-25	
Heat								
Electric								
Water								
Save for House	-95	-100	-100	-100	-100	-100	-100	-100
Health insurance			-85				-85	
Auto/transportation	-25	-25	-25	-25	-25	-25	-25	-25
Gifts/ fun/pets	-5	-5	-5	-5	-5	-5	-5	-5
Car Ins. @ $600 per year.			-50				-50	
Balance in bank	332	493	647	101	255	409	563	50
Paycheck (After approx taxes)	355	355	355	355	355	355	355	355
Balance forward	491	647	101	255	409	563	17	213
Figure Twenty Nine	Notes:							

Chapter 4	16-Jun-23	23-Jun-23	30-Jun-23	7-Jul-23	14-Jul-23	21-Jul-23	28-Jul-23	4-Aug-23
Rent/Mortgage				-500				-500
Groceries	-71	-71	-71	-71	-71	-71	-71	-71
Cell				-40				-40
Internet/Entertainment				-25				-25
Heat								
Electric								
Water								
Save for House	-100	-100	-100	-100	-100	-100	-100	-100
Health insurance				-85				-85
Auto/transportation	-25	-25	-25	-25	-25	-25	-25	-25
Gifts/ fun/pets	-5	-5	-5	-5	-5	-5	-5	-5
Car Ins. @ $600 per year.				-50				-50
Balance in bank	213	367	521	675	129	283	437	682
Paycheck (After approx taxes)	355	355	355	355	355	355	355	355
Balance forward	367	521	675	129	283	437	591	136
Figure Thirty	Notes:							

Chapter 4	11-Aug-23	18-Aug-23	25-Aug-23	1-Sep-23	8-Sep-23	15-Sep-23	22-Sep-23	29-Sep-23
Rent/Mortgage				-500				
Groceries	-71	-71	-71	-71	-71	-71	-71	-71
Cell				-40				
Internet/Entertainment				-25				
Heat								
Electric								
Water								
Save for House	-100	-100	-100	-100	-100	-100	-100	-100
Health insurance				-85				
Auto/transportation	-25	-25	-25	-25	-25	-25	-25	-25
Gifts/ fun/pets	-5	-5	-5	-5	-5	-5	-5	-5
Car Ins. @ $600 per year.				-50				
Balance in bank	153	307	461	615	69	223	377	678
Paycheck (After approx taxes)	355	355	355	355	355	355	355	355
Balance forward	307	461	615	69	223	377	531	832

Figure Thirty One	Notes:

Chapter 4	6-Oct-23	13-Oct-23	20-Oct-23	27-Oct-23	3-Nov-23	10-Nov-23	17-Nov-23	24-Nov-23
Rent/Mortgage	-500				-500			
Groceries	-71	-71	-71	-71	-71	-71	-71	-71
Cell	-40				-40			
Internet/Entertainment	-25				-25			
Heat								
Electric								
Water								
Save for House	-100	-100	-100	-100	-100	-100	-100	-100
Health insurance	-85				-85			
Auto/transportation	-25	-25	-25	-25	-25	-25	-25	-25
Gifts/ fun/pets	-5	-5	-5	-5	-5	-5	-5	-5
Car Ins. @ $600 per year.	-50				-50	-50	-50	-50
Balance in bank	857	311	465	619	773	227	331	468
Paycheck (After approx taxes)	355	355	355	355	355	355	355	355
Balance forward	311	465	619	773	227	331	435	572

Figure Thirty Two	Notes:

Chapter 4	1-Dec-23	8-Dec-23	15-Dec-23	22-Dec-23	29-Dec-23	5-Jan-24	12-Jan-24	19-Jan-23
Rent/Mortgage	-500					-500		
Groceries	-71	-71	-71	-71	-71	-71	-71	-71
Cell	-40					-40		
Internet/Entertainment	-25					-25		
Heat								
Electric								
Water								
Save for House	-100	-100	-100	-100				
Health insurance	-85					-85		
Auto/transportation	-25	-25	-25	-25	-25	-25	-25	-25
Gifts/ fun/pets	-5	-5	-5	-5	-5	-5	-5	-5
Car Ins. @ $600 per year.	-50					-50	-50	-50
Balance in bank	572	26	180	334	488	742	296	500
Paycheck (After approx taxes)	355	355	355	355	355	355	355	355
Balance forward	26	180	334	488	742	296	500	704
Figure Thirty Three	Notes:							

Chapter 4	26-Jan-23	2-Feb-23	9-Feb-23	16-Feb-23	23-Feb-23	2-Mar-23	9-Mar-23	16-Mar-23
Rent/Mortgage	-500					-500		
Groceries	-71	-71	-71	-71	-71	-71	-71	-71
Cell	-40					-40		
Internet/Entertainment	-25					-25		
Heat								
Electric								
Water								
Health insurance	-85					-85		
Auto/transportation	-25	-25	-25	-25	-25	-25	-25	-25
Gifts/ fun/pets	-5	-5	-5	-5	-5	-5	-5	-5
Car Ins. @ $600 per year.	-50	-50	-50	-50	-50	-50	-50	-50
Balance in bank	500	54	258	462	666	870	424	628
Paycheck (After approx taxes)	355	355	355	355	355	355	355	355
Balance forward	54	258	462	666	870	424	628	832
Figure Thirty Four	Notes:							

Chapter 4	23-Mar-23	30-Mar-23	6-Apr-23	13-Apr-23	20-Apr-23	27-Apr-23	4-May-23	11-May-23
Rent/Mortgage			-500				-500	
Groceries	-71	-71	-71	-71	-71	-71	-71	-71
Cell			-40				-40	
Internet/Entertainment			-25				-25	
Heat								
Electric								
Water								
Save for House								
Health insurance			-85				-85	
Auto/transportation	-25	-25	-25	-25	-25	-25	-25	-25
Gifts/ fun/pets	-5	-5	-5	-5	-5	-5	-5	-5
Car Ins. @ $600 per year.	-50	-50	-50	-50	-50	-50	-50	-50
Balance in bank	832	1036	1240	794	998	1202	1406	960
Paycheck (After approx taxes)	355	355	355	355	355	355	355	355
Balance forward	1036	1240	794	998	1202	1406	960	1164

Figure Thirty -Five

CHAPTER FIVE

Living at Home – First Job

This budget is best for a person who still lives at home and has a full time job earning no less than $15.00 per hour, and your goal is to save $15,000.00 to buy a car.

- ◆ Rent to parents or Guardian: If you have a job, it is time to learn to pay rent. $200.00 a month is reasonable for a 'starter' rent. If they won't 'accept' rent, then either add it to your savings or ask them to put it in a separate account for you.

- ◆ Misc. Food: You will probably begin to eat meals away from home, so it is a good idea to budget for it. You can also spend this money on your personal snacks, or add it to savings. You will find a grocery and meal planner at the backof this book.

- ◆ Cell: You can either get your own Discount Mobile plan or reimburse your parents for using theirs.

- ◆ Internet/Entertainment: You may have an on line subscription or something similar, like Hulu or Amazon Prime.

- ◆ Heat, Water, Electric: You probably won't be paying these if you are at home, but it is a good idea to remember you will have to budget for them in the future.

- ◆ Save for Car: This exact amount should be put in to a separate bank account every week. At the end of ONLY 79 weeks you will be able to pay cash for your car. If you put it in a savings account that earns .91% or better, you will have slightly more.

- ◆ Health Insurance: You may have a personal policy that you pay monthly. Your employer may withhold this amount from your check in weekly increments. If you do not have insurance, save this amount in the bank in case you need to see a doctor in the future.

- ◆ Transportation: Even if you skateboard to work, there will be occasional days when you need to take a bus, or ride share.

- ◆ Gifts/Fun: It is going to happen so you need to put it in your budget. You do not have to spend that much, but do not spend more.

- ◆ Emergency Savings: Put this amount aside every week in case of a Real emergency. Medical or a death in the family qualify.

- ◆ Balance in Bank: That is what you should have in your bank account at the end of all transactions in order to stay on your budget. At the beginning of this budget you must start with $200.00 in your bank. That is possible if you deposited half of your pay check the week before.

- ◆ Paycheck: This is an average, because tax laws vary from state to state and even from city to city. You will be shown how to change this number to match your paycheck in the next section

- ◆ Balance forward: This is what is left after you pay your expenses. This money cannot be spent – it is carried forward to the next period. This is the main point of a budget – to not spend every bit of money that comes into your hands.

Chapter 5	4-Jan-19	11-Jan-19	18-Jan-19	25-Jan-19	1-Feb-19	8-Feb-19	15-Feb-19	22-Feb-19
Rent to parents or guardian	-200				-200			
Misc. Food	-50	-50	-50	-50	-50	-50	-50	-50
Cell	-55				-55			
Internet/Entertainment	-25				-25			
Heat								
Electric								
Water								
Save for car		-192	-192	-192	-192	-192	-192	-192
Health insurance	-100				-100			
Transportation	-25	-25	-25	-25	-25	-25	-25	-25
Gifts/ fun/pets		-30	-30	-30	-30	-30	-30	-30
Emergency Savings	-40	-40	-40	-40	-40	-40	-40	-40
Balance in bank	200	139	236	333	430	147	244	341
Paycheck (After approx taxes)	434	434	434	434	434	434	434	434
Balance forward	139	236	333	430	147	244	341	438

Figure One	Notes:							

Chapter 5	1-Mar-19	8-Mar-19	15-Mar-19	22-Mar-19	29-Mar-19	5-Apr-19	12-Apr-19	19-Apr-19
Rent to parents or guardian	-200				-200			
Misc. Food	-50	-50	-50	-50	-50	-50	-50	-50
Cell	-55				-55			
Internet/Entertainment	-25				-25			
Heat								
Electric								
Water								
Save for car	-192	-192	-192	-192	-192	-192	-192	-192
Health insurance	-100				-100			
Transportation	-25	-25	-25	-25	-25	-25	-25	-25
Gifts/ fun/pets	-30	-30	-30	-30	-30	-30	-30	-30
Emergency Savings	-40	-40	-40	-40	-40	-40	-40	-40
Balance in bank	438	155	252	349	446	163	260	357
Paycheck (After approx taxes)	434	434	434	434	434	434	434	434
Balance forward	155	252	349	446	163	260	357	454

Figure Two	Notes:							

Chapter 5	26-Apr-19	3-May-19	10-May-19	17-May-19	24-May-19	31-May-19	7-Jun-19	14-Jun-19
Rent to parents or guardian		-200				-200		
Misc. Food	-50	-50	-50	-50	-50	-50	-50	-50
Cell		-55				-55		
Internet/Entertainment		-25				-25		
Heat								
Electric								
Water								
Save for car	-192	-192	-192	-192	-192	-192	-192	-192
Health insurance		-100				-100		
Transportation	-25	-25	-25	-25	-25	-25	-25	-25
Gifts/ fun/pets	-30	-30	-30	-30	-30	-80	-35	-35
Emergency Savings	-40	-40	-40	-40	-40	-40	-40	-40
Balance in bank	454	551	268	365	462	559	226	318
Paycheck (After approx taxes)	434	434	434	434	434	434	434	434
Balance forward	551	268	365	462	559	226	318	410

Figure Three	Notes:							

Chapter 5	21-Jun-19	28-Jun-19	5-Jul-19	12-Jul-19	19-Jul-19	26-Jul-19	2-Aug-19	9-Aug-19
Rent to parents or guardian		-200					-200	
Misc. Food	-50	-50	-50	-50	-50	-50	-50	-50
Cell		-55					-55	
Internet/Entertainment		-25					-25	
Heat								
Electric								
Water								
Save for car	-192	-192	-192	-192	-192	-192	-192	-192
Health insurance		-100					-100	
Transportation	-25	-25	-25	-25	-25	-25	-25	-25
Gifts/ fun/pets	-35	-35	-80	-35	-35	-35	-35	-35
Emergency Savings	-40	-40	-40	-40	-40	-40	-40	-40
Balance in bank	410	502	214	261	353	445	537	249
Paycheck (After approx taxes)	434	434	434	434	434	434	434	434
Balance forward	502	214	261	353	445	537	249	341

Figure Four	Notes:							

Chapter 5	16-Aug-19	23-Aug-19	30-Aug-19	6-Sep-19	13-Sep-19	20-Sep-19	27-Sep-19	4-Oct-19
Rent to parents or guardian			-200					-200
Misc. Food	-50	-50	-50	-50	-50	-50	-50	-50
Cell				-55				-55
Internet/Entertainment				-25				-25
Heat								
Electric								
Water								
Save for car	-192	-192	-192	-192	-192	-192	-192	-192
Health insurance			-100					-100
Transportation	-25	-25	-25	-25	-25	-25	-25	-25
Gifts/ fun/pets	-35	-35	-70	-35	-35	-35	-35	-35
Emergency Savings	-40	-40	-40	-40	-40	-40	-40	-40
Balance in bank	341	433	525	202	294	386	478	570
Paycheck (After approx taxes)	434	434	434	434	434	434	434	434
Balance forward	433	525	202	294	386	478	570	282

Figure Five	Notes:							

Chapter 5	11-Oct-19	18-Oct-19	25-Oct-19	1-Nov-19	8-Nov-19	15-Nov-19	22-Nov-19	29-Nov-19
Rent to parents or guardian				-200				-200
Misc. Food	-50	-50	-50	-50	-50	-50	-50	-50
Cell				-55				-55
Internet/Entertainment				-25				-25
Heat								
Electric								
Water								
Save for car	-192	-192	-192	-192	-192	-192	-192	-192
Health insurance				-100				-100
Transportation	-25	-25	-25	-25	-25	-25	-25	-25
Gifts/ fun/pets	-35	-35	-35	-60	-35	-35	-50	-35
Emergency Savings	-40	-40	-40	-40	-40	-40	-40	-40
Balance in bank	282	374	466	558	245	337	429	506
Paycheck (After approx taxes)	434	434	434	434	434	434	434	434
Balance forward	374	466	558	245	337	429	506	218

Figure Six	Notes:							

Chapter 5	6-Dec-19	13-Dec-19	20-Dec-19	27-Dec-19	3-Jan-20	10-Jan-20	17-Jan-20	24-Jan-20
Rent to parents or guardian					-200			
Misc. Food	-50	-50	-50	-50	-50	-50	-50	-50
Cell					-55			
Internet/Entertainment					-25			
Heat								
Electric								
Water								
Save for car	-192	-192	-192	-192	-192	-192	-192	-192
Health insurance					-100			
Transportation	-25	-25	-25	-25	-25	-25	-25	-25
Gifts/ fun/pets	-35	-200	-50	-70	-35	-35	-35	-35
Emergency Savings	-40	-40	-40	-40	-40	-40	-40	-40
Balance in bank	218	310	237	314	371	83	175	267
Paycheck (After approx taxes)	434	434	434	434	434	434	434	434
Balance forward	310	237	314	371	83	175	267	359

Figure Seven	Notes:							
	Notes:							

Chapter 5	31-Jan-20	7-Feb-20	14-Feb-20	21-Feb-20	28-Feb-20	6-Mar-20	13-Mar-20	20-Mar-20
Rent to parents or guardian	-200				-200			
Misc. Food	-50	-50	-50	-50	-50	-50	-50	-50
Cell	-55				-55			
Internet/Entertainment	-25				-25			
Heat								
Electric								
Water								
Save for car	-192	-192	-192	-192	-192	-192	-192	-192
Health insurance	-100				-100			
Transportation	-25	-25	-25	-25	-25	-25	-25	-25
Gifts/ fun/pets	-35	-35	-50	-35	-35	-35	-35	-35
Emergency Savings	-40	-40	-40	-40	-40	-40	-40	-40
Balance in bank	359	71	163	240	332	44	136	228
Paycheck (After approx taxes)	434	434	434	434	434	434	434	434
Balance forward	71	163	240	332	44	136	228	320

Figure Eight	Notes:							

Chapter 5	27-Mar-20	3-Apr-20	10-Apr-20	17-Apr-20	24-Apr-20	1-May-20	8-May-20	15-May-20
Rent to parents or guardian	-200					-200		
Misc. Food	-50	-50	-50	-50	-50	-50	-50	-50
Cell	-55					-55		
Internet/Entertainment	-25					-25		
Heat								
Electric								
Water								
Save for car	-192	-192	-192	-192	-192	-192	-192	-192
Health insurance	-100					-100		
Transportation	-25	-25	-25	-25	-25	-25	-25	-25
Gifts/ fun/pets	-35	-35	-35	-40	-40	-40	-40	-40
Emergency Savings	-40	-40	-40	-40	-40	-40	-40	-40
Balance in bank	320	32	124	216	303	390	97	184
Paycheck (After approx taxes)	434	434	434	434	434	434	434	434
Balance forward	32	124	216	303	390	97	184	271

Figure Nine   Notes:

Chapter 5	22-May-20	29-May-20	5-Jun-20	12-Jun-20	19-Jun-20	26-Jun-20	3-Jul-20	10-Jul-20
Rent to parents or guardian		-200					-200	
Misc. Food	-50	-50	-50	-50	-50	-50	-50	
Cell		-55					-55	
Internet/Entertainment		-25					-25	
Heat								
Electric								
Water								
Save for car	-192	-192	-192	-192	-192	-192	-192	-192
Health insurance		-100					-100	
Transportation	-25	-25	-25	-25	-25	-25	-25	-25
Gifts/ fun/pets	-50	-70	-40	-40	-40	-40	-100	-100
Emergency Savings	-40	-40	-40	-40	-40	-40	-40	-40
Balance in bank	271	348	25	112	199	286	373	20
Paycheck (After approx taxes)	434	434	434	434	434	434	434	435
Balance forward	348	25	112	199	286	373	20	98

Figure Ten   Notes:

CHAPTER SIX

Living at Home – Student Debt

This budget is best for a person who has moved back home after completing a minimum of 2-4 years of Trade School or College, has $20,000.00 of student loan debt, and is working at an entry level $15.00 job. Your goal is to pay off the student loans.

♦ Rent to parents or Guardian: You have a job, it is time to learn to pay rent. $200.00 a month is reasonable for a 'starter' rent.

♦ Misc. Food: You will probably begin to eat meals away from home, so it is a good idea to budget for it. You can also spend this money on your personal snacks. You will find a grocery and meal planner at the backof this book.

♦ Cell: You can either get your own Mobile plan or reimburse your parents for using theirs.

♦ Internet/Entertainment: You may have an on line subscription or something similar that you need to pay monthly.

♦ Heat, Water, Electric: You probably won't be paying these if you are at home, but it is a good idea to remember you will have to budget for them in the future.

♦ Pay off Student Loan: This exact amount should be paid on your loan every week. Even though they bill you monthly, if you go ahead and pay them weekly, you will pay off the loan faster because you will be reducing the interest faster. If they have an on-line portal, you can pay there. Otherwise get the correct mailing address and a bunch of stamps and envelopes and go to town. Remember: **weekly payments reduce debt faster** by helping to reduce interest payments. **In only 120 weeks you will have this loan PAID OFF!!!!**

♦ Health Insurance: You may have a personal policy that you pay monthly. Your employer may withhold this amount from your check in weekly increments. If you do not have insurance, save this amount in the bank in case you need to see a doctor in the future.

♦ Transportation: Even if you skateboard to work, there will be occasional days when you need to drive or ride share

♦ Gifts/Fun: It is going to happen so you need to put it in your budget. You do not have to spend that much, but do not spend more.

♦ Emergency Savings: Put this amount aside every week in case of a Real emergency. Medical or a death in the family qualify. When you get to $100,000.00 you can stop.

♦ Balance in Bank: That is what you should have in your bank account at the end of all transactions in order to stay on your budget. At the beginning of this budget you must start with $200.00 in your bank. That is possible if you deposited your first pay check the week before.

♦ Paycheck: This is an average, because tax laws vary from state to state and even from city to city. If you are on salary, your pay will be the same every week. You can copy the exact figure from your pay stub. If you are an hourly worker, your net pay will change from week to week. Some companies give annual or even semi-annual pay increases.

♦ Balance forward: This is what is left after you pay your expenses. This money cannot be spent – it is carried forward to the next period. This is the main point of a budget – to not spend every bit of money that comes into your hands.

Chapter 6	4-Jan-19	11-Jan-19	18-Jan-19	25-Jan-19	1-Feb-19	8-Feb-19	15-Feb-19	22-Feb-19
Rent to parents or guardian	-200				-200			
Misc. Food	-50	-50	-50	-50	-50	-50	-50	-50
Cell	-50				-50			
Internet/Entertainment	-25				-25			
Heat								
Electric								
Water								
Pay Off $20k loan*	-167	-167	-167	-167	-167	-167	-167	-167
Health insurance	-100				-100			
transportation	-30	-30	-30	-30	-30	-30	-30	-30
Gifts/ fun/pets	0	-30	-30	-30	-30	-30	-60	-30
Emergency Savings	0	-25	-25	-25	-25	-25	-25	-25
Balance in bank	200	12	144	276	408	165	297	399
Paycheck (After approx taxes)	434	434	434	434	434	434	434	434
Balance forward	12	144	276	408	165	297	399	531
Figure One	Notes							

Chapter 6	1-Mar-19	8-Mar-19	15-Mar-19	22-Mar-19	29-Mar-19	5-Apr-19	12-Apr-19	19-Apr-19
Rent to parents or guardian	-200				-200			
Misc. Food	-50	-50	-50	-50	-50	-50	-50	-50
Cell	-50				-50			
Internet/Entertainment	-25				-25			
Heat								
Electric								
Water								
Pay Off $20k loan*	-167	-167	-167	-167	-167	-167	-167	-167
Health insurance	-100				-100			
transportation	-30	-30	-30	-30	-30	-30	-30	-30
Gifts/ fun/pets	-30	-30	-30	-50	-50	-50	-50	-50
Emergency Savings	-25	-25	-25	-25	-25	-25	-25	-25
Balance in bank	531	288	420	552	664	401	513	625
Paycheck (After approx taxes)	434	434	434	434	434	434	434	434
Balance forward	288	420	552	664	401	513	625	737
Figure Two	Notes							

Chapter 6	26-Apr-19	3-May-19	10-May-19	17-May-19	24-May-19	31-May-19	7-Jun-19	14-Jun-19
Rent to parents or guardian		-200				-200		
Misc. Food	-50	-50	-50	-50	-50	-50	-50	-50
Cell		-50				-50		
Internet/Entertainment		-25				-25		
Heat								
Electric								
Water								
Pay Off $20k loan*	-167	-167	-167	-167	-167	-167	-167	-167
Health insurance		-100				-100		
transportation	-30	-30	-30	-30	-30	-30	-30	-30
Gifts/ fun/pets	-50	-50	-50	-50	-50	-100	-50	-50
Emergency Savings	-25	-25	-25	-25	-25	-25	-25	-25
Balance in bank	737	849	586	698	810	922	609	721
Paycheck (After approx taxes)	434	434	434	434	434	434	434	434
Balance forward	849	586	698	810	922	609	721	833
Figure Three	Notes							

Chapter 6	21-Jun-19	28-Jun-19	5-Jul-19	12-Jul-19	19-Jul-19	26-Jul-19	2-Aug-19	9-Aug-19
Rent to parents or guardian		-200					-200	
Misc. Food	-50	-50	-50	-50	-50	-50	-50	-50
Cell		-50					-50	
Internet/Entertainment		-25					-25	
Heat								
Electric								
Water								
Pay Off $20k loan*	-167	-167	-167	-167	-167	-167	-167	-167
Health insurance		-100					-100	
transportation	-30	-30	-30	-30	-30	-30	-30	-30
Gifts/ fun/pets	-50	-50	-100	-50	-50	-50	-50	-50
Emergency Savings	-25	-25	-25	-25	-25	-25	-25	-25
Balance in bank	833	945	682	744	856	968	1080	817
Paycheck (After approx taxes)	434	434	434	434	434	434	434	434
Balance forward	945	682	744	856	968	1080	817	929
Figure Four	Notes							

Chapter 6	16-Aug-19	23-Aug-19	30-Aug-19	6-Sep-19	13-Sep-19	20-Sep-19	27-Sep-19	4-Oct-19
Rent to parents or guardian			-200					-200
Misc. Food	-50	-50	-50	-50	-50	-50	-50	-50
Cell			-50					-50
Internet/Entertainment			-25					-25
Heat								
Electric								
Water								
Pay Off $20k loan*	-167	-167	-167	-167	-167	-167	-167	-167
Health insurance			-100					-100
transportation	-30	-30	-30	-30	-30	-30	-30	-30
Gifts/ fun/pets	-50	-50	-100	-50	-50	-50	-50	-50
Emergency Savings	-25	-25	-25	-25	-25	-25	-25	-25
Balance in bank	929	1041	1153	840	952	1064	1176	1288
Paycheck (After approx taxes)	434	434	434	434	434	434	434	434
Balance forward	1041	1153	840	952	1064	1176	1288	1025
Figure Five	Notes							

Chapter 6	11-Oct-19	18-Oct-19	25-Oct-19	1-Nov-19	8-Nov-19	15-Nov-19	22-Nov-19	29-Nov-19
Rent to parents or guardian				-200				-200
Misc. Food	-50	-50	-50	-50	-50	-50	-50	-50
Cell				-50				-50
Internet/Entertainment				-25				-25
Heat								
Electric								
Water								
Pay Off $20k loan*	-167	-167	-167	-167	-167	-167	-167	-167
Health insurance				-100				-100
transportation	-30	-30	-30	-30	-30	-30	-30	-30
Gifts/ fun/pets	-50	-50	-50	-100	-50	-50	-50	-50
Emergency Savings	-25	-25	-25	-25	-25	-25	-25	-25
Balance in bank	1025	1137	1249	1361	1048	1160	1272	1384
Paycheck (After approx taxes)	434	434	434	434	434	434	434	434
Balance forward	1137	1249	1361	1048	1160	1272	1384	1121
Figure Six	Notes							

Chapter 6	6-Dec-19	13-Dec-19	20-Dec-19	27-Dec-19	3-Jan-20	10-Jan-20	17-Jan-20	24-Jan-20
Rent to parents or guardian					-200			
Misc. Food	-50	-50	-50	-50	-50	-50	-50	-50
Cell					-50			
Internet/Entertainment					-25			
Heat								
Electric								
Water								
Pay Off $20k loan*	-167	-167	-167	-167	-167	-167	-167	-167
Health insurance					-100			
transportation	-30	-30	-30	-30	-30	-30	-30	-30
Gifts/ fun/pets	-50	-100	-200	-50	-50	-50	-50	-50
Emergency Savings	-25	-25	-25	-25	-50	-50	-50	-50
Balance in bank	1121	1233	1295	1257	1369	1081	1168	1255
Paycheck (After approx taxes)	434	434	434	434	434	434	434	434
Balance forward	1233	1295	1257	1369	1081	1168	1255	1342
Figure Seven								

Chapter 6	31-Jan-20	7-Feb-20	14-Feb-20	21-Feb-20	28-Feb-20	6-Mar-20	13-Mar-20	20-Mar-20
Rent to parents or guardian	-200				-200			
Misc. Food	-50	-50	-50	-50	-50	-50	-50	-50
Cell	-50				-50			
Internet/Entertainment	-25				-25			
Heat								
Electric								
Water								
Pay Off $20k loan*	-167	-167	-167	-167	-167	-167	-167	-167
Health insurance	-100				-100			
transportation	-30	-30	-30	-30	-30	-30	-30	-30
Gifts/ fun/pets	-50	-50	-100	-50	-50	-50	-50	-50
Emergency Savings	-50	-50	-50	-50	-50	-50	-50	-50
Balance in bank	1342	1054	1141	1178	1265	977	1064	1151
Paycheck (After approx taxes)	434	434	434	434	434	434	434	434
Balance forward	1054	1141	1178	1265	977	1064	1151	1238
Figure Eight								

Chapter 6	27-Mar-20	3-Apr-20	10-Apr-20	17-Apr-20	24-Apr-20	1-May-20	8-May-20	15-May-20
Rent to parents or guardian	-200					-200		
Misc. Food	-50	-50	-50	-50	-50	-50	-50	-50
Cell	-50					-50		
Internet/Entertainment	-25					-25		
Heat								
Electric								
Water								
Pay Off $20k loan*	-167	-167	-167	-167	-167	-167	-167	-167
Health insurance	-100					-100		
transportation	-30	-30	-30	-30	-30	-30	-30	-30
Gifts/ fun/pets	-50	-50	-50	-50	-50	-50	-50	-50
Emergency Savings	-50	-50	-50	-50	-50	-50	-50	-50
Balance in bank	1238	950	1037	1124	1211	1298	1010	1097
Paycheck (After approx taxes)	434	434	434	434	434	434	434	434
Balance forward	950	1037	1124	1211	1298	1010	1097	1184

Figure Nine

Chapter 6	22-May-20	29-May-20	5-Jun-20	12-Jun-20	19-Jun-20	26-Jun-20	3-Jul-20	10-Jul-20
Rent to parents or guardian		-200					-200	
Misc. Food	-50	-50	-50	-50	-50	-50	-50	-50
Cell		-50					-50	
Internet/Entertainment		-25					-25	
Heat								
Electric								
Water								
Pay Off $20k loan*	-167	-167	-167	-167	-167	-167	-167	-167
Health insurance		-100					-100	
transportation	-30	-30	-30	-30	-30	-30	-30	-30
Gifts/ fun/pets	-50	-100	-50	-50	-50	-50	-100	-50
Emergency Savings	-50	-50	-50	-50	-50	-50	-50	-50
Balance in bank	1184	1271	933	1020	1107	1194	1281	943
Paycheck (After approx taxes)	434	434	434	434	434	434	434	434
Balance forward	1271	933	1020	1107	1194	1281	943	1030

Figure Ten

Chapter 6	17-Jul-20	24-Jul-20	31-Jul-20	7-Aug-20	14-Aug-20	21-Aug-20	28-Aug-20	4-Sep-20
Rent to parents or guardian			-200					-200
Misc. Food	-50	-50	-50	-50	-50	-50	-50	-50
Cell			-50					-50
Internet/Entertainment			-25					-25
Heat								
Electric								
Water								
Pay Off $20k loan*	-167	-167	-167	-167	-167	-167	-167	-167
Health insurance			-100					-100
transportation	-30	-30	-30	-30	-30	-30	-30	-30
Gifts/ fun/pets	-50	-50	-50	-50	-50	-50	-50	-100
Emergency Savings	-50	-50	-50	-50	-50	-50	-50	-50
Balance in bank	1030	1117	1204	916	1003	1090	1177	1264
Paycheck (After approx taxes)	434	434	434	434	434	434	434	434
Balance forward	1117	1204	916	1003	1090	1177	1264	926
Figure Eleven								

Chapter 6	11-Sep-20	18-Sep-20	25-Sep-20	2-Oct-20	9-Oct-20	16-Oct-20	23-Oct-20	30-Oct-20
Rent to parents or guardian			-200					-200
Misc. Food	-50	-50	-50	-50	-50	-50	-50	-50
Cell			-50					-50
Internet/Entertainment			-25					-25
Heat								
Electric								
Water								
Pay Off $20k loan*	-167	-167	-167	-167	-167	-167	-167	-167
Health insurance			-100					-100
transportation	-30	-30	-30	-30	-30	-30	-30	-30
Gifts/ fun/pets	-50	-50	-50	-50	-50	-50	-50	-50
Emergency Savings	-50	-50	-50	-50	-50	-50	-50	-50
Balance in bank	926	1013	1100	812	899	986	1073	1160
Paycheck (After approx taxes)	434	434	434	434	434	434	434	434
Balance forward	1013	1100	812	899	986	1073	1160	872
Figure Twelve								

Chapter 6	6-Nov-20	13-Nov-20	20-Nov-20	27-Nov-20	4-Dec-20	11-Dec-20	18-Dec-20	25-Dec-20
Rent to parents or guardian				-200				
Misc. Food	-50	-50	-50	-50	-50	-50	-50	-50
Cell				-50				
Internet/Entertainment				-25				
Heat								
Electric								
Water								
Pay Off $20k loan*	-167	-167	-167	-167	-167	-167	-167	-167
Health insurance				-100				
transportation	-30	-30	-30	-30	-30	-30	-30	-30
Gifts/ fun/pets	-50	-50	-50	-50	-50	-50	-200	-50
Emergency Savings	-50	-50	-50	-50	-50	-50	-50	-50
Balance in bank	872	959	1046	1133	845	932	1019	956
Paycheck (After approx taxes)	434	434	434	434	434	434	434	434
Balance forward	959	1046	1133	845	932	1019	956	1043
Figure Thirteen								

Chapter 6	1-Jan-21	8-Jan-21	15-Jan-21	22-Jan-21	29-Jan-21	5-Feb-21	12-Feb-21	19-Feb-21
Rent to parents or guardian	-200							
Misc. Food	-50	-50	-50	-50	-50		-50	-50
Cell	-50							
Internet/Entertainment	-25							
Heat								
Electric								
Water								
Pay Off $20k loan*	-167	-167	-167	-167	-167	-167	-167	-167
Health insurance	-100					-100		
transportation	-30	-30	-30	-30	-30	-30	-30	-30
Gifts/ fun/pets	-50	-50	-50	-50	-50	-50	-50	-50
Emergency Savings	-75	-75	-75	-75	-75	-75	-75	-75
Balance in bank	1043	730	792	855	919	984	1000	742
Paycheck (After approx taxes)	434	434	435	436	437	438	439	440
Balance forward	730	792	855	919	984	1000	1067	810
Figure Fourteen								

Chapter 6	26-Feb-21	5-Mar-21	12-Mar-21	19-Mar-21	26-Mar-21	2-Apr-21	9-Apr-21	16-Apr-21
Rent to parents or guardian		-200				-200		
Misc. Food	-50	-50	-50	-50	-50	-50	-50	-50
Cell		-50				-50		
Internet/Entertainment		-25				-25		
Heat								
Electric								
Water								
Pay Off $20k loan*	-167	-167	-167	-167	-167	-167	-167	-167
Health insurance		-100				-100		
transportation	-30	-30	-30	-30	-30	-30	-30	-30
Gifts/ fun/pets	-50	-50	-50	-50	-50	-50	-50	-50
Emergency Savings	-75	-75	-75	-75	-75	-75	-75	-75
Balance in bank	810	879	574	645	717	790	489	564
Paycheck (After approx taxes)	441	442	443	444	445	446	447	448
Balance forward	879	574	645	717	790	489	564	640

Figure Fifteen

Chapter 6	23-Apr-21	30-Apr-21	7-May-21					
Rent to parents or guardian			-200					
Misc. Food	-50	-50	-50					
Cell			-50					
Internet/Entertainment			-25					
Heat								
Electric								
Water								
Pay Off $20k loan*	-167							
Health insurance			-100					
transportation	-30	-30	-30					
Gifts/ fun/pets	-50	-50	-50					
Emergency Savings	-75	-75	-75					
Balance in bank	640	640	640					
Paycheck (After approx taxes)	449	449	449					
Balance forward	717	884	509					

Figure Sixteen

CHAPTER SEVEN

Renting -You want to Buy a house

You've just moved into the rental unit you were saving for in **Chapter 3.** Now, you are paying rent on a small apartment or a shared house or condo. You decided that you want to OWN a place, not rent. You own a car. Your goal is to save $36,000.00 for moving expenses and down payment on a $200,000.00 home. You have an entry level $15.00 job.

- Rent : Your $500.00 per month rent includes the few utilities you use when at home

- Groceries: This may not look like a lot, but if you create menus, cook and home and plan your food budget properly you can save yourself a lot of heartache and money. Not to mention eating healthier! Suggested menus and grocery lists are included at the end of the book!

- Cell: You can choose from many good phone plans and a lot of them have discounts.

- Internet/Entertainment: You may have an on line subscription or something similar, like Hulu or Xbox gold.

- Heat, Water, Electric: The presumption is that these are included in your rent. It is a good idea to remember you will have to budget for them in the future.

- Save for Your Home: This exact amount should be put in to a separate bank account every week. This must be a savings account that pays interest. The interest is not likely to be a LOT. It will probably be 1% or less. But as it accumulates in YOUR account it will make certain that you reach your goals faster. In addition to your down payment (which will include closing costs) you need kitchen stuff, a lot of furniture, moving expenses, and some 'fall back' funds in the bank. But, at the end of only 233 weeks, you will have the funds necessary to purchase a home.

- Health Insurance: You may have a personal policy that you pay monthly. Your employer may withhold this amount from your check in weekly increments. If you have no health insurance you should put this amount aside for Emergencies!

- Transportation: Even if you skateboard to work, there will be occasional days when you need to drive or ride share. If you don't spend it...put it in the house fund!

- Gifts/Fun: It is going to happen so you need to put it in your budget. You do not have to spend that much, but do not spend more.

- Emergency Savings: Put this amount aside every week in case of a Real emergency. Medical or a death in the family qualify. (If you NEVER have an emergency...this will turn into your 'early retirement fund'.)

- Balance in Bank: That is what you should have in your bank account at the end of all transactions in order to stay on your budget. At the beginning of this budget you are starting with the $4,300.00 that you had saved for moving at the end of Chapter 3.

- Paycheck: This is an average, because tax laws vary from state to state and even from city to city. If you are on salary, your pay will be the same every week. You can copy the exact figure from your pay stub. If you are an hourly worker, your net pay will change from week to week. Some companies give annual or even semi-annual pay increases.

- Balance forward: This is what is left after you pay your expenses. This money cannot be spent – it is carried forward to the next period. This is why you budget –so you remember to not spend all of your money!

Chapter 7	4-Jan-19	11-Jan-19	18-Jan-19	25-Jan-19	1-Feb-19	8-Feb-19	15-Feb-19	22-Feb-19
Rent/Mortgage	-500				-500			
Security Deposits/ furniture	-2500							
Groceries	-71	-71	-71	-71	-71	-71	-71	-71
Cell	-75				-75			
Internet/ Entertainment	-50				-50			
Heat								
Electric								
Water								
Save for House	-155	-155	-155	-155	-155	-155	-155	-155
Health insurance	-100				-100			
Auto/transportation	-25	-25	-25	-25	-25	-25	-25	-25
Gifts/ fun/pets	-10	-10	-10	-10	-10	-10	-10	-10
Emergency Savings	-5	-5	-5	-5	-5	-5	-5	-5
Car Ins.@ $800 per yr.	-67				-67			
Balance in bank	4,300	1197	1386	1575	1764	1161	1350	1539
Paycheck (After approx taxes)	455	455	455	455	455	455	455	455
Balance forward	1197	1386	1575	1764	1161	1350	1539	1728

Figure One	Notes:							

Chapter 7	1-Mar-19	8-Mar-19	15-Mar-19	22-Mar-19	29-Mar-19	5-Apr-19	12-Apr-19	19-Apr-19
Rent/Mortgage	-500				-500			
Security Deposits/ furniture								
Groceries	-71	-71	-71	-71	-71	-71	-71	-71
Cell	-75				-75			
Internet/ Entertainment	-50				-50			
Heat								
Electric								
Water								
Save for House	-155	-155	-155	-155	-155	-155	-155	-155
Health insurance	-100				-100			
Auto/transportation	-25	-25	-25	-25	-25	-25	-25	-25
Gifts/ fun/pets	-10	-10	-10	-10	-10	-10	-10	-10
Emergency Savings	-5	-5	-5	-5	-5	-5	-5	-5
Car Ins. @ $800 per yr.	-67				-67			
Balance in bank	1728	1125	1314	1503	1692	1089	1278	1467
Paycheck (After approx taxes)	455	455	455	455	455	455	455	455
Balance forward	1125	1314	1503	1692	1089	1278	1467	1656

Figure Two	Notes:							

Chapter 7	26-Apr-19	3-May-19	10-May-19	17-May-19	24-May-19	31-May-19	7-Jun-19	14-Jun-19
Rent/Mortgage		-500				-500		
Security Deposits/ furniture								
Groceries	-71	-71	-71	-71	-71	-71	-71	-71
Cell		-75				-75		
Internet/ Entertainment		-50				-50		
Heat								
Electric								
Water								
Save for House	-155	-155	-155	-155	-155	-155	-155	-155
Health insurance		-100				-100		
Auto/transportation	-25	-25	-25	-25	-25	-25	-25	-25
Gifts/ fun/pets	-10	-10	-10	-10	-10	-10	-15	-15
Emergency Savings	-5	-5	-5	-5	-5	-5	-10	-10
Car Ins. @ $800 per yr.		-67				-67		
Balance in bank	1656	1845	1242	1431	1620	1809	1206	1385
Paycheck (After approx taxes)	455	455	455	455	455	455	455	455
Balance forward	1845	1242	1431	1620	1809	1206	1385	1564

Figure Three	Notes:							

Chapter 7	21-Jun-19	28-Jun-19	5-Jul-19	12-Jul-19	19-Jul-19	26-Jul-19	2-Aug-19	9-Aug-19
Rent/Mortgage		-500					-500	
Security Deposits/ furniture								
Groceries	-71	-71	-71	-71	-71	-71	-71	-71
Cell		-75					-75	
Internet/ Entertainment		-50					-50	
Heat								
Electric								
Water								
Save for House	-155	-155	-155	-155	-155	-155	-155	-155
Health insurance		-100					-100	
Auto/transportation	-25	-25	-25	-25	-25	-25	-25	-25
Gifts/ fun/pets	-15	-15	-15	-15	-15	-15	-15	-15
Emergency Savings	-10	-10	-10	-10	-10	-10	-10	-10
Car Ins. @ $800 per yr.		-67					-67	
Balance in bank	1564	1743	1130	1309	1488	1667	1846	1233
Paycheck (After approx taxes)	455	455	455	455	455	455	455	455
Balance forward	1743	1130	1309	1488	1667	1846	1233	1412

Figure Four	Notes:							

Chapter 7	16-Aug-19	23-Aug-19	30-Aug-19	6-Sep-19	13-Sep-19	20-Sep-19	27-Sep-19	4-Oct-19
Rent/Mortgage			-500					-500
Security Deposits/ furniture								
Groceries	-71	-71	-71	-71	-71	-71	-71	-71
Cell			-75					-75
Internet/ Entertainment			-50					-50
Heat								
Electric								
Water								
Save for House	-155	-155	-155	-155	-155	-155	-155	-155
Health insurance			-100					-100
Auto/transportation	-25	-25	-25	-25	-25	-25	-25	-25
Gifts/ fun/pets	-15	-15	-15	-15	-15	-15	-15	-15
Emergency Savings	-10	-10	-10	-10	-10	-10	-10	-10
Car Ins. @ $800 per yr.			-67					-67
Balance in bank	1412	1591	1770	1157	1336	1515	1694	1873
Paycheck (After approx taxes)	455	455	455	455	455	455	455	455
Balance forward	1591	1770	1157	1336	1515	1694	1873	1260

Figure Five

Chapter 7	11-Oct-19	18-Oct-19	25-Oct-19	1-Nov-19	8-Nov-19	15-Nov-19	22-Nov-19	29-Nov-19
Rent/Mortgage				-500				-500
Security Deposits/ furniture								
Groceries	-71	-71	-71	-71	-71	-71	-71	-71
Cell				-75				-75
Internet/ Entertainment				-50				-50
Heat								
Electric								
Water								
Save for House	-155	-155	-155	-155	-155	-155	-155	-155
Health insurance				-100				-100
Auto/transportation	-25	-25	-25	-25	-25	-25	-25	-25
Gifts/ fun/pets	-15	-15	-15	-15	-15	-15	-15	-15
Emergency Savings	-10	-10	-10	-10	-10	-10	-10	-10
Car Ins. @ $800 per yr.				-67				-67
Balance in bank	1260	1439	1618	1797	1184	1363	1542	1721
Paycheck (After approx taxes)	455	455	455	455	455	455	455	455
Balance forward	1439	1618	1797	1184	1363	1542	1721	1108

Figure Six

Chapter 7	6-Dec-19	13-Dec-19	20-Dec-19	27-Dec-19	3-Jan-20	10-Jan-20	17-Jan-20	24-Jan-20
Rent/Mortgage					-500			
Security Deposits/ furniture								
Groceries	-71	-71	-71	-71	-71	-71	-71	-71
Cell					-75			
Internet/ Entertainment					-50			
Heat								
Electric								
Water								
Save for House	-155	-155	-155	-155	-155	-155	-155	-155
Health insurance					-100			
Auto/transportation	-25	-25	-25	-25	-25	-25	-25	-25
Gifts/ fun/pets	-50	-150	-200	-15	-15	-15	-15	-15
Emergency Savings	-10	-10	-10	-10	-10	-10	-10	-10
Car Ins. @ $800 per yr.					-67			
Balance in bank	1108	1252	1296	1290	1469	856	1035	1214
Paycheck (After approx taxes)	455	455	455	455	455	455	455	455
Balance forward	1252	1296	1290	1469	856	1035	1214	1393

Figure Seven

Chapter 7	31-Jan-20	7-Feb-20	14-Feb-20	21-Feb-20	28-Feb-20	6-Mar-20	13-Mar-20	20-Mar-20
Rent/Mortgage	-500				-500			
Security Deposits/ furniture								
Groceries	-71	-71	-71	-71	-71	-71	-71	-71
Cell	-75				-75			
Internet/ Entertainment	-50				-50			
Heat								
Electric								
Water								
Save for House	-155	-155	-155	-155	-155	-155	-155	-155
Health insurance	-100				-100			
Auto/transportation	-25	-25	-25	-25	-25	-25	-25	-25
Gifts/ fun/pets	-15	-15	-15	-15	-15	-15	-15	-15
Emergency Savings	-10	-10	-10	-10	-10	-10	-10	-10
Car Ins. @ $800 per yr.	-67				-67			
Balance in bank	1393	780	959	1138	1317	704	883	1062
Paycheck (After approx taxes)	455	455	455	455	455	455	455	455
Balance forward	780	959	1138	1317	704	883	1062	1241

Figure Eight

Chapter 7	27-Mar-20	3-Apr-20	10-Apr-20	17-Apr-20	24-Apr-20	1-May-20	8-May-20	15-May-20
Rent/Mortgage	-500					-500		
Security Deposits/ furniture								
Groceries	-71	-71	-71	-71	-71	-71	-71	-71
Cell	-75					-75		
Internet/ Entertainment	-50					-50		
Heat								
Electric								
Water								
Save for House	-155	-155	-155	-155	-155	-155	-155	-155
Health insurance	-100					-100		
Auto/transportation	-25	-25	-25	-25	-25	-25	-25	-25
Gifts/ fun/pets	-15	-20	-20	-20	-20	-20	-20	-20
Emergency Savings	-10	-10	-10	-10	-10	-10	-10	-10
Car Ins. @ $800 per yr.	-67					-67		
Balance in bank	1241	628	812	996	1180	1364	756	940
Paycheck (After approx taxes)	455	465	465	465	465	465	465	465
Balance forward	628	812	996	1180	1364	756	940	1124

Figure Nine — If you have been at your job for more than a year you should get a small COL pay increase

Chapter 7	22-May-20	29-May-20	5-Jun-20	12-Jun-20	19-Jun-20	26-Jun-20	3-Jul-20	10-Jul-20
Rent/Mortgage		-500					-500	
Security Deposits/ furniture								
Groceries	-71	-71	-71	-71	-71	-71	-71	-71
Cell		-75					-75	
Internet/ Entertainment		-50					-50	
Heat								
Electric								
Water								
Save for House	-155	-155	-155	-155	-155	-155	-155	-155
Health insurance		-100					-100	
Auto/transportation	-25	-25	-25	-25	-25	-25	-25	-25
Gifts/ fun/pets	-20	-20	-20	-20	-20	-20	-20	-20
Emergency Savings	-10	-10	-10	-10	-10	-10	-10	-10
Car Ins. @ $800 per yr.		-67					-67	
Balance in bank	1124	1308	700	884	1068	1252	1436	828
Paycheck (After approx taxes)	465	465	465	465	465	465	465	465
Balance forward	1308	700	884	1068	1252	1436	828	1012

Figure Ten

Chapter 7	17-Jul-20	24-Jul-20	31-Jul-20	7-Aug-20	14-Aug-20	21-Aug-20	28-Aug-20	4-Sep-20
Rent/Mortgage			-500					-500
Security Deposits/ furniture								
Groceries	-71	-71	-71	-71	-71	-71	-71	-71
Cell			-75					-75
Internet/ Entertainment			-50					-50
Heat								
Electric								
Water								
Save for House	-155	-155	-155	-155	-155	-155	-155	-155
Health insurance			-100					-100
Auto/transportation	-25	-25	-25	-25	-25	-25	-25	-25
Gifts/ fun/pets	-20	-20	20	20	20	20	20	20
Emergency Savings	-10	-10	-10	-10	-10	-10	-10	-10
Car Ins. @ $800 per yr.			-67					-67
Balance in bank	1012	1196	1380	772	956	1140	1324	1508
Paycheck (After approx taxes)	465	465	465	465	465	465	465	465
Balance forward	1196	1380	772	956	1140	1324	1508	900

Figure Eleven

Chapter 7	11-Sep-20	18-Sep-20	25-Sep-20	2-Oct-20	9-Oct-20	16-Oct-20	23-Oct-20	30-Oct-20
Rent/Mortgage				-500				-500
Security Deposits/ furniture								
Groceries	-71	-71	-71	-71	-71	-71	-71	-71
Cell				-75				-75
Internet/ Entertainment				-50				-50
Heat								
Electric								
Water								
Save for House	-155	-155	-155	-155	-155	-155	-155	-155
Health insurance				-100				-100
Auto/transportation	-25	-25	-25	-25	-25	-25	-25	-25
Gifts/ fun/pets	-20	-20	-20	-20	-20	-20	-20	-20
Emergency Savings	-10	-10	-10	-10	-10	-10	-10	-10
Car Ins. @ $800 per yr.			-67			-67		-67
Balance in bank	900	1084	1268	1385	844	1028	1145	1329
Paycheck (After approx taxes)	465	465	465	465	465	465	465	465
Balance forward	1084	1268	1385	844	1028	1145	1329	721

Figure Twelve

Chapter 7	6-Nov-20	13-Nov-20	20-Nov-20	27-Nov-20	4-Dec-20	11-Dec-20	18-Dec-20	25-Dec-20
Rent/Mortgage				-500				
Security Deposits/ furniture								
Groceries	-71	-71	-71	-71	-71	-71	-71	-71
Cell				-75				
Internet/ Entertainment				-50				
Heat								
Electric								
Water								
Save for House	-155	-155	-155	-155	-155	-155	-155	-155
Health insurance				-100				
Auto/transportation	-25	-25	-25	-25	-25	-25	-25	-25
Gifts/ fun/pets	-20	-20	-20	-20	-20	-150	-100	-50
Emergency Savings	-10	-10	-10	-10	-10	-10	-10	-10
Car Ins. @ $800 per yr.				-67				
Balance in bank	721	905	1089	1273	665	849	903	1007
Paycheck (After approx taxes)	465	465	465	465	465	465	465	465
Balance forward	905	1089	1273	665	849	903	1007	1161

Figure Thirteen

Chapter 7	1-Jan-21	8-Jan-21	15-Jan-21	22-Jan-21	29-Jan-21	5-Feb-21	12-Feb-21	19-Feb-21
Rent/Mortgage	-500				-500			
Security Deposits/ furniture								
Groceries	-71	-71	-71	-71	-71	-71	-71	-71
Cell	-75				-75			
Internet/ Entertainment	-50				-50			
Heat								
Electric								
Water								
Save for House	-155	-155	-155	-155	-155	-155	-155	-155
Health insurance	-100				-100			
Auto/transportation	-25	-25	-25	-25	-25	-25	-25	-25
Gifts/ fun/pets	-25	-25	-25	-25	-25	-25	-25	-25
Emergency Savings	-10	-10	-10	-10	-10	-10	-10	-10
Car Ins. @ $800 per yr.	-67				-67			
Balance in bank	1161	548	727	906	1085	472	651	830
Paycheck (After approx taxes)	465	465	465	465	465	465	465	465
Balance forward	548	727	906	1085	472	651	830	1009

Figure Fourteen

Chapter 7	26-Feb-21	5-Mar-21	12-Mar-21	19-Mar-21	26-Mar-21	2-Apr-21	9-Apr-21	16-Apr-21
Rent/Mortgage		-500				-500		
Security Deposits/ furniture								
Groceries	-71	-71	-71	-71	-71	-71	-71	-71
Cell		-75				-75		
Internet/ Entertainment		-50				-50		
Heat								
Electric								
Water								
Save for House	-155	-155	-155	-155	-155	-155	-155	-155
Health insurance		-100				-100		
Auto/transportation	-25	-25	-25	-25	-25	-25	-25	-25
Gifts/ fun/pets	-25	-25	-25	-25	-25	-25	-25	-25
Emergency Savings	-10	-10	-10	-10	-10	-10	-10	-10
Car Ins. @ $800 per yr.		-67				-67		
Balance in bank	1009	1188	575	754	933	1112	499	678
Paycheck (After approx taxes)	465	465	465	465	465	465	465	465
Balance forward	1188	575	754	933	1112	499	678	857

Figure Fifteen

Chapter 7	23-Apr-21	30-Apr-21	7-May-21	14-May-21	21-May-21	28-May-21	4-Jun-21	11-Jun-21
Rent/Mortgage			-500				-500	
Security Deposits/ furniture								
Groceries	-71	-71	-71	-71	-71	-71	-71	-71
Cell			-75				-75	
Internet/ Entertainment			-50				-50	
Heat								
Electric								
Water								
Save for House	-155	-155	-155	-155	-155	-155	-155	-155
Health insurance			-100				-100	
Auto/transportation	-25	-25	-25	-25	-25	-25	-25	-25
Gifts/ fun/pets	-25	-25	-25	-25	-25	-25	-25	-25
Emergency Savings	-10	-10	-10	-10	-10	-10	-10	-10
Car Ins. @ $800 per yr.			-67				-67	
Balance in bank	857	1036	1215	602	781	960	1139	526
Paycheck (After approx taxes)	465	465	465	465	465	465	465	465
Balance forward	1036	1215	602	781	960	1139	526	705

Figure Sixteen

Chapter 7	18-Jun-21	25-Jun-21	2-Jul-21	9-Jul-21	16-Jul-21	23-Jul-21	30-Jul-21	6-Aug-21
Rent/Mortgage			-500				-500	
Security Deposits/ furniture								
Groceries	-71	-71	-71	-71	-71	-71	-71	-71
Cell			-75				-75	
Internet/ Entertainment			-50				-50	
Heat								
Electric								
Water								
Save for House	-155	-155	-155	-155	-155	-155	-155	-155
Health insurance			-100				-100	
Auto/transportation	-25	-25	-25	-25	-25	-25	-25	-25
Gifts/ fun/pets	-25	-25	-25	-25	-25	-25	-25	-25
Emergency Savings	-10	-10	-10	-10	-10	-10	-10	-10
Car Ins. @ $800 per yr.			-67				-67	
Balance in bank	705	884	1063	450	629	808	987	374
Paycheck (After approx taxes)	465	465	465	465	465	465	465	465
Balance forward	884	1063	450	629	808	987	374	553

Figure Seventeen

Chapter 7	13-Aug-21	20-Aug-21	27-Aug-21	3-Sep-21	10-Sep-21	17-Sep-21	24-Sep-21	1-Oct-21
Rent/Mortgage				-500				-500
Security Deposits/ furniture								
Groceries	-71	-71	-71	-71	-71	-71	-71	-71
Cell				-75				-75
Internet/ Entertainment				-50				-50
Heat								
Electric								
Water								
Save for House	-155	-155	-155	-155	-155	-155	-155	-155
Health insurance				-100				-100
Auto/transportation	-25	-25	-25	-25	-25	-25	-25	-25
Gifts/ fun/pets	-25	-25	-25	-25	-25	-25	-25	-25
Emergency Savings	-10	-10	-10	-10	-10	-10	-10	-10
Car Ins. @ $800 per yr.				-67				-67
Balance in bank	553	732	911	1090	477	656	835	1014
Paycheck (After approx taxes)	465	465	465	465	465	465	465	465
Balance forward	732	911	1090	477	656	835	1014	401

Figure Eighteen

Chapter 7	8-Oct-21	15-Oct-21	22-Oct-21	29-Oct-21	5-Nov-21	12-Nov-21	19-Nov-21	26-Nov-21
Rent/Mortgage				-500				
Security Deposits/ furniture								
Groceries	-71	-71	-71	-71	-71	-71	-71	-71
Cell				-75				
Internet/ Entertainment				-50				
Heat								
Electric								
Water								
Save for House	-155	-155	-155	-155	-155	-155	-155	-155
Health insurance				-100				
Auto/transportation	-25	-25	-25	-25	-25	-25	-25	-25
Gifts/ fun/pets	-25	-25	-25	-25	-25	-25	-25	-25
Emergency Savings	-10	-10	-10	-10	-10	-10	-10	-10
Car Ins. @ $800 per yr.				-67				
Balance in bank	401	580	759	938	325	504	683	862
Paycheck (After approx taxes)	465	465	465	465	465	465	465	465
Balance forward	580	759	938	325	504	683	862	1041

Figure Nineteen

Chapter 7	3-Dec-21	10-Dec-21	17-Dec-21	24-Dec-21	31-Dec-21	7-Jan-22	14-Jan-22	21-Jan-22
Rent/Mortgage	-500				-500			
Security Deposits/ furniture								
Groceries	-71	-71	-71	-71	-71	-71	-71	-71
Cell	-75				-75			
Internet/ Entertainment	-50				-50			
Heat								
Electric								
Water								
Save for House	-155	-155	-155	-155	-155	-155	-155	-155
Health insurance	-100				-100			
Auto/transportation	-25	-25	-25	-25	-25	-25	-25	-25
Gifts/ fun/pets	-25	-125	-225	-50	-25	-25	-25	-25
Emergency Savings	-10	-10	-10	-10	-10	-10	-10	-10
Car Ins. @ $800 per yr.	-67				-67			
Balance in bank	1041	428	507	486	640	27	206	385
Paycheck (After approx taxes)	465	465	465	465	465	465	465	465
Balance forward	428	507	486	640	27	206	385	564

Figure Twenty

Chapter 7	28-Jan-22	4-Feb-22	11-Feb-22	18-Feb-22	25-Feb-22	4-Mar-22	11-Mar-22	18-Mar-22
Rent/Mortgage		-500				-500		
Security Deposits/ furniture								
Groceries	-71	-71				-71		
Cell		-75				-75		
Internet/ Entertainment		-50				-50		
Heat								
Electric								
Water								
Save for House	-155	-155	-155	-155	-155	-155	-155	-155
Health insurance		-100				-100		
Auto/transportation	-25	-25	-25	-25	-25	-25	-25	-25
Gifts/ fun/pets	-25	-25	-25	-25	-25	-25	-25	-25
Emergency Savings	-10	-10	-10	-10	-10	-10	-10	-10
Car Ins.@$800 per yr.		-67				-67		
Balance in bank	564	743	130	380	630	880	267	517
Paycheck (After approx taxes)	465	465	465	465	465	465	465	465
Balance forward	743	130	380	630	880	267	517	767

Figure Twenty One

Chapter 7	25-Mar-22	1-Apr-22	8-Apr-22	15-Apr-22	22-Apr-22	29-Apr-22	6-May-22	13-May-22
Rent/Mortgage		-500				-500		
Security Deposits/ furniture								
Groceries		-71				-71		
Cell		-75				-75		
Internet/ Entertainment		-50				-50		
Heat								
Electric								
Water								
Save for House	-155	-155	-155	-155	-155	-155	-155	-155
Health insurance		-100				-100		
Auto/transportation	-25	-25	-25	-25	-25	-25	-25	-25
Gifts/ fun/pets	-25	-25	-25	-25	-25	-25	-25	-25
Emergency Savings	-10	-10	-10	-10	-10	-10	-10	-10
Car Ins.@$800 per yr.		-67				-67		
Balance in bank	767	1017	404	654	904	1154	541	791
Paycheck (After approx taxes)	465	465	465	465	465	465	465	465
Balance forward	1017	404	654	904	1154	541	791	1041

Figure Twenty Two

Chapter 7	20-May-22	27-May-22	3-Jun-22	10-Jun-22	17-Jun-22	24-Jun-22	1-Jul-22	8-Jul-22
Rent/Mortgage			-500				-500	
Security Deposits/ furniture								
Groceries			-71				-71	
Cell			-75				-75	
Internet/ Entertainment			-50				-50	
Heat								
Electric								
Water								
Save for House	-155	-155	-155	-155	-155	-155	-155	-155
Health insurance			-100				-100	
Auto/transportation	-25	-25	-25	-25	-25	-25	-25	-25
Gifts/ fun/pets	-25	-25	-25	-25	-25	-25	-25	-25
Emergency Savings	-10	-10	-10	-10	-10	-10	-10	-10
Car Ins.@$800 per yr.			-67				-67	
Balance in bank	1041	1291	1541	928	1178	1428	1678	1065
Paycheck (After approx taxes)	465	465	465	465	465	465	465	465
Balance forward	1291	1541	928	1178	1428	1678	1065	1315

Figure Twenty Three

Chapter 7	15-Jul-22	22-Jul-22	29-Jul-22	5-Aug-22	12-Aug-22	19-Aug-22	26-Aug-22	2-Sep-22
Rent/Mortgage			-500					-500
Security Deposits/ furniture								
Groceries			-71					-71
Cell			-75					-75
Internet/ Entertainment			-50					-50
Heat								
Electric								
Water								
Save for House	-155	-155	-155	-155	-155	-155	-155	-155
Health insurance			-100					-100
Auto/transportation	-25	-25	-25	-25	-25	-25	-25	-25
Gifts/ fun/pets	-25	-25	-25	-25	-25	-25	-25	-25
Emergency Savings	-10	-10	-10	-10	-10	-10	-10	-10
Car Ins.@$800 per yr.			-67					-67
Balance in bank	1315	1565	1815	1202	1452	1702	1952	2022
Paycheck (After approx taxes)	465	465	465	465	465	465	465	465
Balance forward	1565	1815	1202	1452	1702	1952	2202	1409

Figure Twenty Four

Chapter 7	9-Sep-22	16-Sep-22	23-Sep-22	30-Sep-22	7-Oct-22	14-Oct-22	21-Oct-22	28-Oct-22
Rent/Mortgage				-500				
Security Deposits/ furniture								
Groceries				-71				
Cell				-75				
Internet/ Entertainment				-50				
Heat								
Electric								
Water								
Save for House	-155	-155	-155	-155	-155	-155	-155	-155
Health insurance				-100				
Auto/transportation	-25	-25	-25	-25	-25	-25	-25	-25
Gifts/ fun/pets	-25	-25	-25	-25	-25	-25	-25	-25
Emergency Savings	-10	-10	-10	-10	-10	-10	-10	-10
Car Ins.@$800 per yr.				-67				
Balance in bank	1409	1659	1909	2159	1546	1796	2046	2296
Paycheck (After approx taxes)	465	465	465	465	465	465	465	465
Balance forward	1659	1909	2159	1546	1796	2046	2296	2546

Figure Twenty Five

Chapter 7	4-Nov-22	11-Nov-22	18-Nov-22	25-Nov-22	2-Dec-22	9-Dec-22	16-Dec-22	23-Dec-22
Rent/Mortgage	-500					-500		
Security Deposits/ furniture								
Groceries	-71					-71		
Cell	-75					-75		
Internet/ Entertainment	-50					-50		
Heat								
Electric								
Water								
Save for House	-155	-155	-155	-155	-155	-155	-155	-155
Health insurance	-100					-100		
Auto/transportation	-25	-25	-25	-25	-25	-25	-25	-25
Gifts/ fun/pets	-25	-25	-25	-25	-25	-25	-25	-25
Emergency Savings	-10	-10	-10	-10	-10	-10	-10	-10
Car Ins.@$800 per yr.	-67					-67		
Balance in bank	2546	1933	2183	2433	2683	2933	2320	2570
Paycheck (After approx taxes)	465	465	465	465	465	465	465	465
Balance forward	1933	2183	2433	2683	2933	2320	2570	2820

Figure Twenty Six

Chapter 7	30-Dec-22	6-Jan-23	13-Jan-23	20-Jan-23	27-Jan-23	3-Feb-23	10-Feb-23	17-Feb-23
Rent/Mortgage		-500				-500		
Security Deposits/ furniture								
Groceries		-71				-71		
Cell		-75				-75		
Internet/ Entertainment		-50				-50		
Heat								
Electric								
Water								
Save for House	-155	-155	-155	-155	-155	-155	-155	-155
Health insurance		-100				-100		
Auto/transportation	-25	-25	-25	-25	-25	-25	-25	-25
Gifts/ fun/pets	-25	-25	-25	-25	-25	-25	-25	-25
Emergency Savings	-10	-10	-10	-10	-10	-10	-10	-10
Car Ins.@$800 per yr.		-67				-67		
Balance in bank	2820	3070	2457	2707	2957	3207	2594	2844
Paycheck (After approx taxes)	465	465	465	465	465	465	465	465
Balance forward	3070	2457	2707	2957	3207	2594	2844	3094

Figure Twenty Seven

Chapter 7	24-Feb-23	3-Mar-23	10-Mar-23	17-Mar-23	24-Mar-23	31-Mar-23	7-Apr-23	14-Apr-23
Rent/Mortgage		-500					-500	
Security Deposits/ furniture								
Groceries		-71					-71	
Cell		-75					-75	
Internet/ Entertainment		-50					-50	
Heat								
Electric								
Water								
Save for House	-155	-155	-155	-155	-155	-155	-155	-155
Health insurance		-100					-100	
Auto/transportation	-25	-25	-25	-25	-25	-25	-25	-25
Gifts/ fun/pets	-25	-25	-25	-25	-25	-25	-25	-25
Emergency Savings	-10	-10	-10	-10	-10	-10	-10	-10
Car Ins.@$800 per yr.		-67					-67	
Balance in bank	3094	3344	2731	2981	3231	3481	3731	3118
Paycheck (After approx taxes)	465	465	465	465	465	465	465	465
Balance forward	3344	2731	2981	3231	3481	3731	3118	3368

Figure Twenty Eight

Chapter 7	21-Apr-23	28-Apr-23	5-May-23	12-May-23	19-May-23	26-May-23	2-Jun-23	9-Jun-23
Rent/Mortgage		-500				-500		
Security Deposits/ furniture								
Groceries		-71				-71		
Cell		-75				-75		
Internet/ Entertainment		-50				-50		
Heat								
Electric								
Water								
Save for House	-155	-155	-155	-155	-155	-155	-155	-155
Health insurance		-100				-100		
Auto/transportation	-25	-25	-25	-25	-25	-25	-25	-25
Gifts/ fun/pets	-25	-25	-25	-25	-25	-25	-25	-25
Emergency Savings	-10	-10	-10	-10	-10	-10	-10	-10
Car Ins.@$800 per yr.		-67				-67		
Balance in bank	3368	3618	3005	3255	3505	3755	3142	3392
Paycheck (After approx taxes)	465	465	465	465	465	465	465	465
Balance forward	3618	3005	3255	3505	3755	3142	3392	3642

Figure Twenty Nine

Chapter 7	16-Jun-23	23-Jun-23	30-Jun-23	7-Jul-23
Rent/Mortgage				-500
Moving Expenses				-2,925.00
Groceries				-71
Cell				-75
Internet/ Entertainment				-50
Heat				
Electric				
Water				
Save for House	-155	-155		
Health insurance				-100
Auto/transportation	-25	-25	-25	-25
Gifts/ fun/pets	-25	-25	-25	-25
Emergency Savings	-10	-10	-10	-10
Car Ins.@$800 per yr.				-67
Balance in bank	3642	3892	4142	4547
Paycheck (After approx taxes)	465	465	465	465
Balance forward	3892	4142	4547	1164

Figure Thirty

CHAPTER EIGHT

You Own Your Home and Want to Get Your Budget Under Control

You've just moved into the Home you were saving for in Chapters 4 and 7. You NOW own your house and you own a car. Your goal is to forecast and plan for expenses for the next two years. You have a $15.00 per hour job.

- Mortgage : Your $1,164.00 per month mortgage is 30 years @3.7% and includes the property tax and insurance. You 'settled' on the 30th so the first Payment is due February.

- Groceries: This may not look like a lot, but if you create menus, cook at home and plan your food budget properly you can save yourself a lot of heartache and money. Not to mention eating healthier! Suggested menus and grocery lists are included at the end of the book!

- Cell: You can choose from many good DISCOUNT phone plans and a lot of them have extra services!

- Internet/Entertainment: You may have an on line subscription or something similar, like Hulu or Xbox gold.

- Heat, Water, Electric: These are an average of average monthly utility expenses. Depending on where you are and what types of appliances you run, these expenses can and will vary.

- Health Insurance: You may have a personal policy that you pay monthly. Your employer may withhold this amount from your check in weekly increments.

- Transportation: Even if you skateboard to work, there will be occasional days when you drive, take a bus, or Uber.

- Gifts/Fun: It is going to happen so you need to put it in your budget. You do not have to spend that much, but do not spend more.

- Emergency Savings: Put this amount aside every week in case of a Real emergency. Medical or a death in the family qualify. If you never spend it - this will become your retirement fund!

- Balance in Bank: That is what you should have in your bank account at the end of all transactions in order to stay on your budget. At the beginning of this budget you are starting with the $1,164.00 in your bank acount that you had 'Left in your account at the end of Chapter 4 or Chapter 7 . your first Month's mortgae will be 'paid' at settlement fromn the funds you previously saved for the home. you mortgage payments will be due the first day of the month thereafter.

- Paycheck: This is an average, because tax laws vary from state to state and even from city to city. An adjustment has been made to the _payroll withholding to account for the mortgage interest deduction that you are now able to take when you file your taxes._   If you are on salary, your pay will be the same every week. You can copy the exact figure from your pay stub. If you are an hourly worker, your net pay will change from week to week. Some companies give annual or even semi-annual pay increases.

- Balance forward: This is what is left after you pay your expenses. This money cannot be spent – it is carried forward to the next period. This is how you keep control of your finances.

Chapter 8	4-Jan-19	11-Jan-19	18-Jan-19	25-Jan-19	1-Feb-19	8-Feb-19	15-Feb-19	22-Feb-19
Rent/Mortgage	0				-1164			
Groceries	-71	-71	-71	-71	-71	-71	-71	-71
Cell	-50				-50			
Internet/Entertainment	-45				-45			
Heat (Yearly averge)	-80				-80			
Electric (Yearly Average)	-80				-80			
Water (Yearly Average)	-60				-60			
Health insurance	-85				-85			
Auto/transportation	-25	-25	-25	-25	-25	-25	-25	-25
Gifts/ fun/ household/pets	-5	-5	-5	-5	-5	-5	-5	-5
Emergency Savings	-10	-10	-10	-10	-10	-10	-10	-10
Car Ins. @ $800 per year.	-67				-67			
Balance in bank	1164	1066	1435	1804	2173	911	1280	1649
Paycheck (After approx taxes)	480	480	480	480	480	480	480	480
Balance forward	1066	1435	1804	2173	911	1280	1649	2018

Figure One

Notes:

Chapter 8	1-Mar-19	8-Mar-19	15-Mar-19	22-Mar-19	29-Mar-19	5-Apr-19	12-Apr-19	19-Apr-19
Rent/Mortgage	-1164				-1164			
Groceries	-71	-71	-71	-71	-71	-71	-71	-71
Cell	-50				-50			
Internet/Entertainment	-45				-45			
Heat (Yearly averge)	-80				-80			
Electric (Yearly Average)	-80				-80			
Water (Yearly Average)	-60				-60			
Health insurance	-85				-85			
Auto/transportation	-25	-25	-25	-25	-25	-25	-25	-25
Gifts/ fun/ household/pets	-5	-5	-5	-5	-5	-5	-5	-5
Emergency Savings	-10	-10	-10	-10	-10	-10	-10	-10
Car Ins. @ $800 per year.	-67				-67			
Balance in bank	2018	756	1125	1494	1863	601	970	1339
Paycheck (After approx taxes)	480	480	480	480	480	480	480	480
Balance forward	756	1125	1494	1863	601	970	1339	1708
Figure Two								

Chapter 8	26-Apr-19	3-May-19	10-May-19	17-May-19	24-May-19	31-May-19	7-Jun-19	14-Jun-19
Rent/Mortgage		-1164				-1164		
Groceries	-71	-71	-71	-71	-71	-71	-71	-71
Cell		-50				-50		
Internet/Entertainment		-45				-45		
Heat (Yearly averge)		-80				-80		
Electric(Yearly Average)		-80				-80		
Water (Yearly Average)		-60				-60		
Health insurance		-85				-85		
Auto/transportation	-25	-25	-25	-25	-25	-25	-25	-25
Gifts/ fun/ household/pets	-5	-5	-5	-5	-5	-5	-5	-5
Emergency Savings	-10	-10	-10	-10	-10	-10	-10	-10
Car Ins.@ $800per year		-67				-67		
Balance in bank	1708	2077	815	1184	1553	1922	660	1029
Paycheck (After approx taxes)	480	480	480	480	480	480	480	480
Balance forward	20177	815	1184	1553	1922	660	1029	1398

Figure Three

Chapter 8	21-Jun-19	28-Jun-19	5-Jul-19	12-Jul-19	19-Jul-19	26-Jul-19	2-Aug-19	9-Aug-19
Rent/Mortgage		-1164					-1164	
Groceries	-71	-71	-71	-71	-71	-71	-71	-71
Cell		-50					-50	
Internet/Entertainment		-45					-45	
Heat (Yearly averge)		-80					-80	
Electric (Yearly Average)		-80					-80	
Water (Yearly Average)		-60					-60	
Health insurance		-85					-85	
Auto/transportation	-25	-25	-25	-25	-25	-25	-25	-25
Gifts/ fun/ household/pets	-5	-5	-5	-5	-5	-5	-5	-5
Emergency Savings	-10	-10	-10	-10	-10	-10	-10	-10
Car Ins.@ $800 per year		-67					-67	
Balance in bank	1398	1767	505	874	1243	1612	1981	719
Paycheck (After approx taxes)	480	480	480	480	480	480	480	480
Balance forward	1767	505	874	1243	1612	1981	719	1088

Figure Four

Chapter 8	16-Aug-19	23-Aug-19	30-Aug-19	6-Sep-19	13-Sep-19	20-Sep-19	27-Sep-19	4-Oct-19
Rent/Mortgage			-1164					-1164
Groceries	-71	-71	-71	-71	-71	-71	-71	-71
Cell			-50					-50
Internet/Entertainment			-45					-45
Heat (Yearly averge)			-80					-80
Electric(Yearly Average)			-80					-80
Water (Yearly Average)			-60					-60
Health insurance			-85					-85
Auto/transportation	-25	-25	-25	-25	-25	-25	-25	-25
Gifts/ fun/ household/pets	-5	-5	-5	-5	-5	-5	-5	-5
Emergency Savings	-10	-10	-10	-10	-10	-10	-10	-10
Car Ins. @ $800 per year.			-67					-67
Balance in bank	1088	1457	1826	564	933	1302	1671	2040
Paycheck (After approx taxes)	480	480	480	480	480	480	480	480
Balance forward	1457	1826	564	933	1302	1671	2040	778
Figure Five								

Chapter 8	11-Oct-19	18-Oct-19	25-Oct-19	1-Nov-19	8-Nov-19	15-Nov-19	22-Nov-19	29-Nov-19
Rent/Mortgage				-1164				-1164
Groceries	-71	-71	-71	-71	-71	-71	-71	-71
Cell				-50				-50
Internet/Entertainment				-45				-45
Heat (Yearly averge)				-80				-80
Electric(Yearly Average)				-80				-80
Water (Yearly Average)				-60				-60
Health insurance				-85				-85
Auto/transportation	-25	-25	-25	-25	-25	-25	-25	-25
Gifts/ fun/ household/pets	-5	-5	-5	-5	-10	-10	-10	-10
Emergency Savings	-10	-10	-10	-10	-10	-10	-10	-10
Car Ins. @ $800 per year.				-67				-67
Balance in bank	778	1147	1516	1885	623	987	1351	1715
Paycheck (After approx taxes)	480	480	480	480	480	480	480	480
Balance forward	1147	1516	1885	623	987	1351	1715	448
Figure Six								

Chapter 8	6-Dec-19	13-Dec-19	20-Dec-19	27-Dec-19	3-Jan-20	10-Jan-20	17-Jan-20	24-Jan-20
Rent/Mortgage					-1164			
Groceries	-71	-71	-71	-71	-71	-71	-71	-71
Cell					-50			
Internet/Entertainment					-45			
Heat (Yearly averge)					-80			
Electric(Yearly Average)					-80			
Water (Yearly Average)					-60			
Health insurance					-85			
Auto/transportation	-25	-25	-25	-25	-25	-25	-25	-25
Gifts/ fun/ household/pets	-75	-100	-75	-10	-10	-10	-10	-10
Emergency Savings	-10	-10	-10	-10	-10	-10	-10	-10
Car Ins.@ $800 per year.					-67			
Balance in bank	448	747	1021	1320	1684	417	781	1145
Paycheck (After approx taxes)	480	480	480	480	480	480	480	480
Balance forward	747	1021	1320	1684	417	781	1145	1509

Figure Seven

Chapter 8	31-Jan-20	7-Feb-20	14-Feb-20	21-Feb-20	28-Feb-20	6-Mar-20	13-Mar-20	20-Mar-20
Rent/Mortgage	-1164				-1164			
Groceries	-71	-71	-71	-71	-71	-71	-71	-71
Cell	-50				-50			
Internet/Entertainment	-45				-45			
Heat (Yearly averge)	-80				-80			
Electric(Yearly Average)	-80				-80			
Water (Yearly Average)	-60				-60			
Health insurance	-85				-85			
Auto/transportation	-25	-25	-25	-25	-25	-25	-25	-25
Gifts/ fun/ household/pets	-10	-10	-10	-10	-10	-10	-10	-10
Emergency Savings	-10	-10	-10	-10	-10	-10	-10	-10
Car Ins. @$800 per year.	-67				-67			
Balance in bank	1509	242	606	990	1374	127	511	895
Paycheck (After approx taxes)	480	480	500	500	500	500	500	500
Balance forward	242	606	990	1374	127	511	895	1279

Figure Eight

If you have been at your job for a year you should receive a small COL raise Reflected here

Chapter 8	27-Mar-20	3-Apr-20	10-Apr-20	17-Apr-20	24-Apr-20	1-May-20	8-May-20	15-May-20
Rent/Mortgage	-1164					-1164		
Groceries	-71	-71	-71	-71	-71	-71	-71	-71
Cell	-50					-50		
Internet/Entertainment	-45					-45		
Heat (Yearly averge)	-80					-80		
Electric(Yearly Average)	-80					-80		
Water (Yearly Average)	-60					-60		
Health insurance	-85					-85		
Auto/transportation	-25	-25	-25	-25	-25	-25	-25	-25
Gifts/ fun/ household/pets	-10	-10	-10	-10	-10	-10	-10	-10
Emergency Savings	-10	-10	-10	-10	-10	-10	-10	-10
Car Ins@$800per year	-67					-67		
Balance in bank	1279	32	416	800	1184	1568	321	705
Paycheck (After approx taxes)	500	500	500	500	500	500	500	500
Balance forward	32	416	800	1184	1568	321	705	1089

Figure Nine

Chapter 8	22-May-20	29-May-20	5-Jun-20	12-Jun-20	19-Jun-20	26-Jun-20	3-Jul-20	10-Jul-20
Rent/Mortgage		-1164					-1164	
Groceries	-71	-71	-71	-71	-71	-71	-71	-71
Cell		-50					-50	
Internet/Entertainment		-45					-45	
Heat (Yearly averge)		-80					-80	
Electric(Yearly Average)		-80					-80	
Water (Yearly Average)		-60					-60	
Health insurance		-85					-85	
Auto/transportation	-25	-25	-25	-25	-25	-25	-25	-25
Gifts/ fun/ household/pets	-10	-10	-10	-10	-10	-10	-10	-10
Emergency Savings	-10	-10	-10	-10	-10	-10	-10	-10
Car Ins@$800per year		-67					-67	
Balance in bank	1089	1473	226	610	994	1378	1762	515
Paycheck (After approx taxes)	500	500	500	500	500	500	500	500
Balance forward	1473	226	610	994	1378	1762	515	899

Figure Ten

Chapter 8	17-Jul-20	24-Jul-20	31-Jul-20	7-Aug-20	14-Aug-20	21-Aug-20	28-Aug-20	4-Sep-20
Rent/Mortgage			-1164					-1164
Groceries	-71	-71	-71	-71	-71	-71	-71	-71
Cell			-50					-50
Internet/Entertainment			-45					-45
Heat (Yearly averge)			-80					-80
Electric(Yearly Average)			-80					-80
Water (Yearly Average)			-60					-60
Health insurance			-85					-85
Auto/transportation	-25	-25	-25	-25	-25	-25	-25	-25
Gifts/ fun/ household/pets	-10	-10	-10	-10	-10	-10	-10	-10
Emergency Savings	-10	-10	-10	-10	-10	-10	-10	-10
Car Ins@$800per year			-67					-67
Balance in bank	899	1283	1667	420	804	1188	1572	1956
Paycheck (After approx taxes)	500	500	500	500	500	500	500	500
Balance forward	1283	1667	420	804	1188	1572	1956	709
Figure Eleven								

Chapter 8	11-Sep-20	18-Sep-20	25-Sep-20	2-Oct-20	9-Oct-20	16-Oct-20	23-Oct-20	30-Oct-20
Rent/Mortgage				-1164				
Groceries	-71	-71	-71	-71	-71	-71	-71	-71
Cell				-50				
Internet/Entertainment				-45				
Heat (Yearly averge)				-80				
Electric(Yearly Average)				-80				
Water (Yearly Average)				-60				
Health insurance				-85				
Auto/transportation	-25	-25	-25	-25	-25	-25	-25	-25
Gifts/ fun/ household/pets	-10	-10	-10	-10	-10	-10	-10	-10
Emergency Savings	-10	-10	-10	-10	-10	-10	-10	-10
Car Ins@$800per year				-67				
Balance in bank	709	1093	1477	1861	614	998	1382	1766
Paycheck (After approx taxes)	500	500	500	500	500	500	500	500
Balance forward	1093	1477	1861	614	998	1382	1766	2150
Figure Twelve								

Chapter 8	6-Nov-20	13-Nov-20	20-Nov-20	27-Nov-20	4-Dec-20	11-Dec-20	18-Dec-20	25-Dec-20
Rent/Mortgage	-1164				-1164			
Groceries	-71	-71	-71	-71	-71	-71	-71	-71
Cell	-50				-50			
Internet/Entertainment	-45				-45			
Heat (Yearly averge)	-80				-80			
Electric(Yearly Average)	-80				-80			
Water (Yearly Average)	-60				-60			
Health insurance	-85				-85			
Auto/transportation	-25	-25	-25	-25	-25	-25	-25	-25
Gifts/ fun/ household/pets	-10	-10	-10	-10	-10	-75	-150	-75
Emergency Savings	-10	-10	-10	-10	-10	-10	-10	-10
Car Ins. @ $800 per year.	-67				-67			
Balance in bank	2150	903	1287	1671	2055	808	1127	1371
Paycheck (After approx taxes)	500	500	500	500	500	500	500	500
Balance forward	903	1287	1671	2055	808	1127	1371	1690
Figure Thirteen								

Chapter 8	1-Jan-21	8-Jan-21
Rent/Mortgage	-1164	
Groceries	-71	-71
Cell	-50	
Internet/Entertainment	-45	
Heat (Yearly averge)	-80	
Electric (Yearly Average)	-80	
Water (Yearly Average)	-60	
Health insurance	-85	
Auto/transportation	-25	-25
Gifts/ fun/ household/pets	-10	-10
Emergency Savings	-10	-10
Car Ins. @ $800 per year.	-67	
Balance in bank	1690	443
Paycheck (After approx taxes)	500	500
Balance forward	443	827
Figure Fourteen		

CHAPTER NINE

Renting - With One Dependent

You are renting a small apartment or sharing a house or condo. You own a car. But NOW, with only a few months notice, you are supporting one dependent - either a child, a partner, a parent or grandparent. You earn $15.00 per hour. You are receiving no public assistance. You claim your dependant on taxes. You had $4,500.00 in the bank (savings) the day you started supporting this person. This two year budget will help you manage your expenses .

- Rent : Your $600.00 per month rent does not include utilities.

- Groceries: $100.00 a week may not look like a lot, but if you create menus, cook and home and plan your food budget properly you can save yourself a lot of heartache and money. Not to mention eating healthier! Suggested menus and grocery lists are included at the end of the book!

- Cell: You can choose from many good phone plans and a lot of them have discounts.

- Internet/Entertainment: You may have an on line subscription or something similar, like Hulu or Xbox gold.

- Heat, Water, Electric: This is an average of an average. Depending on where you live, some of these may be higher or lower or even nonexistent. They will change monthly. So if your electric is $100 in the summer, your Gas may only be $20...then the reverse would be true in winter. Or you may not have gas or oil heat and your entire house may run on Electric

- Health Insurance: You may have a personal policy that you pay monthly. Your employer may withhold this amount from your check in weekly increments.

- Child or Elder Day Care: You need to work to support this person. So you have to pay for day care. You can deduct a portion of this from your taxes every year.

- Transportation: Even if you skateboard to work, there will be occasional days when you need to take a bus, or Uber.

- Gifts/Fun: It is going to happen so you need to put it in your budget. You do not have to spend that much, but do not spend more.

- Emergency Savings: Put this amount aside every week in case of a Real emergency. Medical or a death in the family qualify.

- Balance in Bank: That is what you should have in your bank account at the end of all transactions in order to stay on your budget. At the beginning of this budget you are starting with the $4,500.00 in your bank acount that you had 'saved' in a previous chapter.

-

    Paycheck: This is an average, because tax laws vary from state to state and even from city to city. If you are on salary, your pay will be the same every week. You can copy the exact figure from your pay stub. An adjustment has been made for the tax deduction you will get for your dependent. If you are an hourly worker, your net pay will change from week to week. Some companies give annual or even semi-annual pay increases.

- Balance forward: This is what is left after you pay your expenses. This money cannot be spent – it is carried forward to the next period. This is the main point of a budget – to not spend every bit of money that comes into your hands.

Chapter 9	4-Jan-19	11-Jan-19	18-Jan-19	25-Jan-19	1-Feb-19	8-Feb-19	15-Feb-19	22-Feb-19
Rent/Mortgage	-600				-600			
Groceries	-100	-100	-100	-100	-100	-100	-100	-100
Cell	-60				-60			
Internet/Entertainment	-60				-60			
Heat (Average)	-45				-45			
Electric (Average)	-55				-55			
Water (Average)	-50				-50			
Child Care/Elder Care	-550				-550			
Health insurance	-85				-85			
Auto/transportation	-25	-25	-25	-25	-25	-25	-25	-25
Gifts/ fun	-10	-10	-10	-10	-10	-10	-10	-10
Emergency Savings	-10	-10	-10	-10	-10	-10	-10	-10
Car Ins@ $1000 per yr	-84				-84			
Balance in bank	4,500	3263	3615	3967	4319	3082	3434	3786
Paycheck (After approx taxes)	497	497	497	497	497	497	497	497
Balance forward	3263	3615	3967	4319	3082	3434	3786	4138

Chapter 9	1-Mar-19	8-Mar-19	15-Mar-19	22-Mar-19	29-Mar-19	5-Apr-19	12-Apr-19	19-Apr-19
Rent/Mortgage	-600				-600			
Groceries	-100	-100	-100	-100	-100	-100	-100	-100
Cell	-60				-60			
Internet/Entertainment	-60				-60			
Heat (Average)	-45				-45			
Electric (Average)	-55				-55			
Water (Average)	-50				-50			
Child Care/Elder Care	-550				-550			
Health insurance	-85				-85			
Auto/transportation	-25	-25	-25	-25	-25	-25	-25	-25
Gifts/ fun	-10	-10	-10	-10	-10	-10	-10	-10
Emergency Savings	-10	-10	-10	-10	-10	-10	-10	-10
Car Ins@ $1000 per yr	-84				-84			
Balance in bank	4138	2901	3253	3605	3957	2720	3072	3424
Paycheck (After approx taxes)	497	497	497	497	497	497	497	497
Balance forward	2901	3253	3605	3957	2720	3072	3424	3776

Chapter 9	26-Apr-19	3-May-19	10-May-19	17-May-19	24-May-19	31-May-19	7-Jun-19	14-Jun-19
Rent/Mortgage		-600				-600		
Groceries	-100	-100	-100	-100	-100	-100	-100	-100
Cell		-60				-60		
Internet/Entertainment		-60				-60		
Heat (Average)		-45				-45		
Electric (Average)		-55				-55		
Water (Average)		-50				-50		
Child Care/Elder Care		-550				-550		
Health insurance		-85				-85		
Auto/transportation	-25	-25	-25	-25	-25	-25	-25	-25
Gifts/ fun	-10	-10	-10	-10	-10	-10	-10	-10
Emergency Savings	-10	-10	-10	-10	-10	-10	-5	-10
Car Ins@ $1000 per yr		-84				-84		
Balance in bank	3776	4128	2891	3243	3595	3947	2710	3067
Paycheck (After approx taxes)	497	497	497	497	497	497	497	497
Balance forward	4128	2891	3243	3595	3947	2710	3067	3419

Chapter 9	21-Jun-19	28-Jun-19	5-Jul-19	12-Jul-19	19-Jul-19	26-Jul-19	2-Aug-19	9-Aug-19
Rent/Mortgage		-600					-600	
Groceries	-100	-100	-100	-100	-100	-100	-100	-100
Cell		-60					-60	
Internet/Entertainment		-60					-60	
Heat (Average)		-45					-45	
Electric (Average)		-55					-55	
Water (Average)		-50					-50	
Child Care/Elder Care		-550					-550	
Health insurance		-85					-85	
Auto/transportation	-25	-25	-25	-25	-25	-25	-25	-25
Gifts/ fun	-10	-10	-30	-10	-10	-10	-10	-10
Emergency Savings	-10	-10	-10	-10	-10	-10	-10	-10
Car Ins@ $1000 per yr		-84					-84	
Balance in bank	3419	3771	2534	2866	3218	3570	3922	2685
Paycheck (After approx taxes)	497	497	497	497	497	497	497	497
Balance forward	3771	2534	2866	3218	3570	3922	2685	3037

Chapter 9	16-Aug-19	23-Aug-19	30-Aug-19	6-Sep-19	13-Sep-19	20-Sep-19	27-Sep-19	4-Oct-19
Rent/Mortgage			-600					-600
Groceries	-100	-100	-100	-100	-100	-100	-100	-100
Cell			-60					-60
Internet/Entertainment			-60					-60
Heat (Average)			-45					-45
Electric (Average)			-55					-55
Water (Average)			-50					-50
Child Care/Elder Care			-550					-550
Health insurance			-85					-85
Auto/transportation	-25	-25	-25	-25	-25	-25	-25	-25
Gifts/ fun	-10	-10	-10	-10	-10	-10	-10	-10
Emergency Savings	-10	-10	-10	-10	-10	-10	-10	-5
Car Ins@ $1000 per yr			-84					-84
Balance in bank	3037	3389	3741	2504	2856	3208	3560	3912
Paycheck (After approx taxes)	497	497	497	497	497	497	497	497
Balance forward	3389	3741	2504	2856	3208	3560	3912	2680

Chapter 9	11-Oct-19	18-Oct-19	25-Oct-19	1-Nov-19	8-Nov-19	15-Nov-19	22-Nov-19	29-Nov-19
Rent/Mortgage				-600				-600
Groceries	-100	-100	-100	-100	-100	-100	-100	-100
Cell				-60				-60
Internet/Entertainment				-60				-60
Heat (Average)				-45				-45
Electric (Average)				-55				-55
Water (Average)				-50				-50
Child Care/Elder Care				-550				-550
Health insurance				-85				-85
Auto/transportation	-25	-25	-25	-25	-25	-25	-25	-25
Gifts/ fun	-10	-10	-35	-10	-10	-10	-10	-25
Emergency Savings	-10	-10	-10	-5	-10	-10	-10	-5
Car Ins@ $1000 per yr				-84				-84
Balance in bank	2680	3032	3384	3711	2479	2831	3183	3535
Paycheck (After approx taxes)	497	497	497	497	497	497	497	497
Balance forward	3032	3384	3711	2479	2831	3183	3535	2288

Chapter 9	6-Dec-19	13-Dec-19	20-Dec-19	27-Dec-19	3-Jan-20	10-Jan-20	17-Jan-20	24-Jan-20
Rent/Mortgage					-600			
Groceries	-100	-100	-100	-100	-100	-100	-100	-100
Cell					-60			
Internet/Entertainment					-60			
Heat (Average)					-45			
Electric (Average)					-55			
Water (Average)					-50			
Child Care/Elder Care					-550			
Health insurance					-85			
Auto/transportation	-25	-25	-25	-25	-25	-25	-25	-25
Gifts/ fun	-10	-90	-90	-10	-10	-10	-10	-10
Emergency Savings	-10	-10	-10	-10	-5	-10	-10	-10
Car Ins@ $1000 per yr					-84			
Balance in bank	2288	2640	2912	3184	3536	2304	2656	3008
Paycheck (After approx taxes)	497	497	497	497	497	497	497	497
Balance forward	2640	2912	3184	3536	2304	2656	3008	3360

Chapter 9	31-Jan-20	7-Feb-20	14-Feb-20	21-Feb-20	28-Feb-20	6-Mar-20	13-Mar-20	20-Mar-20
Rent/Mortgage	-600				-600			
Groceries	-100	-100	-100	-100	-100	-100	-100	-100
Cell	-60				-60			
Internet/Entertainment	-60				-60			
Heat (Average)	-45				-45			
Electric (Average)	-55				-55			
Water (Average)	-50				-50			
Child Care/Elder Care	-550				-550			
Health insurance	-85				-85			
Auto/transportation	-25	-25	-25	-25	-25	-25	-25	-25
Gifts/ fun	-10	-10	-10	-10	-10	-10	-10	-10
Emergency Savings	-5	-10	-10	-10	-5	-10	-10	-10
Car Ins@ $1000 per yr	-84				-84			
Balance in bank	3360	2128	2480	2832	3184	1952	2304	2656
Paycheck (After approx taxes)	497	497	497	497	497	497	497	497
Balance forward	2128	2480	2832	3184	1952	2304	2656	3008

Chapter 9	27-Mar-20	3-Apr-20	10-Apr-20	17-Apr-20	24-Apr-20	1-May-20	8-May-20	15-May-20
Rent/Mortgage	-600					-600		
Groceries	-100	-100	-100	-100	-100	-100	-100	-100
Cell	-60					-60		
Internet/Entertainment	-60					-60		
Heat (Average)	-45					-45		
Electric (Average)	-55					-55		
Water (Average)	-50					-50		
Child Care/Elder Care	-550					-550		
Health insurance	-85					-85		
Auto/transportation	-25	-25	-25	-25	-25	-25	-25	-25
Gifts/ fun	-25	-10	-10	-10	-10	-10	-10	-10
Emergency Savings	-5	-10	-10	-10	-10	-5	-25	-25
Car Ins@ $1000 per yr	-84					-84		
Balance in bank	3008	1761	2113	2465	2817	3169	1937	2274
Paycheck (After approx taxes)	497	497	497	497	497	497	497	497
Balance forward	1761	2113	2465	2817	3169	1937	2274	2611

Chapter 9	22-May-20	29-May-20	5-Jun-20	12-Jun-20	19-Jun-20	26-Jun-20	3-Jul-20	10-Jul-20
Rent/Mortgage			-600				-600	
Groceries	-100	-100	-100	-100	-100	-100	-100	-100
Cell			-60				-60	
Internet/Entertainment			-60				-60	
Heat (Average)			-45				-45	
Electric (Average)			-55				-55	
Water (Average)			-50				-50	
Child Care/Elder Care			-550				-550	
Health insurance			-85				-85	
Auto/transportation	-25	-25	-25	-25	-25	-25	-25	-25
Gifts/ fun	-10	-10	-10	-10	-10	-10	-50	-10
Emergency Savings	-25	-25	-25	-25	-25	-25	-25	-25
Car Ins@ $1000 per yr			-84				-84	
Balance in bank	2611	2948	3285	2033	2370	2707	3044	1752
Paycheck (After approx taxes)	497	497	497	497	497	497	497	497
Balance forward	2948	3285	2033	2370	2707	3044	1752	2089

Chapter 9	17-Jul-20	24-Jul-20	31-Jul-20	7-Aug-20	14-Aug-20	21-Aug-20	28-Aug-20	4-Sep-20
Rent/Mortgage				-600				-600
Groceries	-100	-100	-100	-100	-100	-100	-100	-100
Cell				-60				-60
Internet/Entertainment				-60				-60
Heat (Average)				-45				-45
Electric (Average)				-55				-55
Water (Average)				-50				-50
Child Care/Elder Care				-550				-550
Health insurance				-85				-85
Auto/transportation	-25	-25	-25	-25	-25	-25	-25	-25
Gifts/ fun	-10	-10	-10	-10	-10	-10	-10	-10
Emergency Savings	-25	-25	-25	-25	-25	-25	-25	-25
Car Ins@ $1000 per yr			84	-84				-84
Balance in bank	2089	2426	2763	3184	1932	2269	2606	2943
Paycheck (After approx taxes)	497	497	497	497	497	497	497	497
Balance forward	2426	2763	3184	1932	2269	2606	2943	1691

Chapter 9	11-Sep-20	18-Sep-20	25-Sep-20	2-Oct-20	9-Oct-20	16-Oct-20	23-Oct-20	30-Oct-20
Rent/Mortgage				-600				
Groceries	-100	-100	-100	-100	-100	-100	-100	-100
Cell				-60				
Internet/Entertainment				-60				
Heat (Average)				-45				
Electric (Average)				-55				
Water (Average)				-50				
Child Care/Elder Care				-550				
Health insurance				-85				
Auto/transportation	-25	-25	-25	-25	-25	-25	-25	-25
Gifts/ fun	-10	-10	-10	-10	-10	-10	-10	-35
Emergency Savings	-25	-25	-25	-25	-25	-25	-25	-25
Car Ins@ $1000 per yr				-84				
Balance in bank	1691	2028	2365	2702	1450	1787	2124	2461
Paycheck (After approx taxes)	497	497	497	497	497	497	497	497
Balance forward	2028	2365	2702	1450	1787	2124	2461	2773

Chapter 9	6-Nov-20	13-Nov-20	20-Nov-20	27-Nov-20	4-Dec-20	11-Dec-20	18-Dec-20	25-Dec-20
Rent/Mortgage	-600				-600			
Groceries	-100	-100	-100	-100	-100	-100	-100	-100
Cell	-60				-60			
Internet/Entertainment	-60				-60			
Heat (Average)	-45				-45			
Electric (Average)	-55				-55			
Water (Average)	-50				-50			
Child Care/Elder Care	-550				-550			
Health insurance	-85				-85			
Auto/transportation	-25	-25	-25	-25	-25	-25	-25	-25
Gifts/ fun	-25	-10	-10	-10	-25	-85	-150	-30
Emergency Savings	-25	-25	-25	-25	-25	-25	-25	-25
Car Ins@ $1000 per yr	-84				-84			
Balance in bank	2773	1506	1843	2180	2517	1250	1512	1709
Paycheck (After approx taxes)	497	497	497	497	497	497	497	497
Balance forward	1506	1843	2180	2517	1250	1512	1709	2026

Chapter 9	1-Jan-21	8-Jan-21						
Rent/Mortgage	-600							
Groceries	-100	-100						
Cell	-60							
Internet/Entertainment	-60							
Heat (Average)	-45							
Electric (Average)	-55							
Water (Average)	-50							
Child Care/Elder Care	-550							
Health insurance	-85							
Auto/transportation	-25	-25						
Gifts/ fun	-25	-10						
Emergency Savings	-25	-25						
Car Ins@ $1000 per yr	-84							
Balance in bank	2026	759						
Paycheck (After approx taxes)	497	497						
Balance forward	759	1096						

CHAPTER TEN

You Own Your Home and You have Debt

You've just moved into the Home you were saving for in Chapters 4 & 7. You own a car. You have $20,000.00 in credit card debt at 8% interest. You have a $20.00 per hour job. Your goal is to pay off the debt in less than 4 years (208 weeks).

◆ Mortgage : Your $1,164.00 per month mortgage is 30 years @3.7% and includes the property tax and insurance.

◆ Groceries: This may not look like a lot, but if you create menus, cook and home and plan your food budget properly you can save yourself a lot of heartache and money. Not to mention eating healthier! Suggested menus and grocery lists are included at the end of the book!

◆ Cell: You can choose from many good phone plans and a lot of them have discounts.

◆ Internet/Entertainment: You may have an on line subscription or something similar, like Hulu or Xbox gold.

◆ Heat, Water, Electric: These are an average of average monthly utility expenses. Depending on where you are and what types of appliances you run, these expenses can and will vary.

◆ Pay off Debt: This exact amount should be paid on your loan every week. Even though they bill you monthly, if you go ahead and pay them weekly, you will pay off the loan faster because you will be reducing the interest faster. If they have an on-line portal, you can pay there. Otherwise get the correct mailing address and a bunch of stamps and envelopes and go to town. **Remember: weekly payments reduce debt faster by helping to reduce interest charges.** In 160 weeks you will have paid off the debt.

◆ Health Insurance: You may have a personal policy that you pay monthly. Your employer may withhold this amount from your check in weekly increments. If you do not have insurance you may want to put this amount into a health savings account (HSA).

◆ Transportation: If you work you will have transportation expenses of some type.

◆ Gifts/Fun: It is going to happen so you need to put it in your budget. You do not have to spend that much, but do not spend more.

◆ Emergency Savings: Put this amount aside every week in case of a Real emergency. Medical or a death in the family qualify. In 40 years, if not used, this can be added to your retirement account.

◆ Balance in Bank: That is what you should have in your bank account at the end of all transactions in order to stay on your budget. At the beginning of this budget you are starting with $3,600.00 in your bank account.

◆ Paycheck: This is an average, because tax laws vary from state to state and even from city to city. An adjustment has been made to the payroll withholding to account for the mortgage interest deduction that you are now able to take when you file your taxes. If you are on salary, your pay will be the same every week. You can copy the exact figure from your pay stub. If you are an hourly worker, your net pay will change from week to week.

◆ Balance forward: This is what is left after you pay your expenses. This money cannot be spent – it is carried forward to the next period. This is how you keep control of your finances.

Chapter 10	4-Jan-19	11-Jan-19	18-Jan-19	25-Jan-19	1-Feb-19	8-Feb-19	15-Feb-19	22-Feb-19
Rent/Mortgage	-1165				-1165			
Groceries	-75	-75	-75	-75	-75	-75	-75	-75
Cell	-55				-55			
Internet/Entertainment	-50				-50			
Heat (average)	-80				-80			
Electric (average)	-80				-80			
Water (average)	-65				-65			
Paying $20k @ 8%	-125	-125	-125	-125	-125	-125	-125	-125
Health insurance	-85				-85			
Auto/transportation	-30	-30	-30	-30	-30	-30	-30	-30
Household/Gifts/ fun/pets	-5	-5	-5	-5	-5	-5	-5	-5
Emergency Savings	-5	-5	-5	-5	-5	-5	-5	-5
Car Ins.@$1000 per year.	-84				-84			
Balance in bank	3,600	2322	2708	3094	3480	2202	2588	2974
Paycheck (After approx taxes)	626	626	626	626	626	626	626	626
Balance forward	2322	2708	3094	3480	2202	2588	2974	3360

Figure One

Notes:

Chapter 10	1-Mar-19	8-Mar-19	15-Mar-19	22-Mar-19	29-Mar-19	5-Apr-19	12-Apr-19	19-Apr-19
Rent/Mortgage	-1165				-1165			
Groceries	-75	-75	-75	-75	-75	-75	-75	-75
Cell	-55				-55			
Internet/Entertainment	-50				-50			
Heat (average)	-80				-80			
Electric (average)	-80				-80			
Water (average)	-65				-65			
Paying $20k @ 8%	-125	-125	-125	-125	-125	-125	-125	-125
Health insurance	-85				-85			
Auto/transportation	-30	-30	-30	-30	-30	-30	-30	-30
Household/Gifts/ fun/pets	-5	-5	-5	-5	-5	-5	-5	-5
Emergency Savings	-5	-5	-5	-5	-5	-5	-5	-5
Car Ins.@$1000 per year.	-84				-84			
Balance in bank	3360	2082	2468	2854	3240	1962	2348	2734
Paycheck (After approx taxes)	626	626	626	626	626	626	626	626
Balance forward	2082	2468	2854	3240	1962	2348	2734	3120

Figure Two

Notes:

Chapter 10	26-Apr-19	3-May-19	10-May-19	17-May-19	24-May-19	31-May-19	7-Jun-19	14-Jun-19
Rent/Mortgage		-1165				-1165		
Groceries	-75	-75	-75	-75	-75	-75	-75	-75
Cell		-55				-55		
Internet/Entertainment		-50				-50		
Heat (average)		-80				-80		
Electric (average)		-80				-80		
Water (average)		-65				-65		
Paying $20k @ 8%	-125	-125	-125	-125	-125	-125	-125	-125
Health insurance		-85				-85		
Auto/transportation	-30	-30	-30	-30	-30	-30	-30	-30
Household/Gifts/ fun/pets	-5	-5	-5	-5	-5	-5	-5	-5
Emergency Savings	-5	-5	-5	-5	-5	-5	-5	-5
Car Ins.@$1000 per year.		-84				-84		
Balance in bank	3120	3506	2228	2614	3000	3386	2108	2494
Paycheck (After approx taxes)	626	626	626	626	626	626	626	626
Balance forward	3506	2228	2614	3000	3386	2108	2494	2880

Figure Three

Notes:

Chapter 10	21-Jun-19	28-Jun-19	5-Jul-19	12-Jul-19	19-Jul-19	26-Jul-19	2-Aug-19	9-Aug-19
Rent/Mortgage		-1165					-1165	
Groceries	-75	-75	-75	-75	-75	-75	-75	-75
Cell		-55					-55	
Internet/Entertainment		-50					-50	
Heat (average)		-80					-80	
Electric (average)		-80					-80	
Water (average)		-65					-65	
Paying $20k @ 8%	-125	-125	-125	-125	-125	-125	-125	-125
Health insurance		-85					-85	
Auto/transportation	-30	-30	-30	-30	-30	-30	-30	-30
Household/Gifts/ fun/pets	-5	-5	-5	-5	-5	-5	-5	-5
Emergency Savings	-5	-5	-5	-5	-5	-5	-5	-5
Car Ins.@$1000 per year.		-84					-84	
Balance in bank	2880	3266	1988	2374	2760	3146	3532	2254
Paycheck (After approx taxes)	626	626	626	626	626	626	626	626
Balance forward	3266	1988	2374	2760	3146	3532	2254	2640

Figure Four

Notes:

Chapter 10	16-Aug-19	23-Aug-19	30-Aug-19	6-Sep-19	13-Sep-19	20-Sep-19	27-Sep-19	4-Oct-19
Rent/Mortgage			-1165					-1165
Groceries	-75	-75	-75	-75	-75	-80	-80	-80
Cell			-55					-55
Internet/Entertainment			-50					-50
Heat (average)			-80					-80
Electric (average)			-80					-80
Water (average)			-65					-65
Paying $20k @ 8%	-125	-125	-125	-125	-125	-125	-125	-125
Health insurance			-85					-85
Auto/transportation	-30	-30	-30	-30	-30	-30	-30	-30
Household/Gifts/ fun/pets	-5	-5	-5	-5	-5	-5	-5	-5
Emergency Savings	-5	-5	-5	-5	-5	-5	-5	-5
Car Ins.@$1000 per year.			-84					-84
Balance in bank	2640	3026	3412	2134	2520	2906	3287	3668
Paycheck (After approx taxes)	626	626	626	626	626	626	626	626
Balance forward	3026	3412	2134	2520	2906	3287	3668	2385

Figure Five

Notes:

Chapter 10	11-Oct-19	18-Oct-19	25-Oct-19	1-Nov-19	8-Nov-19	15-Nov-19	22-Nov-19	29-Nov-19
Rent/Mortgage				-1165				-1165
Groceries	-80	-80	-80	-80	-80	-80	-80	-80
Cell				-55				-55
Internet/Entertainment				-50				-50
Heat (average)				-80				-80
Electric (average)				-80				-80
Water (average)				-65				-65
Paying $20k @ 8%	-125	-125	-125	-125	-125	-125	-125	-125
Health insurance				-85				-85
Auto/transportation	-30	-30	-30	-30	-30	-30	-30	-30
Household/Gifts/ fun/pets	-5	-5	-25	-10	-10	-10	-25	-10
Emergency Savings	-5	-5	-5	-5	-5	-5	-5	-5
Car Ins.@$1000 per year.				-84				-84
Balance in bank	2385	2766	3147	3508	2220	2596	2972	3333
Paycheck (After approx taxes)	626	626	626	626	626	626	626	626
Balance forward	2766	3147	3508	2220	2596	2972	3333	2045

Figure Six

Notes:

Chapter 10	6-Dec-19	13-Dec-19	20-Dec-19	27-Dec-19	3-Jan-20	10-Jan-20	17-Jan-20	24-Jan-20
Rent/Mortgage					-1165			
Groceries	-80	-80	-80	-80	-80	-80	-80	-80
Cell					-55			
Internet/Entertainment					-50			
Heat (average)					-80			
Electric (average)					-80			
Water (average)					-65			
Paying $20k @ 8%	-125	-125	-125	-125	-125	-125	-125	-125
Health insurance					-85			
Auto/transportation	-30	-30	-30	-30	-30	-30	-30	-30
Household/Gifts/ fun/pets	-10	-100	-10	-10	-10	-10	-10	-10
Emergency Savings	-5	-5	-5	-5	-5	-5	-5	-5
Car Ins.@$1000 per year.					-84			
Balance in bank	2045	2421	2707	3083	3459	2171	2547	2923
Paycheck (After approx taxes)	626	626	626	626	626	626	626	626
Balance forward	2421	2707	3083	3459	2171	2547	2923	3299

Figure Seven

Notes:

Chapter 10	31-Jan-20	7-Feb-20	14-Feb-20	21-Feb-20	28-Feb-20	6-Mar-20	13-Mar-20	20-Mar-20
Rent/Mortgage	-1165				-1165			
Groceries	-80	-80	-80	-80	-80	-80	-80	-80
Cell	-55				-55			
Internet/Entertainment	-50				-50			
Heat (average)	-80				-80			
Electric (average)	-80				-80			
Water (average)	-65				-65			
Paying $20k @ 8%	-125	-125	-125	-125	-125	-125	-125	-125
Health insurance	-85				-85			
Auto/transportation	-30	-30	-30	-30	-30	-30	-30	-30
Household/Gifts/ fun/pets	-10	-10	-10	-10	-10	-10	-10	-10
Emergency Savings	-5	-5	-5	-5	-5	-5	-5	-5
Car Ins.@$1000 per yea	-84				-84			
Balance in bank	3299	2011	2387	2763	3139	1851	2227	2603
Paycheck (After approx taxes)	626	626	626	626	626	626	626	626
Balance forward	2011	2387	2763	3139	1851	2227	2603	2979

Figure Eight

Notes:

Chapter 10	27-Mar-20	3-Apr-20	10-Apr-20	17-Apr-20	24-Apr-20	1-May-20	8-May-20	15-May-20
Rent/Mortgage	-1165					-1165		
Groceries	-80	-80	-80	-80	-80	-80	-80	-80
Cell	-55					-55		
Internet/Entertainment	-50					-50		
Heat (average)	-80					-80		
Electric (average)	-80					-80		
Water (average)	-65					-65		
Paying $20k @ 8%	-125	-125	-125	-125	-125	-125	-125	-125
Health insurance	-85					-85		
Auto/transportation	-30	-30	-30	-30	-30	-30	-30	-30
Household/Gifts/ fun/pets	-10	-10	-10	-10	-10	-10	-10	-10
Emergency Savings	-5	-5	-5	-10	-10	-10	-10	-10
Car Ins.@$1000 per year.	-84					-84		
Balance in bank	2979	1691	2067	2443	2814	3185	1892	2263
Paycheck (After approx taxes)	626	626	626	626	626	626	626	626
Balance forward	1691	2067	2443	2814	3185	1892	2263	2634

Figure Nine

Notes:

Chapter 10	22-May-20	29-May-20	5-Jun-20	12-Jun-20	19-Jun-20	26-Jun-20	3-Jul-20	10-Jul-20
Rent/Mortgage		-1165					-1165	
Groceries	-80	-80	-80	-80	-80	-80	-80	-80
Cell		-55					-55	
Internet/Entertainment		-50					-50	
Heat (average)		-80					-80	
Electric (average)		-80					-80	
Water (average)		-65					-65	
Paying $20k @ 8%	-125	-125	-125	-125	-125	-125	-125	-125
Health insurance		-85					-85	
Auto/transportation	-30	-30	-30	-30	-30	-30	-30	-30
Household/Gifts/ fun/pets	-10	-10	-10	-10	-10	-10	-10	-10
Emergency Savings	-10	-10	-10	-10	-10	-10	-10	-10
Car Ins.@$1000 per year.		-84					-84	
Balance in bank	2634	3005	1712	2083	2454	2825	3196	1903
Paycheck (After approx taxes)	626	626	626	626	626	626	626	626
Balance forward	3005	1712	2083	2454	2825	3196	1903	2274

Figure Ten

Notes:

Chapter 10	17-Jul-20	24-Jul-20	31-Jul-20	7-Aug-20	14-Aug-20	21-Aug-20	28-Aug-20	4-Sep-20
Rent/Mortgage			-1165					-1165
Groceries	-80	-80	-80	-80	-80	-80	-80	-80
Cell			-55					-55
Internet/Entertainment			-50					-50
Heat (average)			-80					-80
Electric (average)			-80					-80
Water (average)			-65					-65
Paying $20k @ 8%	-125	-125	-125	-125	-125	-125	-125	-125
Health insurance			-85					-85
Auto/transportation	-30	-30	-30	-30	-30	-30	-30	-30
Household/Gifts/ fun/pets	-10	-10	-10	-10	-10	-10	-10	-10
Emergency Savings	-10	-10	-10	-10	-10	-10	-10	-10
Car Ins.@$1000 per year.			-84					-84
Balance in bank	2274	2645	3016	1723	2094	2465	2836	3207
Paycheck (After approx taxes)	626	626	626	626	626	626	626	626
Balance forward	2645	3016	1723	2094	2465	2836	3207	1914

Figure Eleven

Notes:

Chapter 10	11-Sep-20	18-Sep-20	25-Sep-20	2-Oct-20	9-Oct-20	16-Oct-20	23-Oct-20	30-Oct-20
Rent/Mortgage				-1165				
Groceries	-80	-80	-80	-80	-80	-80	-80	-80
Cell				-55				
Internet/Entertainment				-50				
Heat (average)				-80				
Electric (average)				-80				
Water (average)				-65				
Paying $20k @ 8%	-125	-125	-125	-125	-125	-125	-125	-125
Health insurance				-85				
Auto/transportation	-30	-30	-30	-30	-30	-30	-30	-30
Household/Gifts/ fun/pets	-10	-10	-10	-10	-10	-10	-10	-25
Emergency Savings	-10	-10	-10	-10	-10	-10	-10	-10
Car Ins.@$1000 per year.				-84				
Balance in bank	1914	2285	2656	3027	1734	2105	2476	2847
Paycheck (After approx taxes)	626	626	626	626	626	626	626	626
Balance forward	2285	2656	3027	1734	2105	2476	2847	3203

Figure Twelve

Notes:

Chapter 10	6-Nov-20	13-Nov-20	20-Nov-20	27-Nov-20	4-Dec-20	11-Dec-20	18-Dec-20	25-Dec-20
Rent/Mortgage	-1165				-1165			
Groceries	-80	-80	-80	-80	-80	-80	-80	-80
Cell	-55				-55			
Internet/Entertainment	-50				-50			
Heat (average)	-80				-80			
Electric (average)	-80				-80			
Water (average)	-65				-65			
Paying $20k @ 8%	-125	-125	-125	-125	-125	-125	-125	-125
Health insurance	-85				-85			
Auto/transportation	-30	-30	-30	-30	-30	-30	-30	-30
Household/Gifts/ fun/pets	-15	-15	-25	-15	-15	-100	-50	-30
Emergency Savings	-10	-10	-10	-10	-10	-10	-10	-10
Car Ins.@$1000 per year.	-84				-84			
Balance in bank	3203	1905	2271	2627	2993	1695	1976	2307
Paycheck (After approx taxes)	626	626	626	626	626	626	626	626
Balance forward	1905	2271	2627	2993	1695	1976	2307	2658

Figure Thirteen

Notes:

Chapter 10	1-Jan-21	8-Jan-21	15-Jan-21	22-Jan-21	29-Jan-21	5-Feb-21	12-Feb-21	19-Feb-21
Rent/Mortgage	-1165					-1165		
Groceries	-80	-80	-80	-80	-80	-80	-80	-80
Cell	-55					-55		
Internet/Entertainment	-50					-50		
Heat (average)	-80					-80		
Electric (average)	-80					-80		
Water (average)	-65					-65		
Paying $20k @ 8%	-125	-125	-125	-125	-125	-125	-125	-125
Health insurance	-85					-85		
Auto/transportation	-30	-30	-30	-30	-30	-30	-30	-30
Household/Gifts/ fun/pets	-15	-15	-15	-15	-15	-15	-15	-15
Emergency Savings	-10	-10	-10	-10	-10	-10	-10	-10
Car Ins.@$1000 per year.	-84					-84		
Balance in bank	2658	1360	1726	2092	2458	2824	1526	1892
Paycheck (After approx taxes)	626	626	626	626	626	626	626	626
Balance forward	1360	1726	2092	2458	2824	1526	1892	2258

Figure Fourteen

Notes:

Chapter 10	26-Feb-21	5-Mar-21	12-Mar-21	19-Mar-21	26-Mar-21	2-Apr-21	9-Apr-21	16-Apr-21
Rent/Mortgage		-1165				-1165		
Groceries	-80	-80	-80	-80	-80	-80	-80	-80
Cell		-55				-55		
Internet/Entertainment		-50				-50		
Heat (average)		-80				-80		
Electric (average)		-80				-80		
Water (average)		-65				-65		
Paying $20k @ 8%	-125	-125	-125	-125	-125	-125	-125	-125
Health insurance		-85				-85		
Auto/transportation	-30	-30	-30	-30	-30	-30	-30	-30
Household/Gifts/ fun/pets	-15	-15	-15	-15	-15	-15	-15	-15
Emergency Savings	-10	-10	-10	-10	-10	-10	-10	-10
Car Ins.@$1000 per year.		-84				-84		
Balance in bank	2258	2624	1326	1692	2058	2424	1126	1492
Paycheck (After approx taxes)	626	626	626	626	626	626	626	626
Balance forward	2624	1326	1692	2058	2424	1126	1492	1858

Figure Fifteen

Notes:

Chapter 10	23-Apr-21	30-Apr-21	7-May-21	14-May-21	21-May-21	28-May-21	4-Jun-21	11-Jun-21
Rent/Mortgage		-1165					-1165	
Groceries	-80	-80	-80	-80	-80	-80	-80	-80
Cell		-55					-55	
Internet/Entertainment		-50					-50	
Heat (average)		-80					-80	
Electric (average)		-80					-80	
Water (average)		-65					-65	
Paying $20k @ 8%	-125	-125	-125	-125	-125	-125	-125	-125
Health insurance		-85					-85	
Auto/transportation	-30	-30	-30	-30	-30	-30	-30	-30
Household/Gifts/ fun/pets	-15	-15	-15	-15	-15	-15	-15	-15
Emergency Savings	-10	-10	-10	-10	-10	-10	-10	-10
Car Ins.@$1000 per year.		-84					-84	
Balance in bank	1858	2224	926	1292	1658	2024	2390	1092
Paycheck (After approx taxes)	626	626	626	626	626	626	626	626
Balance forward	2224	926	1292	1658	2024	2390	1092	1458

Figure Sixteen

Notes:

Chapter 10	18-Jun-21	25-Jun-21	2-Jul-21	9-Jul-21	16-Jul-21	23-Jul-21	30-Jul-21	6-Aug-21
Rent/Mortgage			-1165				-1165	
Groceries	-80	-80	-80	-80	-80	-80	-80	-80
Cell			-55				-55	
Internet/Entertainment			-50				-50	
Heat (average)			-80				-80	
Electric (average)			-80				-80	
Water (average)			-65				-65	
Paying $20k @ 8%	-125	-125	-125	-125	-125	-125	-125	-125
Health insurance			-85				-85	
Auto/transportation	-30	-30	-30	-30	-30	-30	-30	-30
Household/Gifts/ fun/pets	-15	-15	-15	-15	-15	-15	-15	-15
Emergency Savings	-10	-10	-10	-10	-10	-10	-10	-10
Car Ins.@$1000 per year.			-84				-84	
Balance in bank	1458	1824	2190	892	1258	1624	1990	692
Paycheck (After approx taxes)	626	626	626	626	626	626	626	626
Balance forward	1824	2190	892	1258	1624	1990	692	1058

Figure Seventeen

Notes:

Chapter 10	13-Aug-21	20-Aug-21	27-Aug-21	3-Sep-21	10-Sep-21	17-Sep-21	24-Sep-21	1-Oct-21
Rent/Mortgage				-1165				-1165
Groceries	-80	-80	-80	-80	-80	-80	-80	-80
Cell				-55				-55
Internet/Entertainment				-50				-50
Heat (average)				-80				-80
Electric (average)				-80				-80
Water (average)				-65				-65
Paying $20k @ 8%	-125	-125	-125	-125	-125	-125	-125	-125
Health insurance				-85				-85
Auto/transportation	-30	-30	-30	-30	-30	-30	-30	-30
Household/Gifts/ fun/pets	-15	-15	-15	-15	-15	-15	-15	-15
Emergency Savings	-10	-10	-10	-10	-10	-10	-10	-10
Car Ins.@$1000 per year.				-84				-84
Balance in bank	1058	1424	1790	2156	858	1224	1590	1956
Paycheck (After approx taxes)	626	626	626	626	626	626	626	626
Balance forward	1424	1790	2156	858	1224	1590	1956	658

Figure Eighteen

Notes:

Chapter 10	8-Oct-21	15-Oct-21	22-Oct-21	29-Oct-21	5-Nov-21	12-Nov-21	19-Nov-21	26-Nov-21
Rent/Mortgage				-1165				
Groceries	-80	-80	-80	-80	-80	-80	-80	-80
Cell				-55				
Internet/Entertainment				-50				
Heat (average)				-80				
Electric (average)				-80				
Water (average)				-65				
Paying $20k @ 8%	-125	-125	-125	-125	-125	-125	-125	-125
Health insurance				-85				
Auto/transportation	-30	-30	-30	-30	-30	-30	-30	-30
Household/Gifts/ fun/pets	-15	-15	-25	-15	-15	-15	-25	-25
Emergency Savings	-10	-10	-10	-10	-10	-10	-10	-10
Car Ins.@$1000 per year.				-84				
Balance in bank	658	1024	1390	1746	448	814	1180	1536
Paycheck (After approx taxes)	626	626	626	626	626	626	626	626
Balance forward	1024	1390	1746	448	814	1180	1536	1892

Figure Nineteen

Notes:

Chapter 10	3-Dec-21	10-Dec-21	17-Dec-21	24-Dec-21	31-Dec-21	7-Jan-22	14-Jan-22	21-Jan-22
Rent/Mortgage	-1165				-1165			
Groceries	-80	-80	-80	-80	-80	-80	-80	-80
Cell	-55				-55			
Internet/Entertainment	-50				-50			
Heat (average)	-80				-80			
Electric (average)	-80				-80			
Water (average)	-65				-65			
Paying $20k @ 8%	-125	-125	-125	-125	-125	-125	-125	-125
Health insurance	-85				-85			
Auto/transportation	-30	-30	-30	-30	-30	-30	-30	-30
Household/Gifts/ fun/pets	-25	-100	-100	-50	-25	-25	-30	-30
Emergency Savings	-10	-10	-10	-10	-10	-10	-10	-10
Car Ins.@$1000 per year.	-84				-84			
Balance in bank	1892	584	865	1146	1477	169	525	876
Paycheck (After approx taxes)	626	626	626	626	626	626	626	626
Balance forward	584	865	1146	1477	169	525	876	1227

Figure Twenty

Notes:

Chapter 10	28-Jan-22	4-Feb-22	11-Feb-22	18-Feb-22	25-Feb-22	4-Mar-22	11-Mar-22	18-Mar-22
Rent/Mortgage		-1165				-1165		
Groceries	-80	-80	-80	-80	-80	-80	-80	-80
Cell		-55				-55		
Internet/Entertainment		-50				-50		
Heat (average)		-80				-80		
Electric (average)		-80				-80		
Water (average)		-65				-65		
Paying $20k @ 8%	-125	-125	-125	-125	-125	-125	-125	-125
Health insurance		-85				-85		
Auto/transportation	-30	-30	-30	-30	-30	-30	-30	-30
Household/Gifts/ fun/pets	-20	-10	-20	-10	-20	-10	-20	-20
Emergency Savings	-10	-10	-10	-10	-10	-10	-10	-10
Car Ins.@$1000 per year.		-84				-84		
Balance in bank	1227	1588	295	656	1027	1388	95	456
Paycheck (After approx taxes)	626	626	626	626	626	626	626	626
Balance forward	1588	295	656	1027	1388	95	456	817

Figure Twenty One

Notes:

Chapter 10	25-Mar-22	1-Apr-22	8-Apr-22	15-Apr-22	22-Apr-22			
Rent/Mortgage		-1165						
Groceries	-80	-80	-80	-80	-80			
Cell		-55						
Internet/Entertainment		-50						
Heat (average)		-80						
Electric (average)		-80						
Water (average)		-65						
Paying $20k @ 8%	-125	0	0	0	0			
Health insurance		-85						
Auto/transportation	-30	-30	-30	-30	-30			
Household/Gifts/ fun/pets	-10	-10	-30	-30	-30			
Emergency Savings	-10	-10	-10	-10	-10			
Car Ins.@$1000 per year.		-84						
Balance in bank	817	1188	20	496	973			
Paycheck (After approx taxes)	626	626	626	627	628			
Balance forward	1188	20	496	973	1451			

Figure Twenty Two

Notes:

CHAPTER ELEVEN

Renting -You want to Buy a house

You are renting an apartment and you own a car. Your goal is to save $40,000.00 for moving expenses and down payment on a $300,000.00 home. You have a $20.00 per hour job, but to start - you only have $1,200 left in your bank account before you get paid.

♦ Rent : Your rent costs you $1,000.00 per month.

♦ Groceries: This may not look like a lot, but if you create menus, cook and home and plan your food budget properly you can save yourself a lot of heartache and money. Not to mention eating healthier! You will find a grocery and meal planner at the backof this book.

♦ Cell: You can choose from many good phone plans and a lot of them have discounts.

♦ Internet/Entertainment: You may have an on line subscription or something similar, like Hulu or Xbox gold.

♦ Heat, Water, Electric: These are an average of average monthly utility expenses. Depending on where you are and what types of appliances you run, these expenses can and will vary.

♦ Save for Your Home: This exact amount should be put in to a separate bank account every week. This must be a savings account that pays interest. The interest is not likely to be a LOT. It will probably be 1% or less. But as it accumulates in YOUR account it will make certain that you reach your goals faster. In addition to your down payment (which will include closing costs) you need kitchen stuff, a lot of furniture, moving expenses, and some 'fall back' funds in the bank. But, at the end of only 245 weeks, you will have the funds necessary to purchase a home.

♦ Health Insurance: You may have a personal policy that you pay monthly. Your employer may withhold this amount from your check in weekly increments. If you have no insurance - SAVE this amount anyway.

♦ Transportation: Even if you work from home, you will still have transportation expenses from time to time.

♦ Gifts/Fun: It is going to happen so you need to put it in your budget. You do not have to spend that much, but do not spend more.

♦ Emergency Savings: Put this amount aside every week in case of a Real Emergency. Medical or a death in the family qualify.

♦ Balance in Bank: That is what you should have in your bank account at the end of all transactions in order to stay on your budget. At the beginning of this budget you are starting with the $3,600.00 in your bank acount that you have saved.

♦ Paycheck: This is an average, because tax laws vary from state to state and even from city to city. If you are on salary, your pay will be the same every week. You can copy the exact figure from your pay stub. If you are an hourly worker, your net pay will change from week to week. Some companies give annual or even semi-annual pay increases. You will be shown how to change the pay rate figure to match your paycheck in Chapter

♦ Balance forward: This is what is left after you pay your expenses. This money cannot be spent – it is carried forward to the next period. This is why you budget –so you remember to not spend all of your money!

Chapter 11	4-Jan-19	11-Jan-19	18-Jan-19	25-Jan-19	1-Feb-19	8-Feb-19	15-Feb-19	22-Feb-19
Rent/Mortgage	-900				-900			
Groceries	-80	-80	-80	-80	-80	-80	-80	-80
Cell	-55				-55			
Internet/Entertainment	-50				-50			
Heat (averge)	-75				-75			
Electric (average)	-75				-75			
Water (average)	-60				-60			
Saving $40K for house	-150	-150	-150	-150	-150	-150	-150	-150
Health insurance	-100				-100			
Auto/transportation	-30	-30	-30	-30	-30	-30	-30	-30
Gifts/ fun/pets	-5	-5	-5	-5	-5	-5	-5	-5
Emergency Savings	-5	-5	-5	-5	-5	-5	-5	-5
Car Ins.@$1000 per yr.	-84				-84			
Balance in bank	1,200	157	513	869	1225	182	538	894
Paycheck (After approx taxes)	626	626	626	626	626	626	626	626
Balance forward	157	513	869	1225	182	538	894	1250

Figure One
Notes

Chapter 11	1-Mar-19	8-Mar-19	15-Mar-19	22-Mar-19	29-Mar-19	5-Apr-19	12-Apr-19	19-Apr-19
Rent/Mortgage	-900				-900			
Groceries	-80	-80	-80	-80	-80	-80	-80	-80
Cell	-55				-55			
Internet/Entertainment	-50				-50			
Heat (averge)	-75				-75			
Electric (average)	-75				-75			
Water (average)	-60				-60			
Saving $40K for house	-150	-150	-150	-150	-150	-150	-150	-150
Health insurance	-100				-100			
Auto/transportation	-30	-30	-30	-30	-30	-30	-30	-30
Gifts/ fun/pets	-5	-10	-10	-10	-10	-10	-10	-10
Emergency Savings	-5	-10	-10	-10	-10	-10	-10	-10
Car Ins.@$1000 per yr.	-84				-84			
Balance in bank	1250	207	553	899	1245	192	538	884
Paycheck (After approx taxes)	626	626	626	626	626	626	626	626
Balance forward	207	553	899	1245	192	538	884	1230

Figure Two
Notes

Chapter 11	26-Apr-19	3-May-19	10-May-19	17-May-19	24-May-19	31-May-19	7-Jun-19	14-Jun-19
Rent/Mortgage		-900				-900		
Groceries	-80	-80	-80	-80	-80	-80	-80	-80
Cell		-55				-55		
Internet/Entertainment		-50				-50		
Heat (averge)		-75				-75		
Electric (average)		-75				-75		
Water (average)		-60				-60		
Saving $40K for house	-150	-150	-150	-150	-150	-150	-150	-150
Health insurance		-100				-100		
Auto/transportation	-30	-30	-30	-30	-30	-30	-30	-30
Gifts/ fun/pets	-20	-20	-20	-20	-20	-20	-20	-20
Emergency Savings	-10	-10	-10	-10	-10	-10	-10	-10
Car Ins.@$1000 per yr.		-84				-84		
Balance in bank	1230	1566	503	839	1175	1511	448	784
Paycheck (After approx taxes)	626	626	626	626	626	626	626	626
Balance forward	1566	503	839	1175	1511	448	784	1120

Figure Three
Notes

Chapter 11	21-Jun-19	28-Jun-19	5-Jul-19	12-Jul-19	19-Jul-19	26-Jul-19	2-Aug-19	9-Aug-19
Rent/Mortgage		-900					-900	
Groceries	-80	-80	-80	-80	-80	-80	-80	-80
Cell		-55					-55	
Internet/Entertainment		-50					-50	
Heat (averge)		-75					-75	
Electric (average)		-75					-75	
Water (average)		-60					-60	
Saving $40K for house	-150	-150	-150	-150	-150	-150	-150	-150
Health insurance		-100					-100	
Auto/transportation	-30	-30	-30	-30	-30	-30	-30	-30
Gifts/ fun/pets	-20	-20	-20	-20	-20	-20	-20	-20
Emergency Savings	-10	-10	-10	-10	-10	-10	-10	-10
Car Ins.@$1000 per yr.		-84					-84	
Balance in bank	1120	1456	393	729	1065	1401	1737	674
Paycheck (After approx taxes)	626	626	626	626	626	626	626	626
Balance forward	1456	393	729	1065	1401	1737	674	1010

Figure Four
Notes

Chapter 11	16-Aug-19	23-Aug-19	30-Aug-19	6-Sep-19	13-Sep-19	20-Sep-19	27-Sep-19	4-Oct-19
Rent/Mortgage			-900					-900
Groceries	-80	-80	-80	-80	-80	-80	-80	-80
Cell			-55					-55
Internet/Entertainment			-50					-50
Heat (averge)			-75					-75
Electric (average)			-75					-75
Water (average)			-60					-60
Saving $40K for house	-150	-150	-150	-150	-150	-150	-150	-150
Health insurance			-100					-100
Auto/transportation	-30	-30	-30	-30	-30	-30	-30	-30
Gifts/ fun/pets	-20	-20	-20	-20	-20	-20	-20	-20
Emergency Savings	-10	-10	-10	-10	-10	-10	-10	-10
Car Ins.@$1000 per yr.			-84					-84
Balance in bank	1010	1346	1682	619	955	1291	1627	1963
Paycheck (After approx taxes)	626	626	626	626	626	626	626	626
Balance forward	1346	1682	619	955	1291	1627	1963	900
Figure Five								
Notes								
Chapter 11	11-Oct-19	18-Oct-19	25-Oct-19	1-Nov-19	8-Nov-19	15-Nov-19	22-Nov-19	29-Nov-19
Rent/Mortgage				-900				-900
Groceries	-80	-80	-80	-80	-80	-80	-80	-80
Cell				-55				-55
Internet/Entertainment				-50				-50
Heat (averge)				-75				-75
Electric (average)				-75				-75
Water (average)				-60				-60
Saving $40K for house	-150	-150	-150	-150	-150	-150	-150	-150
Health insurance				-100				-100
Auto/transportation	-30	-30	-30	-30	-30	-30	-30	-30
Gifts/ fun/pets	-20	-20	-20	-20	-20	-20	-25	-20
Emergency Savings	-10	-10	-10	-10	-10	-10	-10	-10
Car Ins.@$1000 per yr.				-84				-84
Balance in bank	900	1236	1572	1908	845	1181	1517	1848
Paycheck (After approx taxes)	626	626	626	626	626	626	626	626
Balance forward	1236	1572	1908	845	1181	1517	1848	785
Figure Six								
Notes								

Chapter 11	6-Dec-19	13-Dec-19	20-Dec-19	27-Dec-19	3-Jan-20	10-Jan-20	17-Jan-20	24-Jan-20
Rent/Mortgage					-900			
Groceries	-80	-80	-80	-80	-80	-80	-80	-80
Cell					-55			
Internet/Entertainment					-50			
Heat (averge)					-75			
Electric (average)					-75			
Water (average)					-60			
Saving $40K for house	-150	-150	-150	-150	-150	-150	-150	-150
Health insurance					-100			
Auto/transportation	-30	-30	-30	-30	-30	-30	-30	-30
Gifts/ fun/pets	-30	-50	-100	-20	-20	-20	-20	-20
Emergency Savings	-10	-10	-10	-10	-10	-10	-10	-10
Car Ins.@$1000 per yr.					-84			
Balance in bank	785	1111	1417	1673	2009	946	1282	1618
Paycheck (After approx taxes)	626	626	626	626	626	626	626	626
Balance forward	1111	1417	1673	2009	946	1282	1618	1954

Figure Seven

Notes

Chapter 11	31-Jan-20	7-Feb-20	14-Feb-20	21-Feb-20	28-Feb-20	6-Mar-20	13-Mar-20	20-Mar-20
Rent/Mortgage	-900				-900			
Groceries	-80	-80	-80	-80	-80	-80	-80	-80
Cell	-55				-55			
Internet/Entertainment	-50				-50			
Heat (averge)	-75				-75			
Electric (average)	-75				-75			
Water (average)	-60				-60			
Saving $40K for house	-150	-150	-150	-150	-150	-150	-150	-150
Health insurance	-100				-100			
Auto/transportation	-30	-30	-30	-30	-30	-30	-30	-30
Gifts/ fun/pets	-20	-20	-20	-20	-20	-20	-20	-20
Emergency Savings	-10	-10	-10	-10	-10	-10	-10	-10
Car Ins.@$1000 per yr.	-84				-84			
Balance in bank	1954	891	1227	1563	1899	836	1172	1508
Paycheck (After approx taxes)	626	626	626	626	626	626	626	626
Balance forward	891	1227	1563	1899	836	1172	1508	1844

Figure Eight

Notes

Chapter 11	27-Mar-20	3-Apr-20	10-Apr-20	17-Apr-20	24-Apr-20	1-May-20	8-May-20	15-May-20
Rent/Mortgage	-900					-900		
Groceries	-80	-80	-80	-80	-80	-80	-80	-80
Cell	-55					-55		
Internet/Entertainment	-50					-50		
Heat (averge)	-75					-75		
Electric (average)	-75					-75		
Water (average)	-60					-60		
Saving $40K for house	-150	-150	-150	-150	-150	-150	-150	-150
Health insurance	-100					-100		
Auto/transportation	-30	-30	-30	-30	-30	-30	-30	-30
Gifts/ fun/pets	-20	-20	-20	-20	-20	-20	-20	-20
Emergency Savings	-10	-10	-10	-10	-10	-10	-10	-10
Car Ins.@$1000 per yr.	-84					-84		
Balance in bank	1844	781	1117	1453	1789	2125	1062	1398
Paycheck (After approx taxes)	626	626	626	626	626	626	626	626
Balance forward	781	1117	1453	1789	2125	1062	1398	1734

Figure Nine
Notes

Chapter 11	22-May-20	29-May-20	5-Jun-20	12-Jun-20	19-Jun-20	26-Jun-20	3-Jul-20	10-Jul-20
Rent/Mortgage		-900					-900	
Groceries	-80	-80	-80	-80	-80	-80	-80	-80
Cell		-55					-55	
Internet/Entertainment		-50					-50	
Heat (averge)		-75					-75	
Electric (average)		-75					-75	
Water (average)		-60					-60	
Saving $40K for house	-150	-150	-150	-150	-150	-150	-150	-150
Health insurance		-100					-100	
Auto/transportation	-30	-30	-30	-30	-30	-30	-30	-30
Gifts/ fun/pets	-20	-20	-20	-20	-20	-20	-20	-20
Emergency Savings	-10	-10	-10	-10	-10	-10	-10	-10
Car Ins.@$1000 per yr.		-84					-84	
Balance in bank	1734	2070	1007	1343	1679	2015	2351	1288
Paycheck (After approx taxes)	626	626	626	626	626	626	626	626
Balance forward	2070	1007	1343	1679	2015	2351	1288	1624

Figure Ten
Notes

Chapter 11	17-Jul-20	24-Jul-20	31-Jul-20	7-Aug-20	14-Aug-20	21-Aug-20	28-Aug-20	4-Sep-20
Rent/Mortgage			-900					-900
Groceries	-80	-80	-80	-80	-80	-80	-80	-80
Cell			-55					-55
Internet/Entertainment			-50					-50
Heat (averge)			-75					-75
Electric (average)			-75					-75
Water (average)			-60					-60
Saving $40K for house	-150	-150	-150	-150	-150	-150	-150	-150
Health insurance			-100					-100
Auto/transportation	-30	-30	-30	-30	-30	-30	-30	-30
Gifts/ fun/pets	-20	-20	-20	-20	-20	-20	-20	-20
Emergency Savings	-10	-10	-10	-10	-10	-10	-10	-10
Car Ins.@$1000 per yr.			-84					-84
Balance in bank	1624	1960	2296	1233	1569	1905	2241	2577
Paycheck (After approx taxes)	626	626	626	626	626	626	626	626
Balance forward	1960	2296	1233	1569	1905	2241	2577	1514

Figure Eleven

Notes

Chapter 11	11-Sep-20	18-Sep-20	25-Sep-20	2-Oct-20	9-Oct-20	16-Oct-20	23-Oct-20	30-Oct-20
Rent/Mortgage				-900				
Groceries	-80	-80	-80	-80	-80	-80	-80	-80
Cell				-55				
Internet/Entertainment				-50				
Heat (averge)				-75				
Electric (average)				-75				
Water (average)				-60				
Saving $40K for house	-150	-150	-150	-150	-150	-150	-150	-150
Health insurance				-100				
Auto/transportation	-30	-30	-30	-30	-30	-30	-30	-30
Gifts/ fun/pets	-20	-20	-20	-20	-20	-20	-20	-25
Emergency Savings	-10	-10	-10	-10	-10	-10	-10	-10
Car Ins.@$1000 per yr.				-84				84
Balance in bank	1514	1850	2186	2522	1459	1795	2131	2467
Paycheck (After approx taxes)	626	626	626	626	626	626	626	626
Balance forward	1850	2186	2522	1459	1795	2131	2467	2882

Figure Twelve

Notes

Chapter 11	6-Nov-20	13-Nov-20	20-Nov-20	27-Nov-20	4-Dec-20	11-Dec-20	18-Dec-20	25-Dec-20
Rent/Mortgage	-900				-900			
Groceries	-80	-80	-80	-80	-80	-80	-80	-80
Cell	-55				-55			
Internet/Entertainment	-50				-50			
Heat (averge)	-75				-75			
Electric (average)	-75				-75			
Water (average)	-60				-60			
Saving $40K for house	-150	-150	-150	-150	-150	-150	-150	-150
Health insurance	-100				-100			
Auto/transportation	-30	-30	-30	-30	-30	-30	-30	-30
Gifts/ fun/pets	-20	-20	-25	-20	-30	-75	-125	-30
Emergency Savings	-10	-10	-10	-10	-10	-10	-10	-10
Car Ins.@$1000 per yr.	-84				-84			
Balance in bank	2882	1819	2155	2486	2822	1749	2030	2261
Paycheck (After approx taxes)	626	626	626	626	626	626	626	626
Balance forward	1819	2155	2486	2822	1749	2030	2261	2587

Figure Thirteen
Notes

Chapter 11	1-Jan-21	8-Jan-21	15-Jan-21	22-Jan-21	29-Jan-21	5-Feb-21	12-Feb-21	19-Feb-21
Rent/Mortgage	-900					-900		
Groceries	-80	-80	-80	-80	-80	-80	-80	-80
Cell	-55					-55		
Internet/Entertainment	-50					-50		
Heat (averge)	-75					-75		
Electric (average)	-75					-75		
Water (average)	-60					-60		
Saving $40K for house	-150	-150	-150	-150	-150	-175	-175	-175
Health insurance	-100					-100		
Auto/transportation	-30	-30	-30	-30	-30	-30	-30	-30
Gifts/ fun/pets	-20	-20	-20	-20	-20	-20	-20	-20
Emergency Savings	-10	-10	-10	-10	-10	-10	-10	-10
Car Ins.@$1000 per yr.	-84					-84		
Balance in bank	2587	1524	1860	2196	2532	2868	1780	2091
Paycheck (After approx taxes)	626	626	626	626	626	626	626	626
Balance forward	1524	1860	2196	2532	2868	1780	2091	2402

Figure Fourteen
Notes

Chapter 11	26-Feb-21	5-Mar-21	12-Mar-21	19-Mar-21	26-Mar-21	2-Apr-21	9-Apr-21	16-Apr-21
Rent/Mortgage		-900				-900		
Groceries	-80	-80	-80	-80	-80	-80	-80	-80
Cell		-55				-55		
Internet/Entertainment		-50				-50		
Heat (averge)		-75				-75		
Electric (average)		-75				-75		
Water (average)		-60				-60		
Saving $40K for house	-175	-175	-175	-175	-175	-175	-175	-175
Health insurance		-100				-100		
Auto/transportation	-30	-30	-30	-30	-30	-30	-30	-30
Gifts/ fun/pets	-20	-20	-20	-20	-20	-20	-20	-20
Emergency Savings	-10	-10	-10	-10	-10	-10	-10	-10
Car Ins.@$1000 per yr.		-84				-84		
Balance in bank	2402	2713	1625	1936	2247	2558	1470	1781
Paycheck (After approx taxes)	626	626	626	626	626	626	626	626
Balance forward	2713	1625	1936	2247	2558	1470	1781	2092

Figure Fifteen

Notes

Chapter 11	23-Apr-21	30-Apr-21	7-May-21	14-May-21	21-May-21	28-May-21	4-Jun-21	11-Jun-21
Rent/Mortgage		-900					-900	
Groceries	-80	-80	-80	-80	-80	-80	-80	-80
Cell		-55					-55	
Internet/Entertainment		-50					-50	
Heat (averge)		-75					-75	
Electric (average)		-75					-75	
Water (average)		-60					-60	
Saving $40K for house	-175	-175	-175	-175	-175	-175	-175	-175
Health insurance		-100					-100	
Auto/transportation	-30	-30	-30	-30	-30	-30	-30	-30
Gifts/ fun/pets	-20	-20	-20	-20	-20	-20	-20	-20
Emergency Savings	-10	-20	-20	-20	-20	-20	-20	-20
Car Ins.@$1000 per yr.		-84					-84	
Balance in bank	2092	2403	1305	1606	1907	2208	2509	1411
Paycheck (After approx taxes)	626	626	626	626	626	626	626	626
Balance forward	2403	1305	1606	1907	2208	2509	1411	1712

Figure Sixteen

Notes

Chapter 11	18-Jun-21	25-Jun-21	2-Jul-21	9-Jul-21	16-Jul-21	23-Jul-21	30-Jul-21	6-Aug-21
Rent/Mortgage			-900				-900	
Groceries	-80	-80	-80	-80	-80	-80	-80	-80
Cell			-55				-55	
Internet/Entertainment			-50				-50	
Heat (averge)			-75				-75	
Electric (average)			-75				-75	
Water (average)			-60				-60	
Saving $40K for house	-175	-175	-175	-175	-175	-175	-175	-175
Health insurance			-100				-100	
Auto/transportation	-30	-30	-30	-30	-30	-30	-30	-30
Gifts/ fun/pets	-20	-20	-20	-20	-20	-20	-20	-20
Emergency Savings	-20	-20	-20	-20	-20	-20	-20	-20
Car Ins.@$1000 per yr.			-84				-84	
Balance in bank	1712	2013	2314	1216	1517	1818	2119	1021
Paycheck (After approx taxes)	626	626	626	626	626	626	626	626
Balance forward	2013	2314	1216	1517	1818	2119	1021	1322

Figure Seventeen
Notes

Chapter 11	13-Aug-21	20-Aug-21	27-Aug-21	3-Sep-21	10-Sep-21	17-Sep-21	24-Sep-21	1-Oct-21
Rent/Mortgage				-900				-900
Groceries	-80	-80	-80	-80	-80	-80	-80	-80
Cell				-55				-55
Internet/Entertainment				-50				-50
Heat (averge)				-75				-75
Electric (average)				-75				-75
Water (average)				-60				-60
Saving $40K for house	-175	-175	-175	-175	-175	-175	-175	-175
Health insurance				-100				-100
Auto/transportation	-30	-30	-30	-30	-30	-30	-30	-30
Gifts/ fun/pets	-20	-20	-20	-20	-20	-20	-20	-20
Emergency Savings	-20	-20	-20	-20	-20	-20	-20	-20
Car Ins.@$1000 per yr.				-84				-84
Balance in bank	1322	1623	1924	2225	1127	1428	1729	2030
Paycheck (After approx taxes)	626	626	626	626	626	626	626	626
Balance forward	1623	1924	2225	1127	1428	1729	2030	932

Figure Eighteen
Notes

Chapter 11	8-Oct-21	15-Oct-21	22-Oct-21	29-Oct-21	5-Nov-21	12-Nov-21	19-Nov-21	26-Nov-21
Rent/Mortgage					-900			
Groceries	-80	-80	-80	-80	-80	-80	-80	-80
Cell					-55			
Internet/Entertainment					-50			
Heat (averge)					-75			
Electric (average)					-75			
Water (average)					-60			
Saving $40K for house	-175	-175	-175	-175	-175	-175	-175	-175
Health insurance					-100			
Auto/transportation	-30	-30	-30	-30	-30	-30	-30	-30
Gifts/ fun/pets	-15	-15	-15	-15	-15	-15	-15	-20
Emergency Savings	-15	-15	-15	-15	-15	-15	-15	-20
Car Ins.@$1000 per yr.					-84			
Balance in bank	932	1243	1554	1865	2176	1088	1399	1710
Paycheck (After approx taxes)	626	626	626	626	626	626	626	626
Balance forward	1243	1554	1865	2176	1088	1399	1710	2011

Figure Nineteen

Notes

Chapter 11	3-Dec-21	10-Dec-21	17-Dec-21	24-Dec-21	31-Dec-21	7-Jan-22	14-Jan-22	21-Jan-22
Rent/Mortgage	-900				-900			
Groceries	-80	-80	-80	-80	-80	-80	-80	-80
Cell	-55				-55			
Internet/Entertainment	-50				-50			
Heat (averge)	-75				-75			
Electric (average)	-75				-75			
Water (average)	-60				-60			
Saving $40K for house	-175	-175	-175	-175	-175	-175	-175	-175
Health insurance	-100				-100			
Auto/transportation	-30	-30	-30	-30	-30	-30	-30	-30
Gifts/ fun/pets	-50	-75	-100	-50	-30	-20	-20	-20
Emergency Savings	-15	-15	-15	-15	-15	-15	-15	-15
Car Ins.@$1000 per yr.	-84				-84			
Balance in bank	2011	888	1139	1365	1641	538	844	1150
Paycheck (After approx taxes)	626	626	626	626	626	626	626	626
Balance forward	888	1139	1365	1641	538	844	1150	1456

Figure Twenty

Notes

Chapter 11	28-Jan-22	4-Feb-22	11-Feb-22	18-Feb-22	25-Feb-22	4-Mar-22	11-Mar-22	18-Mar-22
Rent/Mortgage		-900				-900		
Groceries	-80	-80	-80	-80	-80	-80	-80	-80
Cell		-55				-55		
Internet/Entertainment		-50				-50		
Heat (averge)		-75				-75		
Electric (average)		-75				-75		
Water (average)		-60				-60		
Saving $40K for house	-175	-175	-175	-175	-175	-175	-175	-175
Health insurance		-100				-100		
Auto/transportation	-30	-30	-30	-30	-30	-30	-30	-30
Gifts/ fun/pets	-20	-20	-20	-20	-20	-20	-30	-30
Emergency Savings	-20	-20	-20	-20	-20	-20	-20	-20
Car Ins.@$1000 per yr.		-84				-84		
Balance in bank	1456	1757	659	960	1261	1562	464	755
Paycheck (After approx taxes)	626	626	626	626	626	626	626	635
Balance forward	1757	659	960	1261	1562	464	755	1055

Figure Twenty One
Notes

Chapter 11	25-Mar-22	1-Apr-22	8-Apr-22	15-Apr-22	22-Apr-22	29-Apr-22	6-May-22	13-May-22
Rent/Mortgage		-900					-900	
Groceries	-80	-80	-80	-80	-80	-80	-80	-80
Cell		-55					-55	
Internet/Entertainment		-50					-50	
Heat (averge)		-75					-75	
Electric (average)		-75					-75	
Water (average)		-60					-60	
Saving $40K for house	-175	-175	-175	-175	-175	-175	-175	-175
Health insurance		-100					-100	
Auto/transportation	-30	-30	-30	-30	-30	-30	-30	-30
Gifts/ fun/pets	-20	-20	-20	-20	-20	-20	-20	-20
Emergency Savings	-20	-20	-20	-20	-20	-20	-20	-20
Car Ins.@$1000 per yr.		-84					-84	
Balance in bank	1055	1356	283	609	935	1261	1587	514
Paycheck (After approx taxes)	626	651	651	651	651	651	651	651
Balance forward	1356	283	609	935	1261	1587	514	840

Figure Twenty Two | | By this Date:
Notes | | You should receive a pay increase equal to $25.00 per week after taxes

Chapter 11	20-May-22	27-May-22	3-Jun-22	10-Jun-22	17-Jun-22	24-Jun-22	1-Jul-22	8-Jul-22
Rent/Mortgage			-900				-900	
Groceries	-80	-80	-80	-80	-80	-80	-80	-80
Cell			-55				-55	
Internet/Entertainment			-50				-50	
Heat (averge)			-75				-75	
Electric (average)			-75				-75	
Water (average)			-60				-60	
Saving $40K for house	-175	-175	-175	-175	-175	-175	-175	-175
Health insurance			-100				-100	
Auto/transportation	-30	-30	-30	-30	-30	-30	-30	-30
Gifts/ fun/pets	-20	-20	-20	-20	-20	-20	-20	-30
Emergency Savings	-20	-20	-20	-20	-20	-20	-20	-20
Car Ins.@$1000 per yr.			-84				-84	
Balance in bank	840	1166	1492	419	745	1071	1397	324
Paycheck (After approx taxes)	651	651	651	651	651	651	651	651
Balance forward	1166	1492	419	745	1071	1397	324	640

Figure Twenty Three
Notes

Chapter 11	15-Jul-22	22-Jul-22	29-Jul-22	5-Aug-22	12-Aug-22	19-Aug-22	26-Aug-22	2-Sep-22
Rent/Mortgage				-900				
Groceries	-80	-80	-80	-80	-80	-80	-80	-80
Cell				-55				
Internet/Entertainment				-50				
Heat (averge)				-75				
Electric (average)				-75				
Water (average)				-60				
Saving $40K for house	-175	-175	-175	-175	-175	-175	-175	-175
Health insurance				-100				
Auto/transportation	-30	-30	-30	-30	-30	-30	-30	-30
Gifts/ fun/pets	-20	-20	-20	-20	-20	-20	-20	-20
Emergency Savings	-20	-20	-20	-20	-20	-20	-20	-20
Car Ins.@$1000 per yr.				-84				
Balance in bank	640	966	1292	1618	545	871	1197	1453
Paycheck (After approx taxes)	651	651	651	651	651	651	651	651
Balance forward	966	1292	1618	545	871	1197	1523	1779

Figure Twenty Four
Notes

Chapter 11	9-Sep-22	16-Sep-22	23-Sep-22	30-Sep-22	7-Oct-22	14-Oct-22	21-Oct-22	28-Oct-22
Rent/Mortgage	-900				-900			
Groceries	-80	-80	-80	-80	-80	-80	-80	-80
Cell	-55				-55			
Internet/Entertainment	-50				-50			
Heat (averge)	-75				-75			
Electric (average)	-75				-75			
Water (average)	-60				-60			
Saving $40K for house	-175	-175	-175	-175	-175	-175	-175	-175
Health insurance	-100				-100			
Auto/transportation	-30	-30	-30	-30	-30	-30	-30	-30
Gifts/ fun/pets	-10	-20	-20	-20	-20	-10	-10	-10
Emergency Savings	-10	-20	-20	-20	-20	-10	-10	-10
Car Ins.@$1000 per yr.	-84				-84			
Balance in bank	1779	726	1052	1378	1704	631	977	1323
Paycheck (After approx taxes)	651	651	651	651	651	651	651	651
Balance forward	726	1052	1378	1704	631	977	1323	1669

Figure Twenty Five

Notes

Chapter 11	4-Nov-22	11-Nov-22	18-Nov-22	25-Nov-22	2-Dec-22	9-Dec-22	16-Dec-22	23-Dec-22
Rent/Mortgage	-900				-900			
Groceries	-80	-80	-80	-80	-80	-80	-80	-80
Cell	-55				-55			
Internet/Entertainment	-50				-50			
Heat (averge)	-75				-75			
Electric (average)	-75				-75			
Water (average)	-60				-60			
Saving $40K for house	-175	-175	-175	-175	-175	-175	-175	-175
Health insurance	-100				-100			
Auto/transportation	-30	-30	-30	-30	-30	-30	-30	-30
Gifts/ fun/pets	-30	-30	-30	-30	-50	-75	-100	-50
Emergency Savings	-20	-20	-20	-20	-20	-20	-20	-20
Car Ins.@$1000 per yr.	-84				-84			
Balance in bank	1669	586	902	1218	1534	431	702	948
Paycheck (After approx taxes)	651	651	651	651	651	651	651	651
Balance forward	586	902	1218	1534	431	702	948	1244

Figure Twenty Six

Notes

Chapter 11	30-Dec-22	6-Jan-23	13-Jan-23	20-Jan-23	27-Jan-23	3-Feb-23	10-Feb-23	17-Feb-23
Rent/Mortgage		-900				-900		
Groceries	-80	-80	-80	-80	-80	-80	-80	-80
Cell		-55				-55		
Internet/Entertainment		-50				-50		
Heat (averge)		-75				-75		
Electric (average)		-75				-75		
Water (average)		-60				-60		
Saving $40K for house	-175	-175	-175	-175	-175	-175	-175	-175
Health insurance		-100				-100		
Auto/transportation	-30	-30	-30	-30	-30	-30	-30	-30
Gifts/ fun/pets	-20	-20	-20	-20	-20	-20	-20	-20
Emergency Savings	-20	-20	-20	-20	-20	-20	-20	-20
Car Ins.@$1000 per yr.		-84				-84		
Balance in bank	1244	1570	497	823	1149	1475	402	728
Paycheck (After approx taxes)	651	651	651	651	651	651	651	651
Balance forward	1570	497	823	1149	1475	402	728	1054

Figure Twenty Five

Notes

Chapter 11	24-Feb-23	3-Mar-23	10-Mar-23	17-Mar-23	24-Mar-23	31-Mar-23	7-Apr-23	14-Apr-23
Rent/Mortgage		-900					-900	
Groceries	-80	-80	-80	-80	-80	-80	-80	-80
Cell		-55					-55	
Internet/Entertainment		-50					-50	
Heat (averge)		-75					-75	
Electric (average)		-75					-75	
Water (average)		-60					-60	
Saving $40K for house	-175	-175	-175	-175	-175	-175	-175	-175
Health insurance		-100					-100	
Auto/transportation	-30	-30	-30	-30	-30	-30	-30	-30
Gifts/ fun/pets	-20	-20	-20	-20	-20	-20	-20	-20
Emergency Savings	-20	-20	-20	-20	-20	-20	-20	-20
Car Ins.@$1000 per yr.		-84					-84	
Balance in bank	1054	1380	307	633	959	1285	1611	538
Paycheck (After approx taxes)	651	651	651	651	651	651	651	651
Balance forward	1380	307	633	959	1285	1611	538	864

Figure Twenty Six

Notes

Chapter 11	21-Apr-23	28-Apr-23	5-May-23	12-May-23	19-May-23	26-May-23	2-Jun-23	9-Jun-23
Rent/Mortgage			-900				-900	
Groceries	-80	-80	-80	-80	-80	-80	-80	-80
Cell			-55				-55	
Internet/Entertainment			-50				-50	
Heat (averge)			-75				-75	
Electric (average)			-75				-75	
Water (average)			-60				-60	
Saving $40K for house	-175	-175	-175	-175	-175	-175	-175	-175
Health insurance			-100				-100	
Auto/transportation	-30	-30	-30	-30	-30	-30	-30	-30
Gifts/ fun/pets	-30	-30	-30	-30	-30	-30	-30	-30
Emergency Savings	-20	-20	-20	-20	-20	-20	-20	-20
Car Ins.@$1000 per yr.			-84				-84	
Balance in bank	864	1180	1496	413	729	1045	1361	586
Paycheck (After approx taxes)	651	651	651	651	651	651	651	651
Balance forward	1180	1496	413	729	1045	1361	278	902

Figure Twenty Seven

Notes

Chapter 11	16-Jun-23	23-Jun-23	30-Jun-23	7-Jul-23	14-Jul-23	21-Jul-23	28-Jul-23	4-Aug-23
Rent/Mortgage				-900				-900
Groceries	-80	-80	-80	-80	-80	-80	-80	-80
Cell				-55				-55
Internet/Entertainment				-50				-50
Heat (averge)				-75				-75
Electric (average)				-75				-75
Water (average)				-60				-60
Saving $40K for house	-175	-175	-175	-175	-175	-175	-175	-175
Health insurance				-100				-100
Auto/transportation	-30	-30	-30	-30	-30	-30	-30	-30
Gifts/ fun/pets	-30	-30	-30	-30	-30	-30	-30	-30
Emergency Savings	-20	-20	-20	-20	-20	-20	-20	-20
Car Ins.@$1000 per yr.				-84				-84
Balance in bank	902	1218	1534	1850	767	1083	1399	1715
Paycheck (After approx taxes)	651	651	651	651	651	651	651	651
Balance forward	1218	1534	1850	767	1083	1399	1715	632

Figure Twenty Eight

Notes

Chapter 11	11-Aug-23	18-Aug-23	25-Aug-23	1-Sep-23	8-Sep-23		
Rent/Mortgage				-900			
Groceries	-80	-80	-80	-80	-80		
Cell				-55			
Internet/Entertainment				-50			
Heat (averge)				-75			
Electric (average)				-75			
Water (average)				-60			
Saving $40K for house	-175	-175	-175	-175	-175		
Health insurance				-100			
Auto/transportation	-30	-30	-30	-30	-30		
Gifts/ fun/pets	-30	-30	-30	-30	-30		
Emergency Savings	-20	-20	-20	-20	-20		
Car Ins.@$1000 per yr.				-84			
Balance in bank	632	1633	1949	2265	1182		
Paycheck (After approx taxes)	651	651	651	651	651		
Balance forward	1633	1949	2265	1182	1498	.	.

Figure Twenty Nine

Notes

.	.

CHAPTER TWELVE

Renting -You want to Buy a house

You have a spouse and child -2 dependents - and you are renting an apartment. Only one of you works. You own a car. Your goal is to save $26,700.00 for moving expenses and down payment on a $200,000.00 Condo or home. You have a $20.00 per hour job.

♦ Rent : Your Rent is $1,100.00 per month.

♦ Groceries: This may not look like a lot, but if you create menus, cook and home and plan your food budget properly you can save yourself a lot of heartache and money. Not to mention eating healthier! Suggested menus and grocery lists are included at the end of the book!

♦ Cell: You can choose from many good phone plans and a lot of them have discounts.

♦ Internet/Entertainment: You may have an on line subscription or something similar, like Hulu or Xbox gold.

♦ Heat, Water, Electric: These are an average of average monthly utility expenses. Depending on where you are and what types of appliances you run, these expenses can and will vary.

♦ Save for Your Home: This exact amount should be put in to a separate bank account every week. This must be a savings account that pays interest. The interest is not likely to be a LOT. It will probably be 1% or less. But as it accumulates in YOUR account it will make certain that you reach your goals faster. In addition to your down payment (which will include closing costs) you need kitchen stuff, a lot of furniture, moving expenses, and some 'fall back' funds in the bank. But, at the end of only 193 weeks, you will have the funds necessary to start your purchase!

♦ Health Insurance: Your employer may withhold this amount from your check in weekly increments to cover your part of the health insurance coverage. If you do not have insurance save this amount for medical visits.

♦ Transportation: Having two dependents means you need transportation.

♦ Gifts/Fun: It is going to happen so you need to put it in your budget. You do not have to spend that much, but do not spend more.

♦ Emergency Savings: Put this amount aside every week in case of a Real emergency. Medical or a death in the family qualify.

♦ Balance in Bank: That is what you should have in your bank account at the end of all transactions in order to stay on your budget. At the beginning of this budget you are starting with the $3,200.00 in your bank acount that you have saved using another budget.

♦ Paycheck: This is an average, because tax laws vary from state to state and even from city to city. If you are on salary, your pay will be the same every week. You can copy the exact figure from your pay stub. If you are an hourly worker, your net pay will change from week to week. An adjustent has been made to account for the two dependent deduction you will get on your taxes. Some companies give annual or even semi-annual pay increases.

♦ Balance forward: This is what is left after you pay your expenses. This money cannot be spent – it is carried forward to the next period. This is why you budget –so you remember to not spend all of your money!

Chapter 12	4-Jan-19	11-Jan-19	18-Jan-19	25-Jan-19	1-Feb-19	8-Feb-19	15-Feb-19	22-Feb-19
Rent/Mortgage	-1100				-1100			
Groceries	-125	-125	-125	-125	-125	-125	-125	-125
Cell	-50				-50			
Internet/Entertainment	-50				-50			
Heat (average)	-75				-75			
Electric (Average)	-75				-75			
Water (Average)	-60				-60			
Saving $27K to move	-140	-140	-140	-140	-140	-140	-140	-140
Health insurance	-100				-100			
Auto/transportation	-30	-30	-30	-30	-30	-30	-30	-30
Gifts/ fun/pets	-10	-10	-10	-10	-10	-10	-10	-10
Emergency Savings	-10	-10	-10	-10	-10	-10	-10	-10
Car Ins.@$1000 per year.	-84				-84			
Balance in bank	3,200	1966	2326	2686	3046	1812	2172	2532
Paycheck (After approx taxes)	675	675	675	675	675	675	675	675
Balance forward	1966	2326	2686	3046	1812	2172	2532	2892
Figure One								

	Notes:							
Chapter 12	1-Mar-19	8-Mar-19	15-Mar-19	22-Mar-19	29-Mar-19	5-Apr-19	12-Apr-19	19-Apr-19
Rent/Mortgage	-1100				-1100			
Groceries	-125	-125	-125	-125	-125	-125	-125	-125
Cell	-50				-50			
Internet/Entertainment	-50				-50			
Heat (average)	-75				-75			
Electric (Average)	-75				-75			
Water (Average)	-60				-60			
Saving $27K to move	-140	-140	-140	-140	-140	-140	-140	-140
Health insurance	-100				-100			
Auto/transportation	-30	-30	-30	-30	-30	-30	-30	-30
Gifts/ fun/pets	-10	-10	-10	-10	-10	-10	-10	-10
Emergency Savings	-10	-10	-10	-10	-10	-10	-10	-10
Car Ins.@$1000 per year.	-84				-84			
Balance in bank	2892	1658	2018	2378	2738	1504	1864	2224
Paycheck (After approx taxes)	675	675	675	675	675	675	675	675
Balance forward	1658	2018	2378	2738	1504	1864	2224	2584
Figure Two								

Chapter 12	26-Apr-19	3-May-19	10-May-19	17-May-19	24-May-19	31-May-19	7-Jun-19	14-Jun-19
Rent/Mortgage		-1100				-1100		
Groceries	-125	-125	-125	-125	-125	-125	-125	-125
Cell		-50				-50		
Internet/Entertainment		-50				-50		
Heat (average)		-75				-75		
Electric (Average)		-75				-75		
Water (Average)		-60				-60		
Saving $27K to move	-140	-140	-140	-140	-140	-140	-140	-140
Health insurance		-100				-100		
Auto/transportation	-30	-30	-30	-30	-30	-30	-30	-30
Gifts/ fun/pets	-10	-10	-10	-10	-10	-10	-10	-10
Emergency Savings	-10	-10	-10	-10	-10	-10	-10	-10
Car Ins.@$1000 per year.		-84				-84		
Balance in bank	2584	2944	1710	2070	2430	2790	1556	1916
Paycheck (After approx taxes)	675	675	675	675	675	675	675	675
Balance forward	2944	1710	2070	2430	2790	1556	1916	2276
Figure Three								

Chapter 12	21-Jun-19	28-Jun-19	5-Jul-19	12-Jul-19	19-Jul-19	26-Jul-19	2-Aug-19	9-Aug-19
Rent/Mortgage		-1100						
Groceries	-125	-125	-125	-125	-125	-125	-125	-125
Cell		-50						
Internet/Entertainment		-50						
Heat (average)		-75						
Electric (Average)		-75						
Water (Average)		-60						
Saving $27K to move	-140	-140	-140	-140	-140	-140		-140
Health insurance		-100						
Auto/transportation	-30	-30	-30	-30	-30	-30		-30
Gifts/ fun/pets	-10	-10	-10	-10	-10	-10	-10	-10
Emergency Savings	-10	-10	-10	-10	-10	-10	-10	-10
Car Ins.@$1000 per year.		-84						
Balance in bank	2276	2636	1402	1762	2122	2482	2842	3372
Paycheck (After approx taxes)	675	675	675	675	675	675	675	675
Balance forward	2636	1402	1762	2122	2482	2842	3372	3732
Figure Four								

Chapter 12	16-Aug-19	23-Aug-19	30-Aug-19	6-Sep-19	13-Sep-19	20-Sep-19	27-Sep-19	4-Oct-19
Rent/Mortgage			-1100					-1100
Groceries	-125	-125	-125	-125	-125	-125	-125	-125
Cell			-50					-50
Internet/Entertainment			-50					-50
Heat (average)			-75					-75
Electric (Average)			-75					-75
Water (Average)			-60					-60
Saving $27K to move	-140	-140	-140	-140	-140	-140	-140	-140
Health insurance			-100					-100
Auto/transportation	-30	-30	-30	-30	-30	-30	-30	-30
Gifts/ fun/pets	-10	-10	-10	-10	-10	-10	-10	-10
Emergency Savings	-10	-10	-10	-10	-10	-10	-10	-10
Car Ins.@$1000 per year.			-84					-84
Balance in bank	3732	4092	4452	3218	3578	3938	4298	4658
Paycheck (After approx taxes)	675	675	675	675	675	675	675	675
Balance forward	4092	4452	3218	3578	3938	4298	4658	3424
Figure Five								

Chapter 12	11-Oct-19	18-Oct-19	25-Oct-19	1-Nov-19	8-Nov-19	15-Nov-19	22-Nov-19	29-Nov-19
Rent/Mortgage				-1100				-1100
Groceries	-125	-125	-125	-125	-125	-125	-125	-125
Cell				-50				-50
Internet/Entertainment				-50				-50
Heat (average)				-75				-75
Electric (Average)				-75				-75
Water (Average)				-60				-60
Saving $27K to move	-140	-140	-140	-140	-140	-140	-140	-140
Health insurance				-100				-100
Auto/transportation	-30	-30	-30	-30	-30	-30	-30	-30
Gifts/ fun/pets	-10	-10	-10	-10	-10	-10	-25	-10
Emergency Savings	-10	-10	-10	-10	-10	-10	-10	-10
Car Ins.@$1000 per year.				-84				-84
Balance in bank	3424	3784	4144	4504	3270	3630	3990	4335
Paycheck (After approx taxes)	675	675	675	675	675	675	675	675
Balance forward	3784	4144	4504	3270	3630	3990	4335	3101
Figure Six								

Chapter 12	6-Dec-19	13-Dec-19	20-Dec-19	27-Dec-19	3-Jan-20	10-Jan-20	17-Jan-20	24-Jan-20
Rent/Mortgage					-1100			
Groceries	-125	-125	-125	-125	-125	-125	-125	-125
Cell					-50			
Internet/Entertainment					-50			
Heat (average)					-75			
Electric (Average)					-75			
Water (Average)					-60			
Saving $27K to move	-140	-140	-140	-140	-140	-140	-140	-140
Health insurance					-100			
Auto/transportation	-30	-30	-30	-30	-30	-30	-30	-30
Gifts/ fun/pets	-25	-50	-100	-10	-10	-10	-10	-10
Emergency Savings	-10	-10	-10	-10	-10	-10	-10	-10
Car Ins.@$1000 per year.					-84			
Balance in bank	3101	3446	3766	4036	4396	3162	3522	3882
Paycheck (After approx taxes)	675	675	675	675	675	675	675	675
Balance forward	3446	3766	4036	4396	3162	3522	3882	4242

Figure Seven

Chapter 12	31-Jan-20	7-Feb-20	14-Feb-20	21-Feb-20	28-Feb-20	6-Mar-20	13-Mar-20	20-Mar-20
Rent/Mortgage	-1100				-1100			
Groceries	-125	-125	-125	-125	-125	-125	-125	-125
Cell	-50				-50			
Internet/Entertainment	-50				-50			
Heat (average)	-75				-75			
Electric (Average)	-75				-75			
Water (Average)	-60				-60			
Saving $27K to move	-140	-140	-140	-140	-140	-140	-140	-140
Health insurance	-100				-100			
Auto/transportation	-30	-30	-30	-30	-30	-30	-30	-30
Gifts/ fun/pets	-10	-10	-10	-10	-10	-10	-10	-10
Emergency Savings	-10	-10	-10	-10	-10	-10	-10	-10
Car Ins.@$1000 per year.	-84				-84			
Balance in bank	4242	3008	3368	3728	4088	2854	3214	3574
Paycheck (After approx taxes)	675	675	675	675	675	675	675	675
Balance forward	3008	3368	3728	4088	2854	3214	3574	3934

Figure Eight

Chapter 12	27-Mar-20	3-Apr-20	10-Apr-20	17-Apr-20	24-Apr-20	1-May-20	8-May-20	15-May-20
Rent/Mortgage	-1100					-1100		
Groceries	-125	-125	-125	-125	-125	-125	-125	-125
Cell	-50					-50		
Internet/Entertainment	-50					-50		
Heat (average)	-75					-75		
Electric (Average)	-75					-75		
Water (Average)	-60					-60		
Saving $27K to move	-140	-140	-140	-140	-140	-140	-140	-140
Health insurance	-100					-100		
Auto/transportation	-30	-30	-30	-30	-30	-30	-30	-30
Gifts/ fun/pets	-10	-10	-10	-10	-10	-10	-10	-10
Emergency Savings	-10	-10	-10	-10	-10	-10	-10	-10
Car Ins.@$1000 per year.	-84					-84		
Balance in bank	3934	2700	3060	3420	3780	4140	2906	3266
Paycheck (After approx taxes)	675	675	675	675	675	675	675	675
Balance forward	2700	3060	3420	3780	4140	2906	3266	3626

Figure Nine

Chapter 12	22-May-20	29-May-20	5-Jun-20	12-Jun-20	19-Jun-20	26-Jun-20	3-Jul-20	10-Jul-20
Rent/Mortgage		-1100					-1100	
Groceries	-125	-125	-125	-125	-125	-125	-125	-125
Cell		-50					-50	
Internet/Entertainment		-50					-50	
Heat (average)		-75					-75	
Electric (Average)		-75					-75	
Water (Average)		-60					-60	
Saving $27K to move	-140	-140	-140	-140	-140	-140	-140	-140
Health insurance		-100					-100	
Auto/transportation	-30	-30	-30	-30	-30	-30	-30	-30
Gifts/ fun/pets	-10	-10	-10	-10	-10	-10	-10	-10
Emergency Savings	-10	-10	-10	-10	-10	-10	-10	-10
Car Ins.@$1000 per year.		-84					-84	
Balance in bank	3626	3986	2752	3112	3472	3832	4192	2958
Paycheck (After approx taxes)	675	675	675	675	675	675	675	675
Balance forward	3986	2752	3112	3472	3832	4192	2958	3318
Figure Ten								

Chapter 12	17-Jul-20	24-Jul-20	31-Jul-20	7-Aug-20	14-Aug-20	21-Aug-20	28-Aug-20	4-Sep-20
Rent/Mortgage			-1100					-1100
Groceries	-125	-125	-125	-125	-125	-125	-125	-125
Cell			-50					-50
Internet/Entertainment			-50					-50
Heat (average)			-75					-75
Electric (Average)			-75					-75
Water (Average)			-60					-60
Saving $27K to move	-140	-140	-140	-140	-140	-140	-140	-140
Health insurance			-100					-100
Auto/transportation	-30	-30	-30	-30	-30	-30	-30	-30
Gifts/ fun/pets	-10	-10	-10	-10	-10	-10	-10	-10
Emergency Savings	-10	-10	-10	-10	-10	-10	-10	-10
Car Ins. @ $1000 per year.			-84					-84
Balance in bank	3318	3678	4038	2804	3164	3524	3884	4244
Paycheck (After approx taxes)	675	675	675	675	675	675	675	675
Balance forward	3678	4038	2804	3164	3524	3884	4244	3010
Figure Eleven								

Chapter 12	11-Sep-20	18-Sep-20	25-Sep-20	2-Oct-20	9-Oct-20	16-Oct-20	23-Oct-20	30-Oct-20
Rent/Mortgage				-1100				
Groceries	-125	-125	-125	-125	-125	-125	-125	-125
Cell				-50				
Internet/Entertainment				-50				
Heat (average)				-75				
Electric (Average)				-75				
Water (Average)				-60				
Saving $27K to move	-140	-140	-140	-140	-140	-140	-140	-140
Health insurance				-100				
Auto/transportation	-30	-30	-30	-30	-30	-30	-30	-30
Gifts/ fun/pets	-10	-10	-10	-10	-10	-10	-10	-10
Emergency Savings	-10	-10	-10	-10	-10	-10	-10	-10
Car Ins. @ $1000 per year.				-84				84
Balance in bank	3010	3370	3730	4090	2856	3216	3576	3936
Paycheck (After approx taxes)	675	675	675	675	675	675	675	675
Balance forward	3370	3730	4090	2856	3216	3576	3936	4380
Figure Twelve								

Chapter 12	6-Nov-20	13-Nov-20	20-Nov-20	27-Nov-20	4-Dec-20	11-Dec-20	18-Dec-20	25-Dec-20
Rent/Mortgage	-1100				-1100			
Groceries	-125	-125	-125	-125	-125	-125	-125	-125
Cell	-50				-50			
Internet/Entertainment	-50				-50			
Heat (average)	-75				-75			
Electric (Average)	-75				-75			
Water (Average)	-60				-60			
Saving $27K to move	-140	-140	-140	-140	-140	-140	-140	-140
Health insurance	-100				-100			
Auto/transportation	-30	-30	-30	-30	-30	-30	-30	-30
Gifts/ fun/pets	-10	-10	-30	-10	-25	-50	-100	-30
Emergency Savings	-10	-10	-10	-10	-10	-10	-10	-10
Car Ins.@$1000 per year.	-84				-84			
Balance in bank	4380	3146	3506	3846	4206	2957	3277	3547
Paycheck (After approx taxes)	675	675	675	675	675	675	675	675
Balance forward	3146	3506	3846	4206	2957	3277	3547	3887
Figure Thirteen								

Chapter 12	1-Jan-21	8-Jan-21	15-Jan-21	22-Jan-21	29-Jan-21	5-Feb-21	12-Feb-21	19-Feb-21
Rent/Mortgage	-1100					-1100		
Groceries	-125	-125	-125	-125	-125	-125	-125	-125
Cell	-50					-50		
Internet/Entertainment	-50					-50		
Heat (average)	-75					-75		
Electric (Average)	-75					-75		
Water (Average)	-60					-60		
Saving $27K to move	-140	-140	-140	-140	-140	-140	-140	-140
Health insurance	-100					-100		
Auto/transportation	-30	-30	-30	-30	-30	-30	-30	-30
Gifts/ fun/pets	-10	-10	-10	-10	-10	-10	-10	-10
Emergency Savings	-10	-10	-10	-10	-10	-10	-10	-10
Car Ins.@$1000 per year.	-84					-84		
Balance in bank	3887	2653	3013	3373	3733	4093	2859	3219
Paycheck (After approx taxes)	675	675	675	675	675	675	675	675
Balance forward	2653	3013	3373	3733	4093	2859	3219	3579
Figure Fourteen								

Chapter 12	26-Feb-21	5-Mar-21	12-Mar-21	19-Mar-21	26-Mar-21	2-Apr-21	9-Apr-21	16-Apr-21
Rent/Mortgage		-1100				-1100		
Groceries	-125	-125	-125	-125	-125	-125	-125	-125
Cell		-50				-50		
Internet/Entertainment		-50				-50		
Heat (average)		-75				-75		
Electric (Average)		-75				-75		
Water (Average)		-60				-60		
Saving $27K to move	-140	-140	-140	-140	-140	-140	-140	-140
Health insurance		-100				-100		
Auto/transportation	-30	-30	-30	-30	-30	-30	-30	-30
Gifts/ fun/pets	-10	-10	-10	-10	-10	-10	-10	-10
Emergency Savings	-10	-10	-10	-10	-10	-10	-10	-10
Car Ins.@$1000 per year.		-84				-84		
Balance in bank	3579	3939	2705	3065	3425	3785	2551	2911
Paycheck (After approx taxes)	675	675	675	675	675	675	675	675
Balance forward	3939	2705	3065	3425	3785	2551	2911	3271
Figure Fifteen								

Chapter 12	23-Apr-21	30-Apr-21	7-May-21	14-May-21	21-May-21	28-May-21	4-Jun-21	11-Jun-21
Rent/Mortgage		-1100					-1100	
Groceries	-125	-125	-125	-125	-125	-125	-125	-125
Cell		-50					-50	
Internet/Entertainment		-50					-50	
Heat (average)		-75					-75	
Electric (Average)		-75					-75	
Water (Average)		-60					-60	
Saving $27K to move	-140	-140	-140	-140	-140	-140	-140	-140
Health insurance		-100					-100	
Auto/transportation	-30	-30	-30	-30	-30	-30	-30	-30
Gifts/ fun/pets	-10	-10	-10	-10	-10	-10	-10	-10
Emergency Savings	-10	-10	-10	-10	-10	-10	-10	-10
Car Ins.@$1000 per year.		-84					-84	
Balance in bank	3271	3631	2397	2757	3117	3477	3837	2603
Paycheck (After approx taxes)	675	675	675	675	675	675	675	675
Balance forward	3631	2397	2757	3117	3477	3837	2603	2963
Figure Sixteen								

Chapter 12	18-Jun-21	25-Jun-21	2-Jul-21	9-Jul-21	16-Jul-21	23-Jul-21	30-Jul-21	6-Aug-21
Rent/Mortgage			-1100				-1100	
Groceries	-125	-125	-125	-125	-125	-125	-125	-125
Cell			-50				-50	
Internet/Entertainment			-50				-50	
Heat (average)			-75				-75	
Electric (Average)			-75				-75	
Water (Average)			-60				-60	
Saving $27K to move	-140	-140	-140	-140	-140	-140	-140	-140
Health insurance			-100				-100	
Auto/transportation	-30	-30	-30	-30	-30	-30	-30	-30
Gifts/ fun/pets	-20	-20	-20	-20	-20	-20	-20	-20
Emergency Savings	-20	-20	-20	-20	-20	-20	-20	-20
Car Ins.@$1000 per year.			-84				-84	
Balance in bank	2963	3303	3643	2389	2729	3069	3409	2155
Paycheck (After approx taxes)	675	675	675	675	675	675	675	675
Balance forward	3303	3643	2389	2729	3069	3409	2155	2495
Figure Seventeen								

Chapter 12	13-Aug-21	20-Aug-21	27-Aug-21	3-Sep-21	10-Sep-21	17-Sep-21	24-Sep-21	1-Oct-21
Rent/Mortgage				-1100				-1100
Groceries	-125	-125	-125	-125	-125	-125	-125	-125
Cell				-50				-50
Internet/Entertainment				-50				-50
Heat (average)				-75				-75
Electric (Average)				-75				-75
Water (Average)				-60				-60
Saving $27K to move	-140	-140	-140	-140	-140	-140	-140	-140
Health insurance				-100				-100
Auto/transportation	-30	-30	-30	-30	-30	-30	-30	-30
Gifts/ fun/pets	-20	-20	-20	-20	-20	-20	-20	-20
Emergency Savings	-20	-20	-20	-20	-20	-20	-20	-20
Car Ins.@$1000 per year.				-84				-84
Balance in bank	2495	2835	3175	3515	2261	2601	2941	3281
Paycheck (After approx taxes)	675	675	675	675	675	675	675	675
Balance forward	2835	3175	3515	2261	2601	2941	3281	2027
Figure Eighteen								

Chapter 12	8-Oct-21	15-Oct-21	22-Oct-21	29-Oct-21	5-Nov-21	12-Nov-21	19-Nov-21	26-Nov-21
Rent/Mortgage					-1100			
Groceries	-125	-125	-125	-125	-125	-125	-125	-125
Cell					-50			
Internet/Entertainment					-50			
Heat (average)					-75			
Electric (Average)					-75			
Water (Average)					-60			
Saving $27K to move	-140	-140	-140	-140	-140	-140	-140	-140
Health insurance					-100			
Auto/transportation	-30	-30	-30	-30	-30	-30	-30	-30
Gifts/ fun/pets	-20	-20	-20	-20	-20	-20	-30	-10
Emergency Savings	-20	-20	-20	-20	-20	-20	-20	-20
Car Ins.@$1000 per year.				84	-84			
Balance in bank	2027	2367	2707	3047	3471	2217	2557	2887
Paycheck (After approx taxes)	675	675	675	675	675	675	675	675
Balance forward	2367	2707	3047	3471	2217	2557	2887	3237
Figure Nineteen								

Chapter 12	3-Dec-21	10-Dec-21	17-Dec-21	24-Dec-21	31-Dec-21	7-Jan-22	14-Jan-22	21-Jan-22
Rent/Mortgage	-1100				-1100			
Groceries	-125	-125	-125	-125	-125	-125	-125	-125
Cell	-50				-50			
Internet/Entertainment	-50				-50			
Heat (average)	-75				-75			
Electric (Average)	-75				-75			
Water (Average)	-60				-60			
Saving $27K to move	-140	-140	-140	-140	-140	-140	-140	-140
Health insurance	-100				-100			
Auto/transportation	-30	-30	-30	-30	-30	-30	-30	-30
Gifts/ fun/pets	-50	-100	-100	-30	-20	-20	-30	-30
Emergency Savings	-20	-20	-20	-20	-20	-20	-30	-30
Car Ins.@$1000 per year.	-84				-84			
Balance in bank	3237	1953	2213	2473	2803	1549	1889	2209
Paycheck (After approx taxes)	675	675	675	675	675	675	675	675
Balance forward	1953	2213	2473	2803	1549	1889	2209	2529
Figure Twenty								

Chapter 12	28-Jan-22	4-Feb-22	11-Feb-22	18-Feb-22	25-Feb-22	4-Mar-22	11-Mar-22	18-Mar-22
Rent/Mortgage		-1100				-1100		
Groceries	-125	-125	-125	-125	-125	-125	-125	-125
Cell		-50				-50		
Internet/Entertainment		-50				-50		
Heat (average)		-75				-75		
Electric (Average)		-75				-75		
Water (Average)		-60				-60		
Saving $27K to move	-140	-140	-140	-140	-140	-140	-140	-140
Health insurance		-100				-100		
Auto/transportation	-30	-30	-30	-30	-30	-30	-30	-30
Gifts/ fun/pets	-30	-30	-30	-30	-30	-30	-30	-30
Emergency Savings	-30	-30	-30	-30	-30	-30	-30	-30
Car Ins. @ $1000 per year.		-84				-84		
Balance in bank	2529	2849	1575	1895	2215	2535	1261	1581
Paycheck (After approx taxes)	675	675	675	675	675	675	675	675
Balance forward	2849	1575	1895	2215	2535	1261	1581	1901
Figure Twenty One								

Chapter 12	25-Mar-22	1-Apr-22	8-Apr-22	15-Apr-22	22-Apr-22	29-Apr-22	6-May-22	13-May-22
Rent/Mortgage		-1100					-1100	
Groceries	-125	-125	-125	-125	-125	-125	-125	-125
Cell		-50					-50	
Internet/Entertainment		-50					-50	
Heat (average)		-75					-75	
Electric (Average)		-75					-75	
Water (Average)		-60					-60	
Saving $27K to move	-140	-140	-140	-140	-140	-140	-140	-140
Health insurance		-100					-100	
Auto/transportation	-30	-30	-30	-30	-30	-30	-30	-30
Gifts/ fun/pets	-30	-30	-30	-30	-30	-30	-30	-30
Emergency Savings	-30	-30	-30	-30	-30	-30	-30	-30
Car Ins. @ $1000 per year.		-84					-84	
Balance in bank	1901	2221	947	1267	1587	1907	2227	953
Paycheck (After approx taxes)	675	675	675	675	675	675	675	675
Balance forward	2221	947	1267	1587	1907	2227	953	1273
Figure Twenty Two								

Chapter 12	20-May-22	27-May-22	3-Jun-22	10-Jun-22	17-Jun-22	24-Jun-22	1-Jul-22	8-Jul-22
Rent/Mortgage			-1100				-1100	
Groceries	-125	-125	-125	-125	-125	-125	-125	-125
Cell			-50				-50	
Internet/Entertainment			-50				-50	
Heat (average)			-75				-75	
Electric (Average)			-75				-75	
Water (Average)			-60				-60	
Saving $27K to move	-140	-140	-140	-140	-140	-140	-140	-140
Health insurance			-100				-100	
Auto/transportation	-30	-30	-30	-30	-30	-30	-30	-30
Gifts/ fun/pets	-30	-30	-30	-30	-30	-30	-30	-30
Emergency Savings	-30	-30	-30	-30	-30	-30	-30	-30
Car Ins. @ $1000 per year.			-84				-84	
Balance in bank	1273	1593	1913	639	959	1279	1599	325
Paycheck (After approx taxes)	675	675	675	675	675	675	675	675
Balance forward	1593	1913	639	959	1279	1599	325	645
Figure Twenty One								

Chapter 12	15-Jul-22	22-Jul-22	29-Jul-22	5-Aug-22	12-Aug-22	19-Aug-22	26-Aug-22	2-Sep-22
Rent/Mortgage				-1100				-1100
Groceries	-125	-125	-125	-125	-125	-125	-125	-125
Cell				-50				-50
Internet/Entertainment				-50				-50
Heat (average)				-75				-75
Electric (Average)				-75				-75
Water (Average)				-60				-60
Saving $27K to move	-140	-140	-140	-140	-140	-140	-140	-140
Health insurance				-100				-100
Auto/transportation	-30	-30	-30	-30	-30	-30	-30	-30
Gifts/ fun/pets	-30	-30	-30	-30	-30	-30	-30	-30
Emergency Savings	-30	-30	-30	-30	-30	-30	-30	-30
Car Ins. @ $1000 per year.				-84				-84
Balance in bank	645	965	1285	1605	331	651	971	1291
Paycheck (After approx taxes)	675	675	675	675	675	675	675	675
Balance forward	965	1285	1605	331	651	971	1291	17
Figure Twenty Two								

Chapter 12	9-Sep-22	16-Sep-22						
Rent/Mortgage								
Groceries	-125	-125						
Cell								
Internet/Entertainment								
Heat (average)								
Electric (Average)								
Water (Average)								
Saving $27K to move	-140	-140						
Health insurance								
Auto/transportation	-30	-30						
Gifts/ fun/pets	-30	-30						
Emergency Savings	-30	-30						
Car Ins. @ $1000 per year.								
Balance in bank	17	337						
Paycheck (After approx taxes)	675	675						
Balance forward	337	657	.	.	.	.	.	.
Figure Twenty Three								

CHAPTER THIRTEEN

Renting -You want to Buy a house

You have a spouse and child (or elderly parent) - and you are renting an apartment. You work for $20 per hour and your spouse earns $10 per hour. You own one car AND you are making payments on another. Your goal is to save $27,000.00 for moving expenses and down payment   on a $200,000.00 Condo or home. .

♦ Rent : Your Rent is $1,100.00 per month.

♦ Groceries: This may not look like a lot, but if you create menus, cook and home and plan your food budget properly you can save yourself a lot of heartache and money. Not to mention eating healthier!   Suggested menus and grocery lists are included at the end of the book!

♦ Cell: You can choose from many good phone plans and a lot of them have discounts.

♦   Internet/Entertainment: You may have an on line subscription or something similar, like Hulu or Xbox gold.

♦   Heat, Water, Electric: These are an average of average monthly utility expenses. Depending on where you are and what types of appliances you run, these expenses can and will vary.

♦ Save for Your Home: This exact amount should be put in to a separate bank account every week. This must be a savings account that pays interest. The interest is not likely to be a LOT. It will probably be 1% or less. But as it accumulates in YOUR account it will make certain that you reach your goals faster.   In addition to your down payment (which will include closing costs) you need kitchen stuff, a lot of furniture, moving expenses, and some 'fall back' funds in the bank. But, at the end of only 193 weeks, you will have the funds necessary to start your purchase!

♦ Health Insurance: You may have a personal policy that you pay monthly. Your employer may withhold this amount from your check in weekly increments. If you have no insurance - SAVE this amount anyway.

♦   Transportation: Having two jobs means a need for transportation.

♦ Gifts/Fun: It is going to happen so you need to put it in your budget. You do not have to spend that much, but do not spend more.

♦ Emergency Savings: Put this amount aside every week in case of a Real emergency. Medical or a death in the family qualify.

♦   Balance in Bank: That is what you should have in your bank account at the end of all transactions in order to stay on your budget. At the beginning of this budget you are starting with the $3,200.00 in your bank acount that you have saved using another budget.

♦   Paycheck: This is an average, because tax laws vary from state to state and even from city to city. If you are on salary, your pay will be the same every week. You can copy the exact figure from your pay stub. If you are an hourly worker, your net pay will change from week to week. An adjustent has been made to account for the two incomes plus a dependent deduction you will get on your taxes. Some companies give annual or even semi-annual pay increases.

♦ Balance forward: This is what is left after you pay your expenses. This money cannot be spent – it is carried forward to the next period. This is why you budget –so you remember to not spend all of your money!

Chapter 13	4-Jan-19	11-Jan-19	18-Jan-19	25-Jan-19	1-Feb-19	8-Feb-19	15-Feb-19	22-Feb-19
Rent/Mortgage	-1100				-1100			
Groceries	-125	-125	-125	-125	-125	-125	-125	-125
Cell	-70				-70			
Internet/Entertainment	-45				-45			
Heat (Yearly averge)	-65				-65			
Electric (Yearly Average)	-70				-70			
Water (Yearly Average)	-55				-55			
Saving $27K to move	-130	-130	-130	-130	-130	-130	-130	-130
Health insurance	-175				-175			
Child/Elder Care	-550				-550			
Auto/transportation	-45	-45	-45	-45	-45	-45	-45	-45
Car Pmnt (8K@225 per mo)	-225				-225			
Gifts/ fun/pets					-5	-5	-5	-5
Emergency Savings					-5	-5	-5	-5
Car Ins@ $1200 per yr.	-100				-100			
Balance in bank	3200	1318	1891	2464	3037	1145	1708	2271
Paycheck (After approx taxes)	873	873	873	873	873	873	873	873
Balance forward	1318	1891	2464	3037	1145	1708	2271	2834

Figure One

Notes:

Chapter 13	1-Mar-19	8-Mar-19	15-Mar-19	22-Mar-19	29-Mar-19	5-Apr-19	12-Apr-19	19-Apr-19
Rent/Mortgage	-1100				-1100			
Groceries	-125	-125	-125	-125	-125	-125	-125	-125
Cell	-70				-70			
Internet/Entertainment	-45				-45			
Heat (Yearly averge)	-65				-65			
Electric (Yearly Average)	-70				-70			
Water (Yearly Average)	-55				-55			
Saving $27K to move	-130	-130	-130	-130	-130	-130	-130	-130
Health insurance	-175				-175			
Child/Elder Care	-550				-550			
Auto/transportation	-45	-45	-45	-45	-45	-45	-45	-45
Car Pmnt (8K@225 per mo)	-225				-225			
Gifts/ fun/pets	-5	-5	-5	-5	-5	-5	-5	-5
Emergency Savings	-5	-5	-5	-5	-5	-5	-5	-5
Car Ins@ $1200 per yr.	-100				-100			
Balance in bank	2834	942	1505	2068	2631	739	1302	1865
Paycheck (After approx taxes)	873	873	873	873	873	873	873	873
Balance forward	942	1505	2068	2631	739	1302	1865	2428

Figure Two

Chapter 13	26-Apr-19	3-May-19	10-May-19	17-May-19	24-May-19	31-May-19	7-Jun-19	14-Jun-19
Rent/Mortgage		-1100				-1100		
Groceries	-125	-125	-125	-125	-125	-125	-125	-125
Cell		-70				-70		
Internet/Entertainment		-45				-45		
Heat (Yearly averge)		-65				-65		
Electric (Yearly Average)		-70				-70		
Water (Yearly Average)		-55				-55		
Saving $27K to move	-130	-130	-130	-130	-130	-130	-130	-130
Health insurance		-175				-175		
Child/Elder Care		-550				-550		
Auto/transportation	-45	-45	-45	-45	-45	-45	-45	-45
Car Pmnt (8K@225 per mo)		-225				-225		
Gifts/ fun/pets	-5	-5	-5	-5	-5	-5	-5	-5
Emergency Savings	-5	-5	-5	-5	-5	-5	-5	-5
Car Ins@ $1200 per yr.		-100				-100		
Balance in bank	2428	2991	1099	1662	2225	2788	896	1459
Paycheck (After approx taxes)	873	873	873	873	873	873	873	873
Balance forward	2991	1099	1662	2225	2788	896	1459	2022

Figure Three

Chapter 13	21-Jun-19	28-Jun-19	5-Jul-19	12-Jul-19	19-Jul-19	26-Jul-19	2-Aug-19	9-Aug-19
Rent/Mortgage		-1100					-1100	
Groceries	-125	-125	-125	-125	-125	-125	-125	-125
Cell		-70					-70	
Internet/Entertainment		-45					-45	
Heat (Yearly averge)		-65					-65	
Electric (Yearly Average)		-70					-70	
Water (Yearly Average)		-55					-55	
Saving $27K to move	-130	-130	-130	-130	-130	-130	-130	-130
Health insurance		-175					-175	
Child/Elder Care		-550					-550	
Auto/transportation	-45	-45	-45	-45	-45	-45	-45	-45
Car Pmnt (8K@225 per mo)		-225					-225	
Gifts/ fun/pets	-5	-5	-5	-5	-5	-5	-5	-5
Emergency Savings	-5	-5	-5	-5	-5	-5	-5	-5
Car Ins@ $1200 per yr.		-100					-100	
Balance in bank	2022	2585	693	1256	1819	2382	2945	1053
Paycheck (After approx taxes)	873	873	873	873	873	873	873	873
Balance forward	2585	693	1256	1819	2382	2945	1053	1616

Figure Four

Chapter 13	16-Aug-19	23-Aug-19	30-Aug-19	6-Sep-19	13-Sep-19	20-Sep-19	27-Sep-19	4-Oct-19
Rent/Mortgage			-1100					-1100
Groceries	-125	-125	-125	-125	-125	-125	-125	-125
Cell			-70					-70
Internet/Entertainment			-45					-45
Heat (Yearly averge)			-65					-65
Electric (Yearly Average)			-70					-70
Water (Yearly Average)			-55					-55
Saving $27K to move	-130	-130	-130	-130	-130	-130	-130	-130
Health insurance			-175					-175
Child/Elder Care			-550					-550
Auto/transportation	-45	-45	-45	-45	-45	-45	-45	-45
Car Pmnt (8K@225 per mo)			-225					-225
Gifts/ fun/pets	-5	-5	-5	-5	-5	-5	-5	-5
Emergency Savings	-5	-5	-5	-5	-5	-5	-5	-5
Car Ins@ $1200 per yr.			-100					-100
Balance in bank	1616	2179	2742	850	1413	1976	2539	3102
Paycheck (After approx taxes)	873	873	873	873	873	873	873	873
Balance forward	2179	2742	850	1413	1976	2539	3102	1210

Figure Five

Chapter 13	11-Oct-19	18-Oct-19	25-Oct-19	1-Nov-19	8-Nov-19	15-Nov-19	22-Nov-19	29-Nov-19
Rent/Mortgage				-1100				-1100
Groceries	-125	-125	-125	-125	-125	-125	-125	-125
Cell				-70				-70
Internet/Entertainment				-45				-45
Heat (Yearly averge)				-65				-65
Electric (Yearly Average)				-70				-70
Water (Yearly Average)				-55				-55
Saving $27K to move	-130	-130	-130	-130	-130	-130	-130	-130
Health insurance				-175				-175
Child/Elder Care				-550				-550
Auto/transportation	-45	-45	-45	-45	-45	-45	-45	-45
Car Pmnt (8K@225 per mo)				-225				-225
Gifts/ fun/pets	-5	-5	-20	-5	-5	-5	-20	-5
Emergency Savings	-5	-5	-5	-5	-5	-5	-5	-5
Car Ins@ $1200 per yr.				-100				-100
Balance in bank	1210	1773	2336	2884	992	1555	2118	2666
Paycheck (After approx taxes)	873	873	873	873	873	873	873	873
Balance forward	1773	2336	2884	992	1555	2118	2666	774

Figure Six

Chapter 13	6-Dec-19	13-Dec-19	20-Dec-19	27-Dec-19	3-Jan-20	10-Jan-20	17-Jan-20	24-Jan-20
Rent/Mortgage					-1100			
Groceries	-125	-125	-125	-125	-125	-125	-125	-125
Cell					-70			
Internet/Entertainment					-45			
Heat (Yearly averge)					-65			
Electric (Yearly Average)					-70			
Water (Yearly Average)					-55			
Saving $27K to move	-130	-130	-130	-130	-130	-130	-130	-130
Health insurance					-175			
Child/Elder Care					-550			
Auto/transportation	-45	-45	-45	-45	-45	-45	-45	-45
Car Pmnt (8K@225 per mo)					-225			
Gifts/ fun/pets	-5	-50	-200	-5	-5	-5	-5	-5
Emergency Savings	-5	-5	-5	-5	-5	-5	-5	-5
Car Ins@ $1200 per yr.					-100			
Balance in bank	774	1337	1855	2223	2786	894	1457	2020
Paycheck (After approx taxes)	873	873	873	873	873	873	873	873
Balance forward	1337	1855	2223	2786	894	1457	2020	2583

Figure Seven

Chapter 13	31-Jan-20	7-Feb-20	14-Feb-20	21-Feb-20	28-Feb-20	6-Mar-20	13-Mar-20	20-Mar-20
Rent/Mortgage	-1100				-1100			
Groceries	-125	-125	-125	-125	-125	-125	-125	-125
Cell	-70				-70			
Internet/Entertainment	-45				-45			
Heat (Yearly averge)	-65				-65			
Electric (Yearly Average)	-70				-70			
Water (Yearly Average)	-55				-55			
Saving $27K to move	-130	-130	-130	-130	-130	-130	-130	-130
Health insurance	-175				-175			
Child/Elder Care	-550				-550			
Auto/transportation	-45	-45	-45	-45	-45	-45	-45	-45
Car Pmnt (8K@225 per mo)	-225				-225			
Gifts/ fun/pets	-5	-5	-5	-5	-5	-5	-5	-5
Emergency Savings	-5	-5	-5	-5	-5	-5	-5	-5
Car Ins@ $1200 per yr.	-100				-100			
Balance in bank	2583	691	1254	1817	2380	488	1051	1614
Paycheck (After approx taxes)	873	873	873	873	873	873	873	873
Balance forward	691	1254	1817	2380	488	1051	1614	2177

Figure Eight

Chapter 13	27-Mar-20	3-Apr-20	10-Apr-20	17-Apr-20	24-Apr-20	1-May-20	8-May-20	15-May-20
Rent/Mortgage	-1100					-1100		
Groceries	-125	-125	-125	-125	-125	-125	-125	-125
Cell	-70					-70		
Internet/Entertainment	-45					-45		
Heat (Yearly averge)	-65					-65		
Electric (Yearly Average)	-70					-70		
Water (Yearly Average)	-55					-55		
Saving $27K to move	-130	-130	-130	-130	-130	-130	-130	-130
Health insurance	-175					-175		
Child/Elder Care	-550					-550		
Auto/transportation	-45	-45	-45	-45	-45	-45	-45	-45
Car Payment (8K @225 per mo)	-225					-225		
Gifts/ fun/pets	-5	-5	-5	-5	-5	-5	-5	-5
Emergency Savings	-5	-5	-5	-5	-5	-5	-5	-5
Car Ins@ $1200 per yr.	-100					-100		
Balance in bank	2177	285	848	1411	1974	2537	645	1208
Paycheck (After approx taxes)	873	873	873	873	873	873	873	873
Balance forward	285	848	1411	1974	2537	645	1208	1771

Figure Nine

Chapter 13	22-May-20	29-May-20	5-Jun-20	12-Jun-20	19-Jun-20	26-Jun-20	3-Jul-20	10-Jul-20
Rent/Mortgage		-1100					-1100	
Groceries	-125	-125	-125	-125	-125	-125	-125	-125
Cell		-70					-70	
Internet/Entertainment		-45					-45	
Heat (Yearly averge)		-65					-65	
Electric (Yearly Average)		-70					-70	
Water (Yearly Average)		-55					-55	
Saving $27K to move	-130	-130	-130	-130	-130	-130	-130	-130
Health insurance		-175					-175	
Child/Elder Care		-550					-550	
Auto/transportation	-45	-45	-45	-45	-45	-45	-45	-45
Car Payment (8K @225 per mo)		-225					-225	
Gifts/ fun/pets	-5	-5	-5	-5	-5	-5	-5	-5
Emergency Savings	-5	-5	-5	-5	-5	-5	-5	-5
Car Ins@ $1200 per yr.		-100					-100	
Balance in bank	1771	2334	442	1005	1568	2131	2694	802
Paycheck (After approx taxes)	873	873	873	873	873	873	873	873
Balance forward	2334	442	1005	1568	2131	2694	802	1365

Figure Ten

Chapter 13	17-Jul-20	24-Jul-20	31-Jul-20	7-Aug-20	14-Aug-20	21-Aug-20	28-Aug-20	4-Sep-20
Rent/Mortgage			-1100					-1100
Groceries	-125	-125	-125	-125	-125	-125	-125	-125
Cell			-70					-70
Internet/Entertainment			-45					-45
Heat (Yearly averge)			-65					-65
Electric (Yearly Average)			-70					-70
Water (Yearly Average)			-55					-55
Saving $27K to move	-130	-130	-130	-130	-130	-130	-130	-130
Health insurance			-175					-175
Child/Elder Care			-550					-550
Auto/transportation	-45	-45	-45	-45	-45	-45	-45	-45
Car Payment (8K @225 per mo)			-225					-225
Gifts/ fun/pets	-5	-5	-5	-5	-5	-5	-5	-5
Emergency Savings	-5	-5	-5	-5	-5	-5	-5	-5
Car Ins@ $1200 per yr.			-100					-100
Balance in bank	1365	1928	2491	599	1162	1725	2288	2851
Paycheck (After approx taxes)	873	873	873	873	873	873	873	873
Balance forward	1928	2491	599	1162	1725	2288	2851	959

Figure Eleven

Chapter 13	11-Sep-20	18-Sep-20	25-Sep-20	2-Oct-20	9-Oct-20	16-Oct-20	23-Oct-20	30-Oct-20
Rent/Mortgage				-1100				
Groceries	-125	-125	-125	-125	-125	-125	-125	-125
Cell				-70				
Internet/Entertainment				-45				
Heat (Yearly averge)				-65				
Electric (Yearly Average)				-70				
Water (Yearly Average)				-55				
Saving $27K to move	-130	-130	-130	-130	-130	-130	-130	-130
Health insurance				-175				
Child/Elder Care				-550				
Auto/transportation	-45	-45	-45	-45	-45	-45	-45	-45
Car Payment (8K @225 per mo)				-225				
Gifts/ fun/pets	-5	-5	-5	-5	-5	-5	-20	-5
Emergency Savings	-5	-5	-5	-5	-5	-5	-5	-5
Car Ins@ $1200 per yr.				-100				
Balance in bank	959	1522	2085	2648	756	1319	1882	2430
Paycheck (After approx taxes)	873	873	873	873	873	873	873	873
Balance forward	1522	2085	2648	756	1319	1882	2430	2993

Figure Twelve

Chapter 13	6-Nov-20	13-Nov-20	20-Nov-20	27-Nov-20	4-Dec-20	11-Dec-20	18-Dec-20	25-Dec-20
Rent/Mortgage	-1100				-1100			
Groceries	-125	-125	-125	-125	-125	-125	-125	-125
Cell	-70				-70			
Internet/Entertainment	-45				-45			
Heat (Yearly averge)	-65				-65			
Electric (Yearly Average)	-70				-70			
Water (Yearly Average)	-55				-55			
Saving $27K to move	-130	-130	-130	-130	-130	-130	-130	-130
Health insurance	-175				-175			
Child/Elder Care	-550				-550			
Auto/transportation	-45	-45	-45	-45	-45	-45	-45	-45
Car Payment (8K @225 per mo)	-225				-225			
Gifts/ fun/pets	-5	-5	-20	-5	-5	-50	-200	-5
Emergency Savings	-5	-5	-5	-5	-5	-5	-5	-5
Car Ins@ $1200 per yr.	-100				-100			
Balance in bank	2993	1101	1664	2212	2775	883	1401	1769
Paycheck (After approx taxes)	873	873	873	873	873	873	873	873
Balance forward	1101	1664	2212	2775	883	1401	1769	2332

Figure Thirteen

Chapter 13	1-Jan-21	8-Jan-21	15-Jan-21	22-Jan-21	29-Jan-21	5-Feb-21	12-Feb-21	19-Feb-21
Rent/Mortgage	-1100					-1100		
Groceries	-125	-125	-125	-125	-125	-125	-125	-125
Cell	-70					-70		
Internet/Entertainment	-45					-45		
Heat (Yearly averge)	-65					-65		
Electric (Yearly Average)	-70					-70		
Water (Yearly Average)	-55					-55		
Saving $27K to move	-130	-130	-130	-130	-130	-130	-130	-130
Health insurance	-175					-175		
Child/Elder Care	-550					-550		
Auto/transportation	-45	-45	-45	-45	-45	-45	-45	-45
Car Payment (8K @225 per mo)	-225					-225		
Gifts/ fun/pets	-5	-5	-5	-5	-5	-5	-5	-5
Emergency Savings	-5	-5	-5	-5	-5	-5	-5	-5
Car Ins@ $1200 per yr.	-100					-100		
Balance in bank	2332	440	1003	1566	2129	2692	800	1363
Paycheck (After approx taxes)	873	873	873	873	873	873	873	873
Balance forward	440	1003	1566	2129	2692	800	1363	1926

Figure Fourteen

Chapter 13	26-Feb-21	5-Mar-21	12-Mar-21	19-Mar-21	26-Mar-21	2-Apr-21	9-Apr-21	16-Apr-21
Rent/Mortgage		-1100				-1100		
Groceries	-125	-125	-125	-125	-125	-125	-125	-125
Cell		-70				-70		
Internet/Entertainment		-45				-45		
Heat (Yearly averge)		-65				-65		
Electric (Yearly Average)		-70				-70		
Water (Yearly Average)		-55				-55		
Saving $27K to move	-130	-130	-130	-130	-130	-130	-130	-130
Health insurance		-175				-175		
Child/Elder Care		-550				-550		
Auto/transportation	-45	-45	-45	-45	-45	-45	-45	-45
Car Payment (8K @225 per mo)		-225				-225		
Gifts/ fun/pets	-5	-5	-5	-5	-5	-5	-5	-5
Emergency Savings	-5	-5	-5	-5	-5	-5	-5	-5
Car Ins@ $1200 per yr.		-100				-100		
Balance in bank	1926	2489	597	1160	1723	2286	394	957
Paycheck (After approx taxes)	873	873	873	873	873	873	873	873
Balance forward	2489	597	1160	1723	2286	394	957	1520

Figure Fifteen

Chapter 13	23-Apr-21	30-Apr-21	7-May-21	14-May-21	21-May-21	28-May-21	4-Jun-21	11-Jun-21
Rent/Mortgage			-1100				-1100	
Groceries	-125	-125	-125	-125	-125	-125	-125	-125
Cell			-70				-70	
Internet/Entertainment			-45				-45	
Heat (Yearly averge)			-65				-65	
Electric (Yearly Average)			-70				-70	
Water (Yearly Average)			-55				-55	
Saving $27K to move	-130	-130	-130	-130	-130	-130	-130	-130
Health insurance			-175				-175	
Child/Elder Care			-550				-550	
Auto/transportation	-45	-45	-45	-45	-45	-45	-45	-45
Car Payment (8K @225 per mo)			-225				-225	
Gifts/ fun/pets	-5	-5	-5	-5	-5	-5	-5	-5
Emergency Savings	-5	-5	-5	-5	-5	-5	-5	-5
Car Ins@ $1200 per yr.			-100				-100	
Balance in bank	1520	2083	2646	754	1317	1880	2443	551
Paycheck (After approx taxes)	873	873	873	873	873	873	873	873
Balance forward	2083	2646	754	1317	1880	2443	551	1114

Figure Sixteen

Chapter 13	18-Jun-21	25-Jun-21	2-Jul-21	9-Jul-21	16-Jul-21	23-Jul-21	30-Jul-21	6-Aug-21
Rent/Mortgage			-1100				-1100	
Groceries	-125	-125	-125	-125	-125	-125	-125	-125
Cell			-70				-70	
Internet/Entertainment			-45				-45	
Heat (Yearly averge)			-65				-65	
Electric (Yearly Average)			-70				-70	
Water (Yearly Average)			-55				-55	
Saving $27K to move	-130	-130	-130	-130	-130	-130	-130	-130
Health insurance			-175				-175	
Child/Elder Care			-550				-550	
Auto/transportation	-45	-45	-45	-45	-45	-45	-45	-45
Car Payment (8K @225 per mo)			-225				-225	
Gifts/ fun/pets	-5	-5	-5	-5	-5	-5	-5	-5
Emergency Savings	-5	-5	-5	-5	-5	-5	-5	-5
Car Ins@ $1200 per yr.			-100				-100	
Balance in bank	1114	1677	2240	348	911	1474	2037	145
Paycheck (After approx taxes)	873	873	873	873	873	873	873	873
Balance forward	1677	2240	348	911	1474	2037	145	708

Figure Seventeen

Chapter 13	13-Aug-21	20-Aug-21	27-Aug-21	3-Sep-21	10-Sep-21	17-Sep-21	24-Sep-21	1-Oct-21
Rent/Mortgage				-1100				-1100
Groceries	-125	-125	-125	-125	-125	-125	-125	-125
Cell				-70				-70
Internet/Entertainment				-45				-45
Heat (Yearly averge)				-65				-65
Electric (Yearly Average)				-70				-70
Water (Yearly Average)				-55				-55
Saving $27K to move	-130	-130	-130	-130	-130	-130	-130	-130
Health insurance				-175				-175
Child/Elder Care				-550				-550
Auto/transportation	-45	-45	-45	-45	-45	-45	-45	-45
Car Payment (8K @225 per mo)				-225				-225
Gifts/ fun/pets	-5	-5	-5	-5	-5	-5	-5	-5
Emergency Savings	-5	-5	-5	-5	-5	-5	-5	-5
Car Ins@ $1200 per yr.				-100				-100
Balance in bank	708	1271	1834	2397	505	1068	1631	2194
Paycheck (After approx taxes)	873	873	873	873	873	873	873	873
Balance forward	1271	1834	2397	505	1068	1631	2194	302

Figure Eighteen

Chapter 13	8-Oct-21	15-Oct-21	22-Oct-21	29-Oct-21	5-Nov-21	12-Nov-21	19-Nov-21	26-Nov-21
Rent/Mortgage					-1100			
Groceries	-125	-125	-125	-125	-125	-125	-125	-125
Cell					-70			
Internet/Entertainment					-45			
Heat (Yearly averge)					-65			
Electric (Yearly Average)					-70			
Water (Yearly Average)					-55			
Saving $27K to move	-130	-130	-130	-130	-130	-130	-130	-130
Health insurance					-175			
Child/Elder Care					-550			
Auto/transportation	-45	-45	-45	-45	-45	-45	-45	-45
Car Payment (8K @225 per mo)					-225			
Gifts/ fun/pets	-5	-5	-20	-5	-5	-5	-20	-5
Emergency Savings	-5	-5	-5	-5	-5	-5	-5	-5
Car Ins@ $1200 per yr.					-100			
Balance in bank	302	865	1428	1976	2539	647	1210	1758
Paycheck (After approx taxes)	873	873	873	873	873	873	873	873
Balance forward	865	1428	1976	2539	647	1210	1758	2321

Figure Nineteen

Chapter 13	3-Dec-21	10-Dec-21	17-Dec-21	24-Dec-21	31-Dec-21	7-Jan-22	14-Jan-22	21-Jan-22
Rent/Mortgage	-1100					-1100		
Groceries	-125	-125	-125	-125	-125	-125	-125	-125
Cell	-70					-70		
Internet/Entertainment	-45					-45		
Heat (Yearly averge)	-65					-65		
Electric (Yearly Average)	-70					-70		
Water (Yearly Average)	-55					-55		
Saving $27K to move	-130	-130	-130	-130	-130	-130	-130	-130
Health insurance	-175					-175		
Child/Elder Care	-550					-550		
Auto/transportation	-45	-45	-45	-45	-45	-45	-45	-45
Car Payment (8K @225 per mo)	-225					-225		
Gifts/ fun/pets	-5	-50	-200	-5	-5	-5	-5	-5
Emergency Savings	-5	-5	-5	-5	-5	-5	-5	-5
Car Ins@ $1200 per yr.	-100					-100		
Balance in bank	2321	429	947	1315	1878	2441	549	1112
Paycheck (After approx taxes)	873	873	873	873	873	873	873	873
Balance forward	429	947	1315	1878	2441	549	1112	1675

Figure Twenty

Chapter 13	28-Jan-22	4-Feb-22	11-Feb-22	18-Feb-22	25-Feb-22	4-Mar-22	11-Mar-22	18-Mar-22
Rent/Mortgage		-1100				-1100		
Groceries	-125	-125	-125	-125	-125	-125	-125	-125
Cell		-70				-70		
Internet/Entertainment		-45				-45		
Heat (Yearly averge)		-65				-65		
Electric (Yearly Average)		-70				-70		
Water (Yearly Average)		-55				-55		
Saving $27K to move	-130	-130	-180	-180	-180	-180	-180	-180
Health insurance		-175				-175		
Child/Elder Care		-550				-550		
Auto/transportation	-45	-45	-45	-45	-45	-45	-45	-45
Car Payment (8K @225 per mo)								
Gifts/ fun/pets	-5	-5	-5	-5	-5	-5	-5	-5
Emergency Savings	-5	-5	-5	-5	-5	-5	-5	-5
Car Ins@ $1200 per yr.		-100				-100		
Balance in bank	1675	2238	571	1084	1597	2110	393	906
Paycheck (After approx taxes)	873	873	873	873	873	873	873	873
Balance forward	2238	571	1084	1597	2110	393	906	1419

Figure Twenty One

You have just paid off your car loan
NOW extra money goes to your HOUSE fund!

Chapter 13	25-Mar-22	1-Apr-22	8-Apr-22	15-Apr-22	22-Apr-22	29-Apr-22	6-May-22	13-May-22
Rent/Mortgage		-1100				-1100		
Groceries	-125	-125	-125	-125	-125	-125	-125	-125
Cell		-70				-70		
Internet/Entertainment		-45				-45		
Heat (Yearly averge)		-65				-65		
Electric (Yearly Average)		-70				-70		
Water (Yearly Average)		-55				-55		
Saving $27K to move	-180	-180	-180	-180	-180	-180	-180	-180
Health insurance		-175				-175		
Child/Elder Care		-550				-550		
Auto/transportation	-45	-45	-45	-45	-45	-45	-45	-45
Car Payment (8K @225 per mo)								
Gifts/ fun/pets	-5	-5	-5	-5	-5	-5	-5	-10
Emergency Savings	-5	-5	-5	-5	-5	-5	-5	-10
Car Ins. @ $1200 per year.		-100				-100		
Balance in bank	1419	1932	215	728	1241	1754	37	550
Paycheck (After approx taxes)	873	873	873	873	873	873	873	873
Balance forward	1932	215	728	1241	1754	37	550	1053

Figure Twenty Two

Chapter 13	20-May-22	27-May-22	3-Jun-22	10-Jun-22	17-Jun-22	24-Jun-22	1-Jul-22	8-Jul-22
Rent/Mortgage			-1100				-1100	
Groceries	-125	-125	-125	-125	-125	-125	-125	-125
Cell			-70				-70	
Internet/Entertainment			-45				-45	
Heat (Yearly averge)			-65				-65	
Electric (Yearly Average)			-70				-70	
Water (Yearly Average)			-55				-55	
Saving $27K to move	-180	-180	-180	-180	-180	-180	-180	-180
Health insurance			-175				-175	
Child/Elder Care			-550				-550	
Auto/transportation	-45	-45	-45	-45	-45	-45	-45	-45
Car Payment (8K @225 per mo)								
Gifts/ fun/pets	-10	-10	-10	-10	-10	-10	-10	-10
Emergency Savings	-10	-10	-10	-10	-10	-10	-10	-10
Car Ins. @ $1200 per year.			-100				-100	
Balance in bank	1053	1556	2059	332	835	1338	1841	114
Paycheck (After approx taxes)	873	873	873	873	873	873	873	873
Balance forward	1556	2059	332	835	1338	1841	114	617

Figure Twenty Three

Chapter 13	15-Jul-22	22-Jul-22	29-Jul-22	5-Aug-22	12-Aug-22	19-Aug-22	26-Aug-22	2-Sep-22
Rent/Mortgage				-1100				-1100
Groceries	-125	-125	-125	-125	-125	-125	-125	-125
Cell				-70				-70
Internet/Entertainment				-45				-45
Heat (Yearly averge)				-65				-65
Electric (Yearly Average)				-70				-70
Water (Yearly Average)				-55				-55
Saving $27K to move	-180	-180	-180	-180	-180	-180	-180	-180
Health insurance				-175				-175
Child/Elder Care				-550				-550
Auto/transportation	-45	-45	-45	-45	-45	-45	-45	-45
Car Payment (8K @225 per mo)								
Gifts/ fun/pets	-10	-10	-10	-10	-10	-10	-5	-10
Emergency Savings	-10	-10	-10	-10	-10	-10	-5	-10
Car Ins. @ $1200 per year.				-100				-100
Balance in bank	617	1120	1623	2126	399	902	1405	1918
Paycheck (After approx taxes)	873	873	873	873	873	873	873	873
Balance forward	1120	1623	2126	399	902	1405	1918	191

Figure Twenty Four

Chapter 13	9-Sep-22	16-Sep-22	23-Sep-22	30-Sep-22	7-Oct-22	14-Oct-22	21-Oct-22	28-Oct-22
Rent/Mortgage					-1100			
Groceries	-125	-125	-125	-125	-125	-125	-125	-125
Cell					-70			
Internet/Entertainment					-45			
Heat (Yearly averge)					-65			
Electric (Yearly Average)					-70			
Water (Yearly Average)					-55			
Saving $27K to move	-180	-180	-180	-180	-180	-180	-180	-180
Health insurance					-175			
Child/Elder Care					-550			
Auto/transportation	-45	-45	-45	-45	-45	-45	-45	-45
Car Payment (8K @225 per mo)								
Gifts/ fun/pets	-10	-10	-10	-10	-10	-10	-10	-10
Emergency Savings	-10	-10	-10	-10	-10	-10	-10	-10
Car Ins. @ $1200 per year.					-100			
Balance in bank	191	694	1197	1701	2206	482	989	1497
Paycheck (After approx taxes)	873	873	874	875	876	877	878	879
Balance forward	694	1197	1701	2206	482	989	1497	2006

Figure Twenty Five

By October 22, you should have the down payment on the home.
BUT- DO NOT stop saving the same amount until you actually
SIGN the contract and move in. That way you will have extra
cash for furniture or a move in party!

CHAPTER Fourteen

Saving to Start A Business

You have a spouse and 1 dependant - and you have a mortgage. You and your spouse each earn $40,000.00 per year. You own two cars. Your goal is to save $50,000.00 to start a business/buy a franchise.

♦ Rent : Your Mortgage is $1,400.00 per month.

♦ Groceries: This may not look like a lot, but if you create menus, cook and home and plan your food budget properly you can save yourself a lot of heartache and money. Not to mention eating healthier! Suggested menus and grocery lists are included at the end of the book!

♦ Cell: You can choose from many good phone plans and a lot of them have discounts.

♦ Internet/Entertainment: You may have an on line subscription or something similar, like Hulu or Xbox gold.

♦ Heat, Water, Electric: These are an average of average monthly utility expenses. Depending on where you are and what types of appliances you run, these expenses can and will vary.

♦ Save for Business: This exact amount should be put in to a separate bank account every week. This must be a savings account that pays interest. The interest is not likely to be a LOT. It will probably be 1% or less. But as it accumulates in YOUR account it will make certain that you reach your $50,000.00 Business goals faster. Then, at the end of only 177 weeks, YOU will have the cash savings you need to look into a good business investment.

♦ Health Insurance: You may have a personal policy that you pay monthly. Your employer may withhold this amount from your check in weekly increments. If you have no insurance - SAVE this amount anyway.

♦ Transportation: Having two jobs means a need for transportation.

♦ Gifts/Fun: It is going to happen so you need to put it in your budget. You do not have to spend that much. You can even SAVE it for a special treat…. but do not spend more.

♦ Emergency Savings: Put this amount aside every week in case of a Real emergency. Medical or a death in the family qualify. If your car breaks and you need it for work - THAT is an emergency.

♦ Balance in Bank: That is what you should have in your bank account at the end of all transactions in order to stay on your budget. At the beginning of this budget you are starting with $1,500.00 in your bank acount that you have saved using another budget.

♦ Paycheck: This is an average, because tax laws vary from state to state and even from city to city. If you are on salary, your pay will be the same every week. You can copy the exact figure from your pay stub. If you are an hourly worker, your net pay will change from week to week. An adjustent has been made to account for the two incomes plus a dependent deduction you will get on your taxes. Some companies give annual or even semi-annual pay increases.

♦ Balance forward: This is what is left after you pay your expenses. This money cannot be spent – it is carried forward to the next period. This is why you budget –so you remember to not spend all of your money!

Chapter 14	4-Jan-19	11-Jan-19	18-Jan-19	25-Jan-19	1-Feb-19	8-Feb-19	15-Feb-19	22-Feb-19
Rent/Mortgage	-1,400				-1,400			
Groceries	-130	-130	-130	-130	-130	-130	-130	-130
Cell	-125				-125			
Internet/Entertainment	-75				-75			
Heat	-75				-75			
Electric	-75				-75			
Water	-60				-60			
Child care/After School Care	-120	-120	-120	-120	-120	-120	-120	-120
Save for Business	0	-285	-285	-285	-285	-285	-285	-285
Health insurance	-200				-200			
Auto/transportation	-50	-50	-50	-50	-50	-50	-50	-50
Gifts/ fun/pets	-20	-20	-20	-20	-20	-20	-20	-20
Emergency Savings	-25	-25	-25	-25	-25	-25	-25	-25
Car Ins@$1,200 per year.	-100				-100			
Balance in bank	1,500	195	715	1235	1755	165	685	1205
Paychecks (After approx taxes)	1,150	1,150	1,150	1,150	1,150	1,150	1,150	1,150
Balance forward	195	715	1235	1755	165	685	1205	1725
Figure One								

Chapter 14	1-Mar-19	8-Mar-19	15-Mar-19	22-Mar-19	29-Mar-19	5-Apr-19	12-Apr-19	19-Apr-19
Rent/Mortgage	-1,400				-1,400			
Groceries	-130	-130	-130	-130	-130	-130	-130	-130
Cell	-125				-125			
Internet/Entertainment	-75				-75			
Heat	-75				-75			
Electric	-75				-75			
Water	-60				-60			
Child care/After School Care	-120	-120	-120	-120	-120	-120	-120	-120
Save for Business	-285	-285	-285	-285	-285	-285	-285	-285
Health insurance	-200				-200			
Auto/transportation	-50	-50	-50	-50	-50	-50	-50	-50
Gifts/ fun/pets	-20	-20	-20	-20	-20	-20	-20	-20
Emergency Savings	-25	-25	-25	-25	-25	-25	-25	-25
Car Ins@$1,200 per year.	-100				-100			
Balance in bank	1725	135	655	1175	1695	105	625	1145
Paychecks (After approx taxes)	1,150	1,150	1,150	1,150	1,150	1,150	1,150	1,150
Balance forward	135	655	1175	1695	105	625	1145	1665
Figure Two								

Chapter 14	26-Apr-19	3-May-19	10-May-19	17-May-19	24-May-19	31-May-19	7-Jun-19	14-Jun-19
Rent/Mortgage		-1,400				-1,400		
Groceries	-130	-130	-130	-130	-130	-130	-130	-130
Cell		-125				-125		
Internet/Entertainment		-75				-75		
Heat		-75				-75		
Electric		-75				-75		
Water		-60				-60		
Child care/After School Care	-120	-120	-120	-120	-120	-120	-120	-120
Save for Business	-285	-285	-285	-285	-285	-285	-285	-285
Health insurance		-200				-200		
Auto/transportation	-50	-50	-50	-50	-50	-50	-50	-50
Gifts/ fun/pets	-20	-20	-20	-20	-20	-20	-20	-20
Emergency Savings	-25	-25	-25	-25	-25	-25	-25	-25
Car Ins@$1,200 per year.		-100				-100		
Balance in bank	1665	2185	595	1115	1635	2155	565	1085
Paychecks (After approx taxes)	1,150	1,150	1,150	1,150	1,150	1,150	1,150	1,150
Balance forward	2185	595	1115	1635	2155	565	1085	1605

Figure Three

Chapter 14	21-Jun-19	28-Jun-19	5-Jul-19	12-Jul-19	19-Jul-19	26-Jul-19	2-Aug-19	9-Aug-19
Rent/Mortgage		-1,400					-1,400	
Groceries	-130	-130	-130	-130	-130	-130	-130	-130
Cell		-125					-125	
Internet/Entertainment		-75					-75	
Heat		-75					-75	
Electric		-75					-75	
Water		-60					-60	
Child care/After School Care	-120	-120	-120	-120	-120	-120	-120	-120
Save for Business	-285	-285	-285	-285	-285	-285	-285	-285
Health insurance		-200					-200	
Auto/transportation	-50	-50	-50	-50	-50	-50	-50	-50
Gifts/ fun/pets	-20	-20	-20	-20	-20	-20	-20	-20
Emergency Savings	-25	-25	-25	-25	-25	-25	-25	-25
Car Ins@$1,200 per year.		-100					-100	
Balance in bank	1605	2125	535	1055	1575	2095	2615	1025
Paychecks (After approx taxes)	1,150	1,150	1,150	1,150	1,150	1,150	1,150	1,150
Balance forward	2125	535	1055	1575	2095	2615	1025	1545

Figure Four

Chapter 14	16-Aug-19	23-Aug-19	30-Aug-19	6-Sep-19	13-Sep-19	20-Sep-19	27-Sep-19	4-Oct-19
Rent/Mortgage			-1,400					-1,400
Groceries	-130	-130	-130	-130	-130	-130	-130	-130
Cell			-125					-125
Internet/Entertainment			-75					-75
Heat			-75					-75
Electric			-75					-75
Water			-60					-60
Child care/After School Care	-120	-120	-120	-120	-120	-120	-120	-120
Save for Business	-285	-285	-285	-285	-285	-285	-285	-285
Health insurance			-200					-200
Auto/transportation	-50	-50	-50	-50	-50	-50	-50	-50
Gifts/ fun/pets	-20	-20	-20	-20	-20	-20	-20	-20
Emergency Savings	-25	-25	-25	-25	-25	-25	-25	-25
Car Ins@$1,200 per year.			-100					-100
Balance in bank	1545	2065	2585	995	1515	2035	2555	3075
Paychecks (After approx taxes)	1,150	1,150	1,150	1,150	1,150	1,150	1,150	1,150
Balance forward	2065	2585	995	1515	2035	2555	3075	1485
Figure Five								

Chapter 14	11-Oct-19	18-Oct-19	25-Oct-19	1-Nov-19	8-Nov-19	15-Nov-19	22-Nov-19	29-Nov-19
Rent/Mortgage				-1,400				-1,400
Groceries	-130	-130	-130	-130	-130	-130	-130	-130
Cell				-125				-125
Internet/Entertainment				-75				-75
Heat				-75				-75
Electric				-75				-75
Water				-60				-60
Child care/After School Care	-120	-120	-120	-120	-120	-120	-120	-120
Save for Business	-285	-285	-285	-285	-285	-285	-285	-285
Health insurance				-200				-200
Auto/transportation	-50	-50	-50	-50	-50	-50	-50	-50
Gifts/ fun/pets	-20	-20	-50	-20	-20	-20	-20	-20
Emergency Savings	-25	-25	-25	-25	-25	-25	-25	-25
Car Ins@$1,200 per year.				-100				-100
Balance in bank	1485	2005	2525	3015	1425	1945	2465	2985
Paychecks (After approx taxes)	1,150	1,150	1,150	1,150	1,150	1,150	1,150	1,150
Balance forward	2005	2525	3015	1425	1945	2465	2985	1395
Figure Six								

Chapter 14	6-Dec-19	13-Dec-19	20-Dec-19	27-Dec-19	3-Jan-20	10-Jan-20	17-Jan-20	24-Jan-20
Rent/Mortgage					-1,400			
Groceries	-130	-130	-130	-130	-130	-130	-130	-130
Cell					-125			
Internet/Entertainment					-75			
Heat					-75			
Electric					-75			
Water					-60			
Child care/After School Care	-120	-120	-120	-120	-120	-120	-120	-120
Save for Business	-285	-285	-285	-285	-285	-285	-285	-285
Health insurance					-200			
Auto/transportation	-50	-50	-50	-50	-50	-50	-50	-50
Gifts/ fun/pets	-20	-250	-20	-20	-20	-20	-20	-20
Emergency Savings	-25	-25	-25	-25	-25	-25	-25	-25
Car Ins@$1,200 per year.					-100			
Balance in bank	2395	2915	3205	3725	4245	2655	3175	3695
Paychecks (After approx taxes)	1,150	1,150	1,150	1,150	1,150	1,150	1,150	1,150
Balance forward	2915	3205	3725	4245	2655	3175	3695	4215

Figure Seven

Chapter 14	31-Jan-20	7-Feb-20	14-Feb-20	21-Feb-20	28-Feb-20	6-Mar-20	13-Mar-20	20-Mar-20
Rent/Mortgage	-1,400				-1,400			
Groceries	-130	-130	-130	-130	-130	-130	-130	-130
Cell	-125				-125			
Internet/Entertainment	-75				-75			
Heat	-75				-75			
Electric	-75				-75			
Water	-60				-60			
Child care/After School Care	-120	-120	-120	-120	-120	-120	-120	-120
Save for Business	-285	-285	-285	-285	-285	-285	-285	-285
Health insurance	-200				-200			
Auto/transportation	-50	-50	-50	-50	-50	-50	-50	-50
Gifts/ fun/pets	-20	-20	-20	-20	-20	-20	-20	-20
Emergency Savings	-25	-25	-25	-25	-25	-25	-25	-25
Car Ins@$1,200 per year.	-100				-100			
Balance in bank	4215	2625	3145	3665	4185	2595	3115	3635
Paychecks (After approx taxes)	1,150	1,150	1,150	1,150	1,150	1,150	1,150	1,150
Balance forward	2625	3145	3665	4185	2595	3115	3635	4155

Figure Eight

Chapter 14	27-Mar-20	3-Apr-20	10-Apr-20	17-Apr-20	24-Apr-20	1-May-20	8-May-20	15-May-20
Rent/Mortgage	-1,400					-1,400		
Groceries	-130	-130	-130	-130	-130	-130	-130	-130
Cell	-125					-125		
Internet/Entertainment	-75					-75		
Heat	-75					-75		
Electric	-75					-75		
Water	-60					-60		
Child care/After School Care	-120	-120	-120	-120	-120	-120	-120	-120
Save for Business	-285	-285	-285	-285	-285	-285	-285	-285
Health insurance	-200					-200		
Auto/transportation	-50	-50	-50	-50	-50	-50	-50	-50
Gifts/ fun/pets	-20	-20	-20	-20	-20	-20	-20	-20
Emergency Savings	-25	-25	-25	-25	-25	-25	-25	-25
Car Ins@$1,200 per year.	-100					-100		
Balance in bank	4155	2565	3085	3605	4125	4645	3055	3575
Paychecks (After approx taxes)	1,150	1,150	1,150	1,150	1,150	1,150	1,150	1,150
Balance forward	2565	3085	3605	4125	4645	3055	3575	4095
Figure Nine								

Chapter 14	22-May-20	29-May-20	5-Jun-20	12-Jun-20	19-Jun-20	26-Jun-20	3-Jul-20	10-Jul-20
Rent/Mortgage		-1,400					-1,400	
Groceries	-130	-130	-130	-130	-130	-130	-130	-130
Cell		-125					-125	
Internet/Entertainment		-75					-75	
Heat		-75					-75	
Electric		-75					-75	
Water		-60					-60	
Child care/After School Care	-120	-120	-120	-120	-120	-120	-120	-120
Save for Business	-285	-285	-285	-285	-285	-285	-285	-285
Health insurance		-200					-200	
Auto/transportation	-50	-50	-50	-50	-50	-50	-50	-50
Gifts/ fun/pets	-20	-20	-20	-20	-20	-20	-20	-20
Emergency Savings	-25	-25	-25	-25	-25	-25	-25	-25
Car Ins@$1,200 per year.		-100					-100	
Balance in bank	4095	4615	3025	3545	4065	4585	5105	3515
Paychecks (After approx taxes)	1,150	1,150	1,150	1,150	1,150	1,150	1,150	1,150
Balance forward	4615	3025	3545	4065	4585	5105	3515	4035
Figure Ten								

Chapter 14	17-Jul-20	24-Jul-20	31-Jul-20	7-Aug-20	14-Aug-20	21-Aug-20	28-Aug-20	4-Sep-20
Rent/Mortgage			-1,400					-1,400
Groceries	-130	-130	-130	-130	-130	-130	-130	-130
Cell			-125					-125
Internet/Entertainment			-75					-75
Heat			-75					-75
Electric			-75					-75
Water			-60					-60
Child care/After School Care	-120	-120	-120	-120	-120	-120	-120	-120
Save for Business	-285	-285	-285	-285	-285	-285	-285	-285
Health insurance			-200					-200
Auto/transportation	-50	-50	-50	-50	-50	-50	-50	-50
Gifts/ fun/pets	-20	-20	-20	-20	-20	-20	-20	-20
Emergency Savings	-25	-25	-25	-25	-25	-25	-25	-25
Car Ins@$1,200 per year.			-100					-100
Balance in bank	4035	4555	5075	3485	4005	4525	5045	5565
Paychecks (After approx taxes)	1,150	1,150	1,150	1,150	1,150	1,150	1,150	1,150
Balance forward	4555	5075	3485	4005	4525	5045	5565	3975
Figure Eleven								

Chapter 16	11-Sep-20	18-Sep-20	25-Sep-20	2-Oct-20	9-Oct-20	16-Oct-20	23-Oct-20	30-Oct-20
Rent/Mortgage			-1,400					-1,400
Groceries	-130	-130	-130	-130	-130	-130	-130	-130
Cell			-125					-125
Internet/Entertainment			-75					-75
Heat			-75					-75
Electric			-75					-75
Water			-60					-60
Child care/After School Care	-120	-120	-120	-120	-120	-120	-120	-120
Save for Business	-285	-285	-285	-285	-285	-285	-285	-285
Health insurance			-200					-200
Auto/transportation	-50	-50	-50	-50	-50	-50	-50	-50
Gifts/ fun/pets	-20	-20	-20	-20	-20	-20	-50	-20
Emergency Savings	-25	-25	-25	-25	-25	-25	-25	-25
Car Ins@$1,200 per year.			-100					-100
Balance in bank	3975	4495	5015	3425	3945	4465	4985	5475
Paychecks (After approx taxes)	1,150	1,150	1,150	1,150	1,150	1,150	1,150	1,150
Balance forward	4495	5015	3425	3945	4465	4985	5475	3885
Figure Twelve								

Chapter 14	6-Nov-20	13-Nov-20	20-Nov-20	27-Nov-20	4-Dec-20	11-Dec-20	18-Dec-20	25-Dec-20
Rent/Mortgage				-1,400				
Groceries	-130	-130	-130	-130	-130	-130	-130	-130
Cell				-125				
Internet/Entertainment				-75				
Heat				-75				
Electric				-75				
Water				-60				
Child care/After School Care	-120	-120	-120	-120	-120	-120	-120	-120
Save for Business	-285	-285	-285	-285	-285	-285	-285	-285
Health insurance				-200				
Auto/transportation	-50	-50	-50	-50	-50	-50	-50	-50
Gifts/ fun/pets	-20	-20	-20	-20	-20	-300	-35	-35
Emergency Savings	-25	-25	-25	-25	-25	-25	-40	-40
Car Ins@$1,200 per year.				-100				
Balance in bank	3885	4405	4925	5445	3855	4375	4615	5105
Paychecks (After approx taxes)	1,150	1,150	1,150	1,150	1,150	1,150	1,150	1,150
Balance forward	4405	4925	5445	3855	4375	4615	5105	5595
Figure Thirteen								

Chapter 14	1-Jan-21	8-Jan-21	15-Jan-21	22-Jan-21	29-Jan-21	5-Feb-21	12-Feb-21	19-Feb-21
Rent/Mortgage	-1,400				-1,400			
Groceries	-130	-130	-130	-130	-130	-130	-130	-130
Cell	-125				-125			
Internet/Entertainment	-75				-75			
Heat	-75				-75			
Electric	-75				-75			
Water	-60				-60			
Child care/After School Care	-120	-120	-120	-120	-120	-120	-120	-120
Save for Business	-285	-285	-285	-285	-285	-285	-285	-285
Health insurance	-200				-200			
Auto/transportation	-50	-50	-50	-50	-50	-50	-50	-50
Gifts/ fun/pets	-35	-35	-35	-35	-35	-35	-35	-35
Emergency Savings	-40	-40	-40	-40	-40	-40	-40	-40
Car Ins@$1,200 per year.	-100				-100			
Balance in bank	5595	3975	4465	4955	5445	3825	4315	4805
Paychecks (After approx taxes)	1,150	1,150	1,150	1,150	1,150	1,150	1,150	1,150
Balance forward	3975	4465	4955	5445	3825	4315	4805	5295
Figure Fourteen								

Chapter 14	26-Feb-21	5-Mar-21	12-Mar-21	19-Mar-21	26-Mar-21	2-Apr-21	9-Apr-21	16-Apr-21
Rent/Mortgage		-1,400				-1,400		
Groceries	-130	-130	-130	-130	-130	-130	-130	-130
Cell		-125				-125		
Internet/Entertainment		-75				-75		
Heat		-75				-75		
Electric		-75				-75		
Water		-60				-60		
Child care/After School Care	-120	-120	-120	-120	-120	-120	-120	-120
Save for Business	-285	-285	-285	-285	-285	-285	-285	-285
Health insurance		-200				-200		
Auto/transportation	-50	-50	-50	-50	-50	-50	-50	-50
Gifts/ fun/pets	-35	-35	-35	-35	-35	-35	-35	-35
Emergency Savings	-40	-40	-40	-40	-40	-40	-40	-40
Car Ins@$1,200 per year.		-100				-100		
Balance in bank	5295	5785	4165	4655	5145	5635	4015	4505
Paychecks (After approx taxes)	1,150	1,150	1,150	1,150	1,150	1,150	1,150	1,150
Balance forward	5785	4165	4655	5145	5635	4015	4505	4995
Figure Fifteen								

Chapter 14	23-Apr-21	30-Apr-21	7-May-21	14-May-21	21-May-21	28-May-21	4-Jun-21	11-Jun-21
Rent/Mortgage			-1,400				-1,400	
Groceries	-130	-130	-130	-130	-130	-130	-130	-130
Cell			-125				-125	
Internet/Entertainment			-75				-75	
Heat			-75				-75	
Electric			-75				-75	
Water			-60				-60	
Child care/After School Care	-120	-120	-120	-120	-120	-120	-120	-120
Save for Business	-285	-285	-285	-285	-285	-285	-285	-285
Health insurance			-200				-200	
Auto/transportation	-50	-50	-50	-50	-50	-50	-50	-50
Gifts/ fun/pets	-35	-35	-35	-35	-35	-35	-35	-35
Emergency Savings	-40	-40	-40	-40	-40	-40	-40	-40
Car Ins@$1,200 per year.			-100				-100	
Balance in bank	4995	5485	5975	4355	4845	5335	5825	4205
Paychecks (After approx taxes)	1,150	1,150	1,150	1,150	1,150	1,150	1,150	1,150
Balance forward	5485	5975	4355	4845	5335	5825	4205	4695
Figure Sixteen								

Chapter 14	18-Jun-21	25-Jun-21	2-Jul-21	9-Jul-21	16-Jul-21	23-Jul-21	30-Jul-21	6-Aug-21
Rent/Mortgage			-1,400				-1,400	
Groceries	-130	-130	-130	-130	-130	-130	-130	-130
Cell			-125				-125	
Internet/Entertainment			-75				-75	
Heat			-75				-75	
Electric			-75				-75	
Water			-60				-60	
Child care/After School Care	-120	-120	-120	-120	-120	-120	-120	-120
Save for Business	-285	-285	-285	-285	-285	-285	-285	-285
Health insurance			-200				-200	
Auto/transportation	-50	-50	-50	-50	-50	-50	-50	-50
Gifts/ fun/pets	-35	-35	-35	-35	-35	-35	-35	-35
Emergency Savings	-40	-40	-40	-40	-40	-40	-40	-40
Car Ins@$1,200 per year.			-100				-100	
Balance in bank	4695	5185	5675	4055	4545	5035	5525	3905
Paychecks (After approx taxes)	1,150	1,150	1,150	1,150	1,150	1,150	1,150	1,150
Balance forward	5185	5675	4055	4545	5035	5525	3905	4395
Figure Seventeen								

Chapter 14	13-Aug-21	20-Aug-21	27-Aug-21	3-Sep-21	10-Sep-21	17-Sep-21	24-Sep-21	1-Oct-21
Rent/Mortgage				-1,400				-1,400
Groceries	-130	-130	-130	-130	-130	-130	-130	-130
Cell				-125				-125
Internet/Entertainment				-75				-75
Heat				-75				-75
Electric				-75				-75
Water				-60				-60
Child care/After School Care	-120	-120	-120	-120	-120	-120	-120	-120
Save for Business	-285	-285	-285	-285	-285	-285	-285	-285
Health insurance				-200				-200
Auto/transportation	-50	-50	-50	-50	-50	-50	-50	-50
Gifts/ fun/pets	-35	-35	-35	-35	-35	-35	-35	-35
Emergency Savings	-40	-40	-40	-40	-40	-40	-40	-40
Car Ins@$1,200 per year.				-100				-100
Balance in bank	4395	4885	5375	5865	4245	4735	5225	5715
Paychecks (After approx taxes)	1,150	1,150	1,150	1,150	1,150	1,150	1,150	1,150
Balance forward	4885	5375	5865	4245	4735	5225	5715	4095
Figure Eighteen								

Chapter 14	8-Oct-21	15-Oct-21	22-Oct-21	29-Oct-21	5-Nov-21	12-Nov-21	19-Nov-21	26-Nov-21
Rent/Mortgage				-1,400				
Groceries	-130	-130	-130	-130	-130	-130	-130	-130
Cell				-125				
Internet/Entertainment				-75				
Heat				-75				
Electric				-75				
Water				-60				
Child care/After School Care	-120	-120	-120	-120	-120	-120	-120	-120
Save for Business	-285	-285	-285	-285	-285	-285	-285	-285
Health insurance				-200				
Auto/transportation	-50	-50	-50	-50	-50	-50	-50	-50
Gifts/ fun/pets	-35	-35	-50	-35	-35	-35	-35	-35
Emergency Savings	-40	-40	-40	-40	-40	-40	-40	-40
Car Ins@$1,200 per year.				-100				
Balance in bank	4095	4585	5075	5550	3930	4420	4910	5400
Paychecks (After approx taxes)	1,150	1,150	1,150	1,150	1,150	1,150	1,150	1,150
Balance forward	4585	5075	5550	3930	4420	4910	5400	5890
Figure Nineteen								

Chapter 14	3-Dec-21	10-Dec-21	17-Dec-21	24-Dec-21	31-Dec-21	7-Jan-22	14-Jan-22	21-Jan-22
Rent/Mortgage	-1,400				-1,400			
Groceries	-130	-130	-130	-130	-130	-130	-130	-130
Cell	-125				-125			
Internet/Entertainment	-75				-75			
Heat	-75				-75			
Electric	-75				-75			
Water	-60				-60			
Child care/After School Care	-120	-120	-120	-120	-120	-120	-120	-120
Save for Business	-285	-285	-285	-285	-285	-285	-285	-285
Health insurance	-200				-200			
Auto/transportation	-50	-50	-50	-50	-50	-50	-50	-50
Gifts/ fun/pets	-35	-250	-40	-40	-40	-40	-40	-40
Emergency Savings	-40	-40	-50	-50	-50	-50	-50	-50
Car Ins@$1,200 per year.	-100				-100			
Balance in bank	5890	4270	4545	5020	5495	3860	4335	4810
Paychecks (After approx taxes)	1,150	1,150	1,150	1,150	1,150	1,150	1,150	1,150
Balance forward	4270	4545	5020	5495	3860	4335	4810	5285
Figure Twenty								

Chapter 14	28-Jan-22	4-Feb-22	11-Feb-22	18-Feb-22	25-Feb-22	4-Mar-22	11-Mar-22	18-Mar-22
Rent/Mortgage		-1,400				-1,400		
Groceries	-130	-130	-130	-130	-130	-130	-130	-130
Cell		-125				-125		
Internet/Entertainment		-75				-75		
Heat		-75				-75		
Electric		-75				-75		
Water		-60				-60		
Child care/After School Care	-120	-120	-120	-120	-120	-120	-120	-120
Save for Business	-285	-285	-285	-285	-285	-285	-285	-285
Health insurance		-200				-200		
Auto/transportation	-50	-50	-50	-50	-50	-50	-50	-50
Gifts/ fun/pets	-40	-40	-40	-40	-40	-40	-40	-40
Emergency Savings	-50	-50	-50	-50	-50	-50	-50	-50
Car Ins@$1,200 per year.		-100	-100	-100	-100	-100	-100	-100
Balance in bank	5285	5760	4125	4501	4878	5256	3625	4005
Paychecks (After approx taxes)	1,150	1,150	1,151	1,152	1,153	1,154	1,155	1,156
Balance forward	5760	4125	4501	4878	5256	3625	4005	4386
Figure Twenty One								

Chapter 14	25-Mar-22	1-Apr-22	8-Apr-22	15-Apr-22	22-Apr-22	29-Apr-22	6-May-22	13-May-22
Rent/Mortgage		-1,400					-1,400	
Groceries	-130	-130	-130	-130	-130	-130	-130	-130
Cell		-125					-125	
Internet/Entertainment		-75					-75	
Heat		-75					-75	
Electric		-75					-75	
Water		-60					-60	
Child care/After School Care	-120	-120	-120	-120	-120	-120	-120	-120
Save for Business	-285	-285	-285	-285	-285	-285	-285	-285
Health insurance		-200					-200	
Auto/transportation	-50	-50	-50	-50	-50	-50	-50	-50
Gifts/ fun/pets	-40	-40	-40	-40	-40	-40	-40	-40
Emergency Savings	-50	-50	-50	-50	-50	-50	-50	-50
Car Ins@$1,200 per year.	-100	-100	-100	-100	-100	-100	-100	-100
Balance in bank	4386	4768	3141	3525	3910	4296	4683	3061
Paychecks (After approx taxes)	1,157	1,158	1,159	1,160	1,161	1,162	1,163	1,164
Balance forward	4768	3141	3525	3910	4296	4683	3061	3450
Figure Twenty Two								

Groceries

The best way to save money is to cook yourself filling and nutritious meals. When you feed yourself at home and you learn to prepare food yourself, you don't spend extra cash in restaurants and you avoid Doctor's visits because you stay healthy.

Unfortunately , very many people have never learned how to live with and use a kitchen properly. Neither have they learned how to stock a kitchen and shop for groceries in a meal based manner.

This section will be of help to folks who are setting up a kitchen and grocery budget for the first time.

Must Have Items	Cost
Crockpot	35.00
Food Storage- freezer safe	10.00
Toilet paper	3.00
Laundry Soap	5.00
Dryer Sheets	3.00
Dish Soap	2.00
Spray Cleaner	3.00
Papertowels	3.00
5lbs all purpose flour	3.00
can of baking soda	2.00
can of baking powder	2.00
2lbs white sugar	3.00
2lbs confectioners sugar	3.00
coco powder	4.00
Vanilla extract	5.00
Katsup	2.00
mustard	2.00
mayonaise	3.00
pickle relish	2.00
Corn Meal	5.00
Coffee/tea/etc	10.00
eggs	3.00
butter	4.00
olive oil	4.00
aluminium foil	3.00
canola oil	2.00
salt	1.00
black pepper	2.00
bullion cubes	2.00
cinnamon	4.00
Chili Powder	3.00
Cumin	3.00
italian seasoning	3.00
basil	4.00
oregano	4.00
Total	**152**

Groceries	Cost
1/2 gal milk	3.00
2 box cereal	6.00
Bread	3.00
Fresh carrots	1.49
lettuce	2.99
Tomatoes	3.00
Potatoes 3 lbs for 3	3.00
Onions 3lbs @ 3	3.00
Chicken 4lbs@1.39	5.56
garlic	1.59
Cheese	3.00
pasta sauce	2.25
eggnoodles	1.79
London Broil	3.49
Can of tuna	1.49
1/4 lb sliced turkey	3.00
pasta	1.00
apples	3.00
brownie mix	3.00
Sweet potatoes	3.00
Butter	4.00
Gravey	1.35
green beans	1.09
Sweet pepper	2.99
Adobo	5.59
Celery	1.79
Bay Leaf	3.59
Stew packet	1.29
italian seasoning	2.49
Salt	2.39
Black Pepper	2.49
Stuffing mix	2.49
Dark brown sugar	1.29
Olive oil	6.00
	96.49

Date	Breakfast	Lunch	Dinner	Snack
1/3/2019	Cereal and fruit	Sandwich & drink	Beef Stew	brownies
1/4/2019	Cereal and fruit	Tuna Sandwich	Pasta & Salad	brownies
1/5/2019	Cereal and fruit	Turkey Sandwich	Baked Chicken	brownies
1/6/2019	Cereal and fruit	Chicken Sandwich	Beef Stew & pasta	brownies
1/7/2019	Cereal and fruit	Tuna Sandwich	Leftover Chicken	brownies
1/8/2019	Cereal and fruit	Turkey Sandwich	beef stew	brownies
1/9/2019	Cereal and fruit	Chicken Sandwich	Chicken soup	brownies

Easy Baked Chicken

Buy These Groceries:

2	pounds sweet potatoes	1.50	3.00
1	4 lb Chicken	5.56	5.56
1	pound butter	4.00	4.00
1	can chicken gravey	1.35	1.35
1	can green beans	1.09	1.09
1	small sweet red pepper	2.99	2.99
1	Jar Adobo Seasoning	5.59	5.59
1	Salt	2.39	2.39
1	Ground Black Pepper	2.49	2.49
1	Box Complete Stuffing mix	2.49	2.49
1	pound dark brown sugar	1.29	1.29
1	Bottle olive oil	6.00	6.00
	Makes about 4 meals and a bonus!		38.24

Beef Stew

Buy These Groceries:

1	3 lb bag potatoes	1.99	1.99
1	lb beef (london broil/stew meat)	3.49	3.49
2	Medium Tomatoes	1.00	2.00
1	2 lb Bag carrots	1.49	1.49
1	1 lb celery	1.49	1.49
1	2 lb yellow onion	1.99	1.99
1	Jar bay leaf	3.59	3.59
1	Salt	2.39	2.39
1	Ground Black Pepper	2.49	2.49
1	Garlic Powder	2.49	2.49
1	Packet McCormick Stew Season	1.49	1.49
1	Bottle olive oil	6.00	6.00
	Makes 6 meals		30.90

Easy Chicken Noodle Soup

Use These 'Baked Chicken' Leftovers for 'cheap' meals!

Chicken Bones, ETC from 'Baked Chicken'
Chicken drippings from 'baked chicken'
Olive oil, Sea salt & black pepper

Buy These Groceries:

1	Bag egg noodles	##	2.00
2	Fresh Carrots	##	2.98
1	yellow onion	##	4.00
1	garlic	##	
1	Celery	##	1.79
1	large potato	##	1.00
Makes about 4 servings!			11.77

Groceries	Cost	
1/2 gal milk		3.00
2 box cereal		6.00
Bread		3.00
Frozen peas and carrots		2.39
lettuce		3.00
Can Tomatoes		1.00
White Beans		1.09
Dried onion		2.79
1 lb ground beef		4.00
black beans		0.89
Cheese		5.00
pasta sauce		2.25
1 lb chicken		4.00
Can of tuna		2.00
1/4 lb sliced turkey		3.00
bananas		2.00
apples		3.00
Biscuit roll		3.00
Chicken Bullion		1.09
yellow onion		1.00
Corn Starch		1.49
Sweet red pepper		2.99
Box of cookies		2.99
		60.97

Date	Breakfast	Lunch	Dinner	Snack
1/10/2019	Cereal and fruit	Sandwich & drink	Beef Stew from Last week	cookies
1/11/2019	Cereal and fruit	Tuna Sandwich	Chicken Soup from last week	cookies
1/12/2019	Cereal and fruit	Turkey Sandwich	Chili & Salad	cookies
1/13/2019	Cereal and fruit	Chicken Soup	Pasta	cookies
1/14/2019	Cereal and fruit	Tuna Sandwich	Chicken and Dumplings	cookies
1/15/2019	Cereal and fruit	Turkey Sandwich	Leftover Chili	cookies
1/16/2019	Cereal and fruit	Leftovers	Chicken & Dumplings	cookies

Easy Chicken & Dumplings

1	Pillsburys buttermilk biscuits	2.99	2.99
1	lb Boneless chicken breast or thighs	4.39	4.39
2	32 oz Cans chicken bullion	2.00	4.00
1	1 lb yellow onion	1.00	1.00
1	bag frozen peas and carrots	2.49	2.49
1	small sweet red pepper	2.99	2.99
1	Jar Italian Seasoning	4.59	4.59
1	Salt	2.39	2.39
1	Ground Black Pepper	4.39	4.39
1	Garlic	1.59	1.59
1	Bottle olive oil	6.00	6.00
1	16 oz cornstarch	1.49	1.49
1	Box chicken bullion cubes	1.09	1.09
*Makes about 6 meals			39.40

Beef Chili

1	8 oz bag grated cheddar cheese	2.99	2.99
1	lb ground beef	4.00	4.00
1	Can petite diced tomatoes	1.00	1.00
1	1 Can Black Beans	0.89	0.89
1	1 Can Cannalini (white) beans	1.29	1.29
1	jar dried onion	2.79	2.79
1	Jar Chili powder	2.49	2.49
1	Jar Salt	2.39	2.39
1	Jar Ground Black Pepper	2.49	2.49
1	Jar Minced-dried Garlic	2.49	2.49
1	Packet McCormick Chili Seasoning	1.49	1.49
1	Bottle olive oil	6.00	6.00
*Makes 6 meals			30.31

Groceries	Cost
1/2 gal milk	3.00
1 box cereal/1bx bars	6.00
Bread	3.00
Fresh carrots	1.49
lettuce	3.00
Tomatoes	4.00
beets	1.49
Onions	2.00
Frozen Meatballs	3.79
Whole oats regular oatmeal	3.39
Cheese	5.00
pasta sauce 2@2.50	5.00
squash	1.00
Can of tuna	1.49
1/4 lb sliced turkey	3.00
bananas	2.00
apples	3.00
grapes	1.00
yogurt	3.00
Cookies or treats	2.50
Red Cabbage	1.49
white beans	1.00
Red wine	7.99
	68.63

Date	Breakfast	Lunch	Dinner	Snack
1/17/2019	Cereal and fruit	Fruit and bars and cheese	Veggie Soup	cookies
1/18/2019	Bars and yogurt	Tuna Sandwich	Chili (leftover)& Salad	cookies
1/19/2019	Cereal and fruit	Turkey Sandwich	Chicken & Dumplings (last week)	cookies
1/20/2019	Bars and yogurt	Veggie Soup	Meatballs & Pasta	cookies
1/21/2019	Cereal and fruit	Tuna Sandwich	Veggie Soup	cookies
1/22/2019	Bars and yogurt	Turkey Sandwich	Meatballs	cookies
1/23/2019	Cereal and fruit	Veggie Soup	Chicken Dumplings	cookies

Hearty Veggie Soup

Buy These Groceries:

	Item		
1	3 lb bag potatoes	1.99	1.99
1	lb beets	1.49	1.49
3	Medium Tomatoes	1.00	3.00
1	2 lb Bag carrots	1.49	1.49
1	1 lb celery	1.49	1.49
1	2 lb yellow onion	1.99	1.99
1	Can White Beans (Cannalini)	1.00	1.00
1	Jar bay leaf	3.59	3.59
1	Salt	2.39	2.39
1	Ground Black Pepper	4.39	4.39
1	Whole oats regular oatmeal	3.39	3.39
1	Jar Oregano	2.39	2.39
1	Jar Basil	2.39	2.39
1	Garlic	1.59	1.59
1	1/2 small head of red cabbage	1.49	1.49
1	Bottle olive oil	6.00	6.00
1	Bottle Red Wine (Barefoot)	8.99	8.99
1	Medium Yellow Squash	1.00	1.00
	*Makes 6 meals		50.06

Easy Tasty Meatballs for Pasta or Subs

	Item		
1	8 oz bag grated Parmesan cheese	2.99	2.99
1	Bag of Frozen Meatballs (about 1	3.79	3.79
1	Jar of Marinara sauce	2.29	2.29
1	jar dried onion	2.99	2.99
1	Salt	2.39	2.39
1	Jar Ground Black Pepper	2.49	2.49
1	Garlic	1.49	1.49
1	Jar Italian Seasoning	2.39	2.39
1	Bottle olive oil	6.00	6.00
	*Makes 8 meals		26.82

Groceries	Cost
1/2 gal milk	3.00
1 box cereal/1bx bars	6.00
Bread	3.00
Fresh carrots	1.49
lettuce	2.00
Tomato	1.50
Pasta	2.00
Onions	2.00
Frozen Peas and Carrots	2.39
Pie Crust	3.98
Cheese	3.00
pasta sauce 1@2.50	2.50
potatoes	2.00
1/4 lb sliced chicken	3.00
1/4 lb sliced turkey	3.00
bananas	2.00
apples	3.00
grapes	1.00
yogurt	3.00
garlic	1.59
Celery	1.49
white beans	1.00
2 cans tuna	2.98
squash	1.00
Kale or spinach	1.49
	59.41

Date	Breakfast	Lunch	Dinner	Snack
1/24/2019	Cereal and fruit	Fruit and bars and cheese	Meatballs Left Overs	cookies
1/25/2019	Bars and yogurt	Chicken Sandwich	Pot Pies	cookies
1/26/2019	Cereal and fruit	Meatballs	Pasta	cookies
1/27/2019	Bars and yogurt	Potpies	Tuna Mac Salad	cookies
1/28/2019	Cereal and fruit	Chicken Sandwich	Meatballs (Left overs)	cookies
1/29/2019	Bars and yogurt	Turkey Sandwich	Tuna Mac Salad	cookies
1/30/2019	Cereal and fruit	Meatballs (Leftovers)	Potpies	cookies

Tuna Mac Salad

1	16 oz box Box elbow macaroni	1.25	1.25
2	5 oz cans Tuna	1.49	2.98
1	32 oz jar mayonaise	2.99	2.99
1	2 lb Bag carrots	1.49	1.49
1	1 lb celery	1.49	1.49
1	1 lb yellow onion	1.00	1.00
1	medium tomato	1.00	1.00
1	Jar celery seed	4.59	4.59
1	Salt	2.39	2.39
1	Ground Black Pepper	2.49	2.49
1	Minced-dried Garlic	2.39	2.39
1	8oz Shreadded cheese (optional)	3.00	3.00
1	Bottle olive oil	6.00	6.00
	Makes 4 meals or 6 side dishes		**33.06**

Hearty Veggie Pot Pies

1	3 lb bag potatoes	1.99	1.99
1	bag frozen peas and carrots	2.39	2.39
2	Packages refrigerated pie crust (2 pe	1.99	3.98
1	1 lb celery	1.49	1.49
1	lb spinach or kale	1.99	1.99
1	2 lb yellow onion	1.99	1.99
1	Can White Beans (Cannalini)	1.00	1.00
1	Box Cornstarch	1.49	1.49
1	Flaked Sea Salt	2.39	2.39
1	Ground Black Pepper	2.49	2.49
1	Jar Oregano	4.39	4.39
1	Jar Basil	4.39	4.39
1	Garlic	1.59	1.59
1	Bottle olive oil	6.00	6.00
	Makes 6 meals		37.57

Create Your Own Spreadsheets

How to set up, update and edit your spreadsheets:

*Open a new (blank) spreadsheet on your computer or pad.

*In column A starting on line 2 enter your budget items in a single column (see sample above)

*In column B enter your start date on line 1

*In column B – starting on line 2 enter your budget items. Remember to enter your bank balance and income as NEGATIVE NUMBERS (see sample above)

*In column B under your paycheck amount enter =SUM(B2:B15) NOTE: In some cases you will have more or less than 15 lines of budget items including your paycheck. For the second 'B' number you must enter the number of the line where you put your paycheck amount – so that could be - B8, B17, or B23

*In column C line one enter =B1+7. That will make the spreadsheet give you a date one week from the first date- allowing you to have a weekly budget. NEXT – HIGHLIGHT then DRAG the formula to column C, D, E…all away across the page to create a one, two, five or even ten year budget.

*At the bottom of column B highlight then DRAG the formula to column C. Now that will calculate automatically. You can continue to DRAG the formula across the columns to create a two, three, five or even ten year budget calculator.

*Now you can go back and enter weekly budget amounts in the spaces and your new tool will automatically calculate everything for you.

*If the amount of your Paycheck, rent, or anything changes, just enter the changes on your budget sheet and your budget sheet will calculate for you!

A	B	C	D	E
This will be BLANK	1/3/2014	=B1+7	=C1+7	=D1+7
Rent	-200			
Food	-50	-50	-50	-50
Cell	-35			
Internet/ Entertainment	-25			
Heat	-25			
Electric	-25			
Water	-25			
Save	-96	-96	-96	-96
Health insurance	-85			
Transportation	-25	-25	-25	-25
Gifts/ fun/pets	-20	-20	-20	-20
Emergency Savings	-25	-25	-25	-25
Balance in bank	300	300	300	300
Paycheck (After approx taxes)	310	310	310	310
	=SUM(B2:B15)	=SUM(C2:C15)	=SUM(D2:D15)	=SUM(E2:E15)